KILLING TIME

ARCHAEOLOGY
AND THE
FIRST WORLD WAR

Nicholas J. Saunders

The History Press

In memory of Bob Craig (1950–2006)

Cover illustrations: front (from top): The Grimsby Chums (© Reuters/Corbis); Canadian troops on the Ancre Heights, 1916 (Imperial War Museum).

First published in 2007
This edition published in 2010

The History Press
The Mill, Brimscombe Port
Stroud, Gloucestershire, GL5 2QG
www.thehistorypress.co.uk

© Nicholas J. Saunders, 2007, 2010

British Library Cataloguing in Publication Data.
A catalogue record for this book is available from the British Library.

ISBN 978 0 7524 5602 7

Typesetting and origination by The History Press
Printed in Great Britain

Contents

Acknowledgements

It is inevitable that a book such as this relies to an overwhelming extent on the professional work, advice, comments and goodwill of many colleagues from a wide range of disciplines, as well as on the support of family, and the companionship of personal friends. I owe a great debt to all the individuals listed below, whose cooperation, expertise, insights and friendship have greatly influenced my own work, and made this book possible. None of them is responsible for what I have made of their many generosities.

As it would be invidious as well as impossible to rank these individuals according to my gratitude, I list them here in alphabetical order: Frédéric Adam, Zeyad al-Salameen, Stéphane Audoin-Rouzeau, Marco Balbi, Annette Becker, Barbara Bender, Bob Bewley, Franky Bostyn, Jean Bourgeois, Isabelle Brandauer, James Brazier, Andy Brockman, Graham Brown, Martin Brown, David Cameron, John Carman, Piet Chielens, Željko Cimpric, Hugh Clout, David Cohen, Thomas Compère-Morel, Paul Cornish, Susan Daniels, Janiek Degryse, Anna Gow, Armando De Guio, Mark Dennis, Roger De Smul, Dominiek Dendooven, Aleks Deseyne, Yves Desfossés, Jan Dewilde, Marc Dewilde, Mike Dolamore, Nils Fabiansson, Hani Falahat, Neil Faulkner, David Field, Paola Filippucci, Philippe Gorczynski, Paul Gough, Fabio Gygi, Andy Hawkins, Italo Hellmann, Gary Hollingsworth, Patrik Indevuyst, Alain Jacques, David Kenyon, Arlene King, Joe Lahae, Mathieu de Meyer, Tom Morgan, Richard Osgood, Jon Price, Pedro Pype, Paul Reed, Rik Ryon, Jacques Schier, John Schofield, Aurel Sercu, Mansour Shqiarat, Ivan Sinnaeve, Tony Spagnoly, Harald Stadler, Birger Stichelbaut, David Thorpe, Christopher Tilley, Senior Captain A. Vander Mast, Johan Vandewalle, Gabriel Versavel, Carol Walker, Roger Ward, Patrice Warin, the late Marian Wenzel, John Winterburn, and John Woolsgrove, as well as www.greatwar.be and www.suffolkchurches.co.uk.

As always, I owe a great debt to my wife, Pauline, my children, Roxanne and Alexander, my parents, Geoff and Pat Saunders, and, ultimately, to my grandfathers, Alfred William Saunders of the King's Own Royal Regiment (Lancaster) and Matthew Inkerman Chorley of the South Lancashire Regiment. Both fought in the First World War and survived. I can only imagine what they would have thought about the idea that the war that forged them as young men would, almost within their own lifetimes, become a part of archaeology.

Introduction

The First World War remains ambiguously 'recent' in the European imagination – hovering above the border where oral history, military history and cultural history meet individual and collective memories. Its objects live on in people's homes, in museums and in salesrooms, and its legacies permeate the tortuous politics of identity, via nationalism and ethnicity, across Europe and beyond. The war exists also in the conjoined worlds of tourism and heritage, with ever-increasing numbers of visitors to its battlefields and museums, especially along the old Western Front of Belgium and France – the focus of this book.

Yet, until recently, almost nothing that we knew of the First World War (the Great War) had come from beneath the soil, from innumerable kilometres of now subterranean trenches, dugouts, hospitals, bomb craters, tunnels and impromptu battlefield graves. It is as if the idea of an archaeology of the war was somehow beyond reach, or perhaps not worth bothering about, as everything we needed to know could be gleaned from the historical accounts of its many battles, and their tragic cost in human lives and suffering. Was the First World War suitable for archaeological excavation? Was it not too recent? Could archaeology tell us anything new?

Times change, and ideas and attitudes change with them. The past ten years have seen extraordinary developments in what can now be called, without fear of contradiction, the archaeology of the First World War. A decade ago it seemed to me, and to others, that here was a vast new field of archaeological (and anthropological) research that had hardly been considered, far less acted upon. I remember tramping the battlefields of the Western Front in all weathers, searching for examples of curious objects called trench art – three-dimensional items made by soldiers and civilians (often as souvenirs) during and after the war – and encountering landscapes and material culture that had only ever been in the background of the great military histories of the war.

I heard dark rumours of clandestine battlefield digging, of soldiers' bodies torn from the earth and stripped of their equipment and personal possessions, and of almost mythical private collections of the trench art I sought, and of other objects from the war. I wandered through museums, large and small, in which there was a wealth of objects waiting to be studied, and across old battlefield landscapes whose archaeology had only fleetingly been touched, and whose anthropological dimension had hardly even been considered. And, in countless interviews, I came across ideas, stories, insights and attitudes that seemed to move effortlessly back and forth between the trench art I had come to study, family experiences and memories of the war, and the surface worlds and underground landscapes of the conflict. Running through all these varied aspects like an electric current were the lives of real people. They had names, signatures and faces, and their letters, photographs and objects seemed to me to announce a new kind of archaeology – that of the recent historical past in time of conflict.

Great War archaeology is a complex endeavour. In one sense, it is a kind of industrial archaeology, whose strata are saturated with mass-produced artefacts of the twentieth century – an overwhelming sea of materiality that seems to mock the archaeologist's quest for meaningful patternings of objects. In another sense, it is historical archaeology, informed by a wealth of written documents on every conceivable aspect of the conflict, from trench life to global military strategy, from the personal meanings of memorabilia to the international consequences of its aftermath. It is also social archaeology, public archaeology, and anthropological archaeology, and one of the many so-called 'archaeologies of the contemporary past'.

Great War archaeology is all of these and more, for it deals with the actions and consequences of modern industrialised war on a global scale. It is the archaeology of new worlds brought into being at terrible cost between 1914 and 1918 – worlds that have transformed themselves ever since, within which we still live today, and with whose legacies we still struggle, whether in Bosnia, Gaza or Iraq.

This book focuses mainly on the old battlefields of the Western Front, for it is here that most archaeology and anthropology has been carried out, and it is here also that the issues of heritage and tourism are currently most accessible. It is here, too, that younger generations are being motivated as much by what lies beneath the battlefields, and what this tells us of the human experience of war, as previous generations were (and still are) by the more traditional historical accounts of the First World War's many iconic battles. Great War archaeology is, ultimately, the archaeology of us, and it is only just beginning.

CHAPTER 1

Excavating Memories: Great War Archaeology

The passage of time has all but extinguished any living memory of the Great War of 1914-1918, but the experiences of those who fought in the trenches of the Somme in northern France, and around the town of Ypres in Belgian Flanders, have since become epic history and the stuff of legend.

The archaeology of recent ancestors. Three veterans of the First World War at the Menin Gate memorial to the missing, Ypres, on 11 November 2002. From left to right, Jack Davies, 108 (died 2003), Arthur Halestrap, 104 (died 2004), and Harry Patch, 111 (died 2009). *(Courtesy and © www.greatwar.be)*

Today, hardly a month passes without some dramatic and often poignant discovery along the old killing fields of the Western Front in France and Belgium. Evocative burials of British, French or German soldiers buried during battle and then forgotten – lying in rows seemingly arm in arm, interred in a makeshift shell-crater grave, or found still crouching after eighty-five years at the entrance to a dugout. Whole 'underground cities' of trenches, dugouts, galleries and shelters lie preserved beneath the mud of Flanders – sometimes with newspapers, blankets and socks scattered where they were left. Underground field hospitals carved into the chalk country of Artois and Picardy in France also survive, as do hundreds of kilometres of tunnels scratched with graffiti by long-dead hands. Most threatening of all, countless tons of volatile bombs and gas canisters still wait for a chance to explode. Almost a century after the war ended, on 11 November 1918, there is an annual loss of life caused by this deadly legacy of the 'war to end all wars'.

The living reality of the First World War today belongs increasingly to archaeology. When the last old soldier passes away, anything new about the war will, almost by definition, belong in the realm of the archaeologist. Yet, while there are innumerable books on the military history of the war, its battles, its generals, and its cultural and economic legacies, there is not a single book on the modern scientific archaeology of the world's first industrialised global conflict.

This book, unique today, but surely not for long, brings together for the first time widely scattered archaeological discoveries of the First World War (many not published in English), and offers new insights into the human dimension of the conflict. It shows how the archaeology of the war is a new kind of archaeology – one that includes not only the excavation of battlefields, but also its personal and emotional dimensions – a social archaeology that excavates people's lives, and that can take place in their own homes, museums, car-boot sales, on the Internet, and in public and private collections of war memorabilia.

Unlike other kinds of archaeology, Great War archaeology connects directly to virtually every family in Britain, France, Belgium, Italy, Australia, New Zealand, Canada, Germany and Austria, as well as to hundreds of thousands of others around the world, whose great-grandfathers and great-uncles fought in the trenches of the Western Front and beyond. Countless families preserve photographs, diaries and souvenirs of the First World War – objects as eloquent as anything found on the battlefields today – and all speak of ordinary men living extraordinary lives in momentous times.

During the past thirty years, archaeology has changed beyond all recognition. Today, archaeologists are concerned as much with what is called the 'contemporary past' as with deep prehistory or the worlds of classical antiquity. The archaeology of conflict, much influenced by anthropology, offers unique perspectives on the recent past by investigating the physical remains of everyday life – of battles won and lost, of national tragedy and individual struggle. Modern archaeology yields surprising personal and often poignant insights into people's lives over the past hundred years as well as in ancient times.

The archaeology of the First World War is the newest of these archaeologies of the contemporary or recent past. It tells a different story of the war from unexpected points of view, and shows how we create the past we desire. It is also a fast-developing subject, and one that is spearheading the advance to a greater goal – the archaeology of all twentieth-century conflict. The picture that archaeology reveals of war illustrates what it means to be human in that most fundamental and ironic invention of modern civilisation – industrialised conflict.

ARCHAEOLOGY AND THE FIRST WORLD WAR

The birth and development of a modern archaeology of the First World War is a curiously tangled affair, lasting almost a century, and, appropriately, not without its own internal conflicts and rivalries. Here, four notional phases are identified, less as a strict chronology that all must agree upon, and more as a way of beginning to understand Great War archaeology. Each of these phases is as notable for its broader anthropological dimension as it is for its contribution to the archaeology of conflict. The first phase belongs to the period of the war itself, 1914–18, the second to the years 1919–90, the third to the decade of the 1990s and the early 2000s, and the fourth from 2002 to the present. In this book, this timeline relates mainly, but not exclusively, to the Western Front (and includes different developments in France and Belgium). Although some examples are taken from other theatres of the war, similar chronologies for the Eastern Front, Italy, the Balkans, Gallipoli, and the Middle East have not yet been suggested. The outline offered here is neither hard and fast, nor universally applicable, and it is not meant to be. It is a general framework, designed to throw light on the complex origins and development of Great War archaeology, its connections with anthropology, history and other disciplines, and its potential for changing our ideas of what modern archaeology is about, and what it can achieve.

Phase 1: 1914–18

The Western Front was, in effect, a parallel set of the two longest archaeological trenches in history – one Allied, the other German. These stretched some 500km from the Belgian coast to the Swiss border, and were supplemented by dugouts, underground tunnels and extensive systems of support trenches cut at right angles to the front line. It is estimated that the French army alone dug 10,000km of trenches (Barbusse 2003: 25). It is possible that more earth was dug, more archaeological sites uncovered, more stratigraphy revealed, and more ancient artefacts discovered during the four years of the war than at any time before or since. To this must be added the devastation of landscape and towns caused by four years of artillery bombardment by both sides, which itself, and ironically, opened up previously unknown (or long-forgotten) archaeological areas. Nevertheless, in both instances, war conditions meant that much of this newly discovered archaeological data went unrecorded or was subsequently lost.

This was clearly a different kind of archaeology. It was not the archaeology of the ongoing war itself, but rather a miscellany of discoveries of traditional archaeological kinds, revealed as a byproduct of industrialised conflict. Never before had there been the strategic conditions or the weapons that cut open the landscape across such vast areas as happened between 1914 and 1918.

Artillery barrage and the digging of trenches uncovered Gallo-Roman and medieval remains in built-up areas, and revealed traces of older prehistory in open country. This early relationship between war and archaeology is illustrated by the link between the intensity of fighting and the discovery of archaeological remains. Prominent in this respect was the rapid German advance across the Somme battlefield in spring 1918 – part of the so-called *Kaiserschlacht* (Kaiser's Battle).

In response to the German advance, Captain J.B. Frost of the Royal Engineers dug defensive trenches at Harponville on the Somme in April, and discovered a Neolithic axe, which is now in the Imperial War Museum, London. Similarly, Captain Francis Buckley of the Northumberland Fusiliers supervised the digging of trenches at Coigneux, some 6 miles behind the British lines southwest of Arras. Coigneux was reinforced by these trenches, known as the 'Red Line', though, as Buckley observed, they were never used. Inspecting these freshly dug and empty Red Line trenches, Buckley discovered Palaeolithic (Mousterian) artefacts, and noted that that, 'For about 15 or 20 yards along the parapets there was a good sprinkling of implements, some recently broken and some whole. . . . [including] a hand axe . . ., a typical Levallois flake and

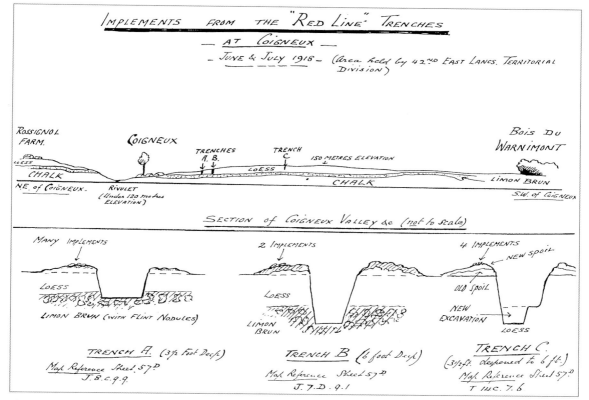

Captain Francis Buckley's section drawing of the 'Red Line' trenches dug at Coigneux on the Somme in 1918.

a number of scrapers' (Buckley 1920–1: 4). Buckley would spend over three years in France and Belgium, during which time he collected many prehistoric 'flints'.

The German offensive failed, and in August the Allies began pushing them back east across the Somme battlefield to the defensive position known as the Hindenburg Line. As the Germans retreated, artillery fire left new landscapes pitted with craters, in one of which, at Richcourt-les-Bapaume, a British soldier picked up a prehistoric flint tool. A photograph of this implement, labelled 'War Souvenir Flint' and 'French microlith (Late Cave Period)', is now in the Tolson Memorial Museum in Huddersfield.

German and French soldiers were also involved in similar activities. At Juvincourt-Damary, in the French department of the Aisne, German soldiers digging trenches under cover of night kept an eagle eye on their excavations, hoping to find metal scrap from enemy bombardments that they could sell or

German officer and soldier uncover a carved Roman monument during the digging of a trench in northern France. (© *Author's collection*)

exchange for a profit. On one occasion, they discovered a Bronze Age trove of axe-heads, projectiles, knives and jewellery, which they quickly divided up among themselves and eventually took back to Germany (Niethammer 1923; Jockenhövel and Smolla 1975: 289–90).

An equally dramatic discovery was recorded by the French soldier-author Henri Barbusse, whose literary account of his war experiences was published as

Under Fire in 1917, and became a bestseller. In one passage, where Barbusse and his comrade Tulacque are digging tunnels, Tulacque shows him a Neolithic or Bronze Age bone-hafted flint axe which he had found in a subterranean gallery the previous night, and which he was using in preference to the standard-issue army axe (Barbusse 1988: 10; 2003: 12). In this instance, the war had led to the discovery of a prehistoric artefact that had originally been used to dig subterranean galleries, and was now being reused for the same purpose, in war conditions, more than three thousand years later.

On the Eastern Front also, digging trenches, dugouts and fortifications uncovered numerous archaeological remains, from prehistoric tools and burials to caches of more recent coins, often only centimetres beneath the surface. Dynamiting the ground for laying fortification foundations produced showers of Bronze Age and Iron Age bones and artefacts, and numerous army newspapers reported on the prehistoric artefacts that were found during trench digging (Liulevicius 2000: 37–8). The battlezone landscape itself was a virtually untouched (and uninvestigated) palimpsest of prehistoric remains – hundreds of hillforts, and innumerable survivals of pre-Christian beliefs commemorated as Christianised roadside crosses (*ibid.*) and other expressions of peasant soldier Christian faith. In Macedonia, in northern Greece – then still part of the Ottoman Empire – the wartime activities of Allied forces (particularly the French and British) based in and around Thessaloniki (Salonica) not only uncovered previously unknown archaeological sites, but actively stimulated serious archaeological research as well as the inevitable looting (Saunders n.d.).

The French and British, though wartime allies, could not resist competing with each other in the guise of archaeology. The French set up a wartime archaeological service, identified and excavated many sites, and displayed the finds to their troops (Mazower 2004: 316–17). The British High Command responded in kind, and ordered that all discoveries made while digging trenches and dugouts be reported to military headquarters. Meanwhile, the soldiers themselves scavenged the prehistoric tumuli of the region (*ibid.*). Soldiers of the Black Watch, Cheshires and Wiltshires discovered whole prehistoric cemeteries, burials with jewellery, and innumerable artefacts. Even rock-cut tombs above the ancient Macedonian city of Amphipolis by the River Strymon were investigated by the Royal Army Medical Corps when an enemy artillery barrage unexpectedly opened up a Hellenistic tomb dating to around 200 BC (Saunders n.d.).

Discoveries were also made away from the battlefields, in areas that were, nevertheless, still places affected by conflict. Arguably one of the best-known examples was the investigation by the archaeologist and writer Jacquetta

Effigy of Greek Orthodox saint left by Russian soldiers in their abandoned trench on the Eastern Front. *(© Author's collection)*

British officer carrying a prehistoric ceramic pot on the Salonica Front in northern Greece. *(© Author's collection)*

Hawkes of an archaeological site first revealed by the construction of a prisoner-of-war camp on Jersey in the Channel Islands (Finn 2005: 126–7). Hawkes published her findings in 1939, and included a drawing of flints from 'chipping areas' within a prisoner-of-war camp at Les Blanches Banques that had been used between 1915 and 1919. The ground had been disturbed by building, occupation and abandonment of the camp, and revealed a large area of prehistoric occupation with flints, pottery, stone implements and shell middens dating to the end of what was then called the megalithic period (i.e. the late Neolithic, early Bronze Age) (Hawkes 1939: 66 n. 9, 179–80, n. 9). In the same way as in the battlezones, wartime activity had served to 'excavate' archaeological remains.

From the Western and Eastern fronts, south to Turkey, Mesopotamia and Egypt, the war was conducted above and below ground in landscapes of imposing (and sometimes hitherto unknown) archaeological monuments. These archaeological discoveries were incidental, confined to sites and artefacts revealed only by wartime activities. Events during this period had a direct relationship to archaeology itself, and to the beginnings of Great War archaeology. The war had uncovered large numbers of previously unknown archaeological sites and significant quantities of artefacts, and so added to traditional archaeology's knowledge of the past.

Importantly, the conflict also randomly mixed pre-war archaeological strata with levels of destruction of historic and contemporary buildings, war materiel, unexploded ordnance and human remains. This hybrid layer could take many forms. The constants were traces of war-related activities, destruction, bodies and weaponry; while the variables were the older remains of the Palaeolithic, Mesolithic, Neolithic, Bronze Age or Iron Age periods, either on their own, or in combination. This new, infinitely variable (and sometimes potentially lethal) hybrid layer belonged to the war itself, and is the focus of Great War archaeology.

Phase 2: 1919–90

In the war's aftermath, the old battlezones of the Western Front were gradually reclaimed through bomb clearance and reconstruction – activities that together created a new shallow layer of civilian reoccupation overlying the war level, and dating mainly to the 1920s and 1930s (Clout 1996). In addition, the Imperial War Graves Commission, now the Commonwealth War Graves Commission (CWGC), scoured the battlefields locating individual bodies for identification and burial, and consolidating small battlefield cemeteries into larger ones (Longworth 1985). Much of this activity is what today would be called forensic archaeology, although it was not seen in this way at the time. The bodies located during these official activities were respectfully reburied in CWGC cemeteries, but there were other, more clandestine and less respectful activities that occurred alongside them.

Refugees returning to their destroyed villages and poisoned farmlands were confronted with dire economic circumstances in which they were unable immediately to resume their pre-war lives, and had to find alternative ways of making a living. One quickly acquired habit was searching the battlefields for military scrap, unfired munitions and miscellaneous war materiel, which could be sold to the authorities, or – sometimes in its raw state, sometimes made into 'trench-art' objects – sold as souvenirs to the burgeoning numbers of battlefield pilgrims and tourists who began arriving in 1919. During the 1920s and 1930s, searching and clearing the battlefields became a newly invented 'tradition' for the local inhabitants of an area, begun in childhood, continued when adult, and passed on in turn to their own children.

While the war was far too recent for professional archaeologists to consider it worthy of study, and while local digging and collecting of battlefield objects was probably never seen in any sense as archaeology, these activities helped lay the foundations for the modern archaeology of the war that is now emerging. Some individuals during this time (and still today) specialised in locating human remains and stripping them of their military equipment and personal belongings – German helmets, firearms, uniforms, regimental badges and insignia were especially sought, and became increasingly valuable over time. By virtue of the clandestine nature of this activity, the authorities were usually not informed, and the human remains themselves were quickly and unceremoniously reburied. It is not surprising that little is known about these activities, and even less written.

Over some seventy years, from 1919 to around 1990, purposeful digging on battlefields in order to find Great War objects was mainly the preserve of French and Belgians, who knew and often owned their local landscapes, traded their finds through regional networks of militaria fairs, and put together often impressive personal collections of objects. These individuals often formed the nucleus of informal groups of like-minded friends who would go to dig a promising spot in search of saleable items. These groups were the precursors of a new generation which, during the 1990s, would establish more formal 'associations' whose interest was as much in Great War history as it was in finding objects to sell. Partly stimulated by the expanding market in such memorabilia (and an increasing general interest in the war itself), the 1960s saw numbers of British enthusiasts visiting the battlefields, parking their cars by the side of a field, and setting to work with shovels, and occasionally a metal-detector.

Throughout this whole period, professional and academic archaeology did not recognise the First World War as archaeological heritage. The partial exception to this was in France, where rescue digs in advance of the construction of motorways, the high-speed TGV rail link to Paris and urban development occasionally required formal excavation of a Great War site. It was during the last decade of this period, the 1980s, that an unofficial kind of battlefield archaeology began to take shape, distinguished by the fact that the diggers (mainly local people and a few British enthusiasts) were amateurs, whose enthusiasm stemmed from their knowledge of military history, not archaeology. The term 'battlefield archaeologist' began to be heard along the Western Front, though in fact their activities often amounted to little more than a weekend hobby.

These individuals were not looters, and their digging had a serious purpose. Yet they did not replace the opportunistic battlefield scavengers who continued their search for bodies and artefacts. Indeed, by opening up and publicising their digs, amateur groups often alerted the less scrupulous, who would hover out of sight until the diggers left, and then raid the site under cover of darkness. The idea that these latter individuals were, in a general sense, desecrating their own ancestors' remains, or destroying a virtually pan-European archaeological heritage, seems not to have occurred to them. It seems that annually mourning the dead on 11 November was not seen as inconsistent with despoiling the remains of 'the missing' in pursuit of profit.

Serious-minded, but still informal, amateur groups, as well as the battlefield scavengers, could both, on occasion, describe themselves as 'battlefield archaeologists' – though the term had little to do with archaeology. It seems to have become increasingly popular towards the end of the 1980s, adopted by, and indiscriminately applied to, all who 'investigated' battlefields. It is likely that the reputations of the more serious-minded amateurs suffered by sharing this designation with the looters.

Whatever their intentions, the increasing numbers and different kinds of 'battlefield archaeologists' drew support and inspiration from the publication in 1987 of a book entitled *Battlefield Archaeology* by the war historian John Laffin. While Laffin's extensive knowledge of the war was undeniable (he was a prolific author of military history), his knowledge of archaeology was lamentable, and his definition of the subject little more than a self-serving looter's charter. His view that there was nothing sacreligious about digging up battlefield relics was reinforced by a belief that a tourist needed only a guidebook to become an archaeologist, and that battlefield archaeologists should search for the places where Victoria Crosses were won (Laffin 1987: 10, 70). Such bizarre notions were tastelessly illustrated by a photograph of two human teeth and a finger bone that he had dug up, alongside a poem inspired by their discovery. While it was no surprise that the book lacked a single archaeological reference, it was more worrying that it passed virtually unnoticed and uncriticised by professional archaeologists, who still at this time did not regard the war as an appropriate subject for archaeological investigation.

Phase 3: 1990–2001

The penultimate phase in the development of Great War archaeology began during the early 1990s, when the hitherto loose-knit groups of amateur diggers in Belgian Flanders began to adopt a more formal identity, sometimes as associations. These groups were composed of a heterogeneous mix of enthusiasts: some just liked digging, others specialised in military history; some were experts in military uniforms and equipment, others in weapons and munitions, and some in the development of military technologies. Several were motivated by a sense of moral responsibility to find the remains of those who had fallen on the battlefields. All freely admitted they were amateurs, not professionals, and diggers rather than excavators.

Interestingly, while this period saw a quickening of the pace of digging battlefields, this development took a different path in Belgium than it did in France. Also important at this time was the international dissemination of a scattered literature on the many large and small investigations occurring along the old Western Front – a service made possible only by the developing technology of the Internet. In August 2000, the Swedish archaeologist Nils Fabiansson launched a website called 'The Archaeology of the Western Front 1914–1918' which was to last until August 2005 (Fabiansson 2000–2005). For these critical five years in the development of Great War archaeology, Fabiansson chronicled almost every activity that took place, and the website played a central role in bringing together and informing everyone concerned with excavating Great War sites.

In Belgium, there were several semi-formal groups of amateur 'battlefield archaeologists' that thrived in part because at that time there was little official archaeological involvement in war heritage. It was, in a sense, a free market, where, once the landowner's permission was obtained, digging could take place almost anywhere, constrained only by manpower, enthusiasm, finances and the weather. Near Ypres, in the centre of the old Ypres Salient battlefield, one local group made a virtue of necessity, and called themselves 'The Diggers'. They began digging in 1992, and soon focused their attention on an area of open fields opposite the town of Boezinge, north of Ypres, part of an expanding industrial estate. This area, which had not been developed since the end of the First World War, was the site of the first German gas attack in 1915.

The Diggers worked under licence from Belgium's Institute for Archaeological Heritage (IAP), whose professional archaeologists kept a watching brief on their activities. The Diggers used metal-detectors in their investigations, kept the local police informed of any discovery of human remains, and handed over these remains to the Commonwealth War Graves Commission for reburial in military cemeteries. They also maintained a good working relationship with the In Flanders Fields Museum in Ypres, to which they donated some of their artefacts (Sercu 2001; and see Smith 1999). The Diggers were not alone in conducting such excavations. Another group, calling itself the 'Association for Battlefield Archaeology in Flanders' (ABAF), began its own ad hoc series of digs in the Ypres Salient in 1999. ABAF was more international in its composition, with some members having worked with The Diggers; others were local Great War enthusiasts, and several also came from the United Kingdom. While none of ABAF's members were professional archaeologists, several had academic training in other disciplines.

ABAF dug at various locations around Ypres, notably at Bayernwald (Croonaert Wood) near Wijtschate, and 'Beecham Dugout', near Tyne Cot cemetery outside Passchendaele. On both occasions, the group published detailed accounts of their researches in the form of Dutch-language books that brought together archival and archaeological data (Bostyn 1999; Bostyn and Vancoillie 2000). They made detailed plans, collected and numbered their finds, and kept an often eerily beautiful photographic record of their work underground. Nevertheless, differences of opinion between ABAF, The Diggers and other influential bodies, as well within these groups, soon came to the fore, and in late 2000, ABAF ceased its fieldwork investigations. Only several years later, and after several personnel changes, would a 'new' reconstituted ABAF again be archaeologically active, by which time the official attitudes and legal constraints had changed considerably.

Also, in late 2000, The Diggers' activities were scandalised in a British television programme and in the British press (Tyson 2000; Harvey 2000a,

Remains of a French soldier found by The Diggers at the Boezinge site, near Ypres.
(Courtesy and © Aurel Sercu)

Shaving brush and the remains of a harmonica found by The Diggers at Boezinge, near Ypres. *(Courtesy and © Aurel Sercu)*

2000b; Tweedie 2000). This led to official statements by the Belgian government, and talk of an inquiry by the British government. The situation was disappointing for Great War archaeology. For over eighty years, unauthorised battlefield diggings had attracted little comment or official sanction. Long-ignored issues concerning who should excavate what and how, and the treatment of the dead and their artefacts, had suddenly exploded, dramatically politicising the archaeology of the First World War in Belgium. Further dissension followed when ABAF personnel investigated extensive Great War tunnels and dugouts beneath the Belgian coastal town of Nieuwpoort that had serious implications for subsidence and compensation (Doyle *et al.* 2001). However, disagreements between the investigators, military experts, and local and national Belgian politicians led to rancorous exchanges and little has happened since.

The passions aroused by the activities of The Diggers and ABAF during the 1990s were the background for a decisive shift in official attitudes towards acknowledging the region's Great War remains as a valued and valuable part of Belgian Flanders' archaeological heritage. This change, while restricted to Belgium, nevertheless marks the beginning of phase 4.

In France during the 1990s, events took a different course from those in Belgium. Regional Archaeological Services in France operate as part of the local Direction régionale des affaires culturelles (DRAC). Their responsibility is for their region's total archaeological heritage, from prehistory to recent times. French attitudes to Great War sites have been shaped by the practical experience of carrying out their duty to investigate all archaeological heritage. This has not been a proactive interest inasmuch as there has never been an official group of professional DRAC archaeologists dedicated to excavating First World War remains. Great War sites have been investigated as part of rescue excavations – most commonly during the construction of the TGV train link from Calais to Paris, and various motorways that have cut across the old Somme battlefield and elsewhere (Desfossés 1999). Occasionally, traditional archaeology and Great War archaeology have become entangled, as when the remains of twenty-four Royal Fusiliers were found by archaeologists investigating a multi-period (though mainly Gallo-Roman) site at Monchy-le-Preux near Arras.

The attitude of French professional archaeologists has been pragmatic, and they have developed a unique expertise in excavating such sites and publishing the results (Historial de la Grande Guerre 1999; Desfossés and Jacques 2000). The most publicised investigation to date is the 1991 excavation of twenty-one bodies of French soldiers at Saint-Rémy-la-Calonne, where the investigation was contentious because of the presence among the dead of the French novelist Alain-Fournier (Adam 1991, 1999). More recently, the remains of German soldiers have been found at Gavrelle, and of British soldiers at Le Point du Jour, both outside Arras (Desfossés and Jacques 2000: 35). These discoveries are discussed in Chapter 5.

The French experience has differed from the Belgian one in this respect, and, while there are many specialist groups in France, their interest lies in various aspects of Great War military history, rather than in forming groups of amateur 'battlefield archaeologists'. The only similar group is the Association Souvenir Bataille de Fromelles, which includes French and Belgian enthusiasts who investigate remains near the French village of Fromelles, and maintain a small but important museum in the local town hall. Occasionally, isolated finds occur whose investigation crosses the boundary between military history and archaeology. The most famous example was the discovery of a British tank near the village of Flesquières, which was excavated in 1998 and is awaiting restoration.

Unlike in Belgium (until 2002–3), professional, amateur and mixed professional–amateur groups have coexisted in France since the 1990s. What has been noticeable is the presence of foreign groups, often with a core of professionals, who have been involved in more sustained research. The Durand Group of mainly British expert military and civilian volunteers has been investigating underground tunnels at Vimy Ridge since 1997. They have specialised in archaeological and photographic surveying and mapping, the defusing of unexploded mines, and the pioneering of non-destructive remote sensing surveys of battlefields (Watkins 1998; Dolamore 2000).

Perhaps the best-known foreign excavation in France has been the 'Ocean Villas Project' at Auchonvillers on the Somme (OVPW 2001). It was conducted by a British team composed of a professional archaeologist, several military historians, and volunteers. Its aim was to investigate communication trenches and a cellar used by British soldiers during the war, and to reconstruct and present them as part of a tourist feature associated with a tearoom and guest house for battlefield visitors. Nearby, at Beaumont-Hamel, a joint Canadian and French team excavated the site of a proposed car park adjacent to the preserved battlefield landscape of Newfoundland Memorial Park in 1998 (Piédalue 1998). In both instances, it was battlefield tourism that stimulated archaeological investigation, and that itself became part of a wider debate on Great War heritage and cultural memory. Anthropological concerns lay at the heart of these archaeological developments.

As the 1990s drew to a close, it was a sign of changing times and attitudes in France that the French First World War scholarly journal, *14/18: Aujourd'hui. Today. Heute*, dedicated its second issue almost exclusively to the beginnings of an archaeology of the war (Historial de la Grande Guerre 1999). Although it provided a snapshot of ideas and discoveries rather than an in-depth analysis, it was nevertheless a landmark publication that presented original and creative thinking about what an archaeology of the First World War might look like. Every article raised important points, a fact made more remarkable in that half of the authors were historians not archaeologists, and those who were archaeologists were not Great War specialists (although they were becoming so). Eminent scholars such as Alain Schnapp, Annette Becker, Stéphane Audoin-Rouzeau and Gerd Krumeich argued the need for an archaeology of the First World War, while archaeologists Yves Desfossés and Frédéric Adam offered timely archaeological case studies that illustrated this need, and these were commented on from an anthropological perspective by Claire Reverchon, Pierre Gaudin and Henri Duday. Considered together, these diverse articles were a powerful call to arms.

Phase 4: 2002–present

By the end of 2001, Great War archaeology had temporarily stalled in Belgium with the adverse publicity surrounding the amateur groups, but continued in France on the same path as during the 1990s. Now, new forces were coming into play: the professionalisation of Great War archaeology in Belgium, and the advent of 'television archaeology' in France and Belgium.

In Belgium, the initial stimulus for a dramatic change of attitude was the survey and excavation by the Institute for Archaeological Heritage in the area known as Pilckem Ridge in the middle of the Ypres Salient battlefield. Pilckem Ridge saw fierce fighting and terrible losses on both sides during the Third Battle of Ypres (Passchendaele) between July and August 1917, and lay on the route of an extension to the A19 motorway.

The Institute's archaeologists began conducting reconnaissance in the area in 2002, and the results quickly demonstrated the need for a fully fledged professional archaeological investigation. Their preliminary research involved an extensive survey of the literature, trench maps and contemporary 1914–18 aerial photographs. Discovered trench systems, barbed-wire entanglements and dugouts were plotted on modern maps, and fieldwalking filled in the picture by locating the remains of bunkers and concentrations of other wartime material. This work, along with information gained by interviewing local residents, identified nine zones for detailed archaeological along the route of the planned A19 extension. The effect of the Pilckem Ridge survey was to usher in a new, official, legally constituted and totally professional archaeology of the war under the aegis of the Institute for Archaeological Heritage.

On 10 November 2003, the Belgian minister Paul van Grembergen officially opened the Department of First World War Archaeology as part of the Institute for Archaeological Heritage (Dewilde *et al.* 2004). The new department had the support of Flemish universities, the Belgian Army's Service for the Disposal and Demolition of Explosives (DOVO), as well as groups of amateur diggers and historians, and a wide range of international collaborators. Its aim was to undertake archaeological research, compile inventories and manage Great War sites, as well as direct, monitor and coordinate the various private activities and initiatives undertaken by museums, amateur diggers, historians and other interested parties.

In this way, the hitherto fragmented wealth of expertise and specialised knowledge of individuals and amateur groups would not be lost, but rather made available to the department's legal and professional framework for conducting modern scientific archaeological investigations. It was further hoped that recognition of the heritage value of the region's Great War remains would stimulate different kinds of cultural and tourism-related initiatives. The year 2003 saw the culmination of digging activities in Belgian Flanders that had begun between 1914 and 1918. More widely, it was arguably the most important single advance in investigating the material culture of the First World War along the Western Front in over eighty years.

An integral part of this development was the work carried on within the A19 Project by research students from Ghent University. The study of aerial photographs taken at various times from before, during and after the war, and their correlation with wartime trench maps and documentary records, was an especially promising approach. What made it more innovative was the integration (and analysis) of these images with Geographical Information System (GIS) technology in ways that offered unique insights not only into Great War archaeology, but also for the parent discipline of archaeology itself. Such developments showed that the archaeology of the First World War was slowly becoming part of mainstream archaeology, and was fast losing its amateur status.

The second development was the arrival of a distinctive 'television archaeology' of the war in France and Belgium. There had long been occasional television interest in the Great War, especially around the 11 November commemorations on the Somme and in Ypres. More recently, programmes such as *The Underground War* (1998) and *The Trench* (2002) had catered for the rising public interest in the conflict. Even *Battlefield Scavengers* (2000) – the programme that attacked the activities of The Diggers, and a BBC follow-up, *The Forgotten Battlefield* (2002), which had taken a more even-handed approach, were, in a sense, traditional kinds of coverage of inherently interesting events. What occurred from 2003 onwards, however, was a quite different phenomenon.

Instead of filming ongoing excavations of Great War sites by archaeologists following an established research agenda, several Canadian television companies directly sponsored excavations to an extent beyond the restricted financial resources available to academic and professional archaeology. Television was now actively creating and formulating archaeological projects, driven by time, finances, broadcasting schedules, and the potential for dramatic and telegenic on-screen discoveries. The Canadian companies planned not single programmes but short series of episodes involving professional and volunteer archaeologists digging at a variety of sites along the northern sector of the Western Front.

One episode in the series entitled *Finding the Fallen* (YAP Films 2005) was called *Passchendaele 1917: Drowning in Mud*. It epitomised an approach that was, at least in part, an updated televisual version of the books of soldiers' personal accounts published by Lyn Macdonald during the 1980s and 1990s (e.g. 1993a, 1993b), albeit focused on archaeological discoveries, and drawing strong connections between human beings, landscape and objects.

Publicity card for the Yap Films series *Finding the Fallen*, first transmitted in 2005, and again as *Battlefield Detectives* in 2006. *(Courtesy and © Yap Films)*

The episode built a profile of a soldier, identified as Second Lieutenant John Humphrey England, 14th Battalion, Welsh Regiment, who lived in south Wales, and died in the Ypres Salient aged 20. The reconstructed early life of John England and the discovery of a wristwatch (which it was suggested may have belonged to him) were intercut with accounts of the dreadful weather the soldiers endured, and the tracking down of a great-nephew, Richard England. The programme's narrative wove these different aspects together to make strong and meaningful human connections for its audience, illustrating the potential of this new kind of television archaeology to enlighten and educate, as well as to entertain (see Clack 2006: 91–2).

The professional archaeologists and military historians involved in these and other programmes were understandably grateful for the opportunity to conduct well-funded research that would otherwise have been impossible. Nevertheless, contracts had to be signed that stipulated an embargo on publishing results until the programmes had been broadcast, and lines of responsibility for such publications remain unclear. Meanwhile, new programmes are planned, and may well be filmed and broadcast before the results of the earlier series are published. It is clear that fast-moving, television-driven archaeological agendas have already played a significant role in the early stages of this fourth phase of Great War archaeology's development. It remains to be seen whether this is a short-term phenomenon or a long-term trend, and to what extent it strengthens the archaeology of conflict or compromises its integrity.

For almost eighty years, between 1914 and the early 1990s, most professional archaeologists regarded the First World War as too young (and too historically well documented) to be appropriate for archaeological investigation. The Great War's significance was, by and large, seen in terms of the havoc and destruction it had brought to the traditional pre-war archaeological heritage, notably to medieval towns and cities such as Ypres, Arras, Péronne, Rheims and Verdun, as well as more generally to Gallo-Roman and prehistoric remains. By 2003, attitudes were changing rapidly, and layers of war destruction were seen in a new and positive light – as a vast, virtually untouched and uniquely hybrid archaeological level, whose investigation had captured the public imagination, and become a kind of commemorative act in its own right.

France and Belgium had taken different paths on the road to a modern archaeology of the First World War, and each made its own distinctive contribution. What unites them is the fact that the speed of much postwar reconstruction has left innumerable war landscapes intact. Systems of trenches, dugouts, tunnels, craters, weapons and munitions, personal belongings and human remains are often well preserved, and sometimes only just beneath the modern land surface. Yet, while preservation is an advantage, urban development is a growing and constant threat, particularly on the outskirts of major towns and cities. Nowhere along the Western Front is there currently a long-term, professional and fully funded research programme of Great War archaeology.

In order to develop and mature, this archaeology (and eventually the archaeology of all modern conflicts) must draw on the wealth of expertise held not only by archaeologists and anthropologists, but also by military historians, cultural historians and art historians, as well as geographers, geologists, and museum and heritage professionals. Only by combining these varied talents will the archaeology of the First World War achieve a distinctive shape and identity that will permit it to investigate the multifaceted nature and legacy of modern war.

ANTHROPOLOGY AND THE MATERIAL CULTURE OF WAR

The ninety-year-long relationship between archaeology and the First World War – from 1914 until today – forcefully illustrates two points: that all archaeology is 'social archaeology', and that the emerging modern archaeology of the Great War is deeply embedded in anthropological issues concerning memory, identity, race, religion and spirituality, as well as with looting, landscape, treatment of the dead, museums, tourism, art and heritage.

The anthropological dimension of Great War archaeology is also revealed by the fact that Allied armies were international in composition, and thus the archaeological record is multi-ethnic and multi-faith in nature. On the Western Front, the war involved not just British, French, Belgian and German soldiers, but American, Russian, Australian, New Zealand, South African and Canadian troops as well. Furthermore, many non-white, indigenous peoples from all over the world took part, such as African-Americans, African-Caribbean peoples (Howe 2002; Smith 2004), men from African tribal societies, and Native Americans (Barton 1997), Hindus (Omissi 1999), Sikhs (Anon. 1999),

West Indian soldiers stacking shells near Ypres. *(Courtesy and © Imperial War Museum, E 2078)*

Representatives of the Sikh community at the Menin Gate, Ypres. *(Courtesy and © www.greatwar.be)*

Chinese labourers and British soldiers by a battlefield calvary on the Western Front in France in 1919. *(Courtesy and © Imperial War Museum, Q 390)*

Maoris, Vietnamese ('Annamites') and Chinese (Bailey 2000). The involvement of these groups (and of their descendants or representatives) in the war and its aftermath illustrates that Great War archaeology is a complex and many-layered interdisciplinary endeavour, not just a new sub-discipline where scientific techniques are applied to excavating the physical remains of war.

In recent years, the study of the First World War has become increasingly sensitive in responding to changing public attitudes and expectations, as well as to advances in academic scholarship and understanding. It is one of many ironies that, as the generations who had first-hand experience of the war and interwar years are disappearing, so archaeology and anthropology are becoming increasingly interested in the physical remains of the conflict. As history becomes archaeology before our eyes, the boundaries of archaeology are extending – and overlapping, especially with anthropology's renewed interest in material culture and landscape (see Miller 1994 and 1998 for anthropological approaches to material culture).

The anthropological study of material culture is a major influence on archaeology's concern with the objects and physical remains that are excavated from war-related sites. Both disciplines seek to explore the relationships

Representative of Native American peoples at the Canadian Memorial, Sint Juliaan, in the middle of the Ypres Salient on 1 November 2005. *(Courtesy and © www.greatwar.be)*

between people, objects and landscape today, as well as in the past. The material culture of war is not restricted to such obvious wartime items as weaponry and ammunition, uniforms, personal belongings, devastated buildings and defensive structures. It also includes memorabilia, souvenirs, and the architecture and objects produced during the postwar era, from war cemeteries to museums, whole towns to individual monuments. Most of all, perhaps, it includes the battlezone landscapes within which all these features are located.

Landscape, of course, is itself a cultural artefact, tied irrevocably to a sense of identity, and subject to changing attitudes towards war and memory. The increasing number of battlezones that see places in the landscape – virtually 'empty' a few years ago – become the focus of well-attended commemorative events are themselves a natural field of study for both archaeology and anthropology. In developing and defining a modern archaeology of the First World War, it is often these broader anthropological kinds of relationships that embody many important, and often unacknowledged and uninvestigated, issues. The potential and responsibility of archaeology to throw new light on the First World War is illustrated by the sobering thought that

> The human cost of creating First World War battlefield landscapes was described day-by-day, sometimes hour-by-hour, in memoirs and regimental war diaries. This surely produced the most exhaustively documented, intimately personalized, and spiritualized areas ever to be subject to, or considered for, archaeological investigation. (Saunders 2002a: 106)

The anthropological focus on the material culture of the First World War takes us to places that until recently were not the obvious locations to conduct archaeology. We journey into people's homes, to art exhibitions, war cemeteries, war-themed shops and guest houses in France and Belgium, car-boot sales and militaria fairs, re-enactment events and war commemorations, as well as to the battlefields themselves and their museums. All preserve an aspect of the First World War, and its legacy of cherished personal memories, scholarly research and commercial activities. The broad framework of Great War archaeology illustrates the material ways in which the 'war to end all wars' has shaped many subsequent twentieth-century wars, affected people's lives for almost a century, and is itself being constantly reshaped in an ever-changing world.

The anthropological dimension of Great War archaeology embraces many complex issues that hover between archaeology, anthropology, history and politics. Illustrating the variety of such issues are the following:

- An increasing awareness of the battlefields as national and trans-national cultural heritage
- The commercialisation of battlefield regions stimulated by burgeoning tourism
- The creation and rejuvenation of war-related museums and heritage sites in battlefield areas
- The incorporation of places and commemorative events into a widening trend for public war remembrance activities
- The ambiguous survival of large areas saturated with unexploded munitions
- The existence of private collections of war artefacts; a vigorous international trade in such items, and the stimulus this provides to further despoil battlefields
- The development of a methodology specifically tailored to investigate industrialised battlezones.

These are just some of the broader topics that Great War archaeology must address, over and above the excavation of sites and the post-excavation analysis of artefacts. Yet, as archaeology comes to terms with the First World War, it is venturing into a terrain already occupied, to a greater or lesser degree, by many other specialists. Military and cultural historians, art historians, tourism professionals, heritage specialists, museum curators, cultural geographers and geologists have long since laid claim to parts of the war's physical and symbolic legacy. There is no doubt that archaeology is a latecomer to the study of the First World War (and, indeed, to the investigation of all twentieth-century conflicts).

Neverthless, two features of modern archaeology stand out for their ability to justify and integrate archaeology into the wider study of conflict. First, sophisticated forensic techniques developed by anthropologists and archaeologists now have the potential to identify the war dead (military and civilian), and, with the expertise of historians, to reclaim them from lists of 'the missing', to restore their humanity, and to reunite them with their families. From First World War battlefields to the mass graves of Bosnia and Rwanda, and around the world, forensic studies and techniques such as DNA profiling can often identify the victims of conflict in ways that were previously impossible.

Second, archaeology's critical relationship with anthropology through a shared focus on material culture and landscape unites it with the diversity of other specialists who have been studying the First World War ever since (if

A typical war souvenir. A matchbox cover made from scrap metal and engraved with the insignia of the Lancashire Fusiliers, whose badge stands next to it. *(© Author's collection, with thanks to Philipe Oosterlinck)*

not before) the war ended. Illustrating this relationship is the study of what anthropologists have called the 'social life' of objects, where artefacts are not simply identified as a bullet, an artillery shell, a trench or a souvenir, but rather are investigated for their social origins, multiple uses and reuses, and the continuing cultural and personal relevance they possess long after their original purpose has ended.

One example of this approach (explored in depth in Chapter 2) is a war souvenir bought or made by a soldier during the war, and sent home to his wife, sweetheart or family. Whatever it meant for the soldier in the trenches, it became a cherished memory-object for the family, and could have been displayed with pride in the home for decades afterwards, before eventually being sold to a militaria collector by a distant relative for whom it had no obvious personal value. The item could then have been resold (or donated) to a museum where it is seen by countless schoolchildren, and perhaps studied by future generations of scholars. Rather than simply being an artefact of war with one original use, these various episodes, stretching over ninety years, show how a biography of the object begins to unfold.

From an anthropological perspective, each of these episodes can be studied on its own, or with other episodes. For example, what role did the war souvenir play for the family in whose home it resided for thirty years or more? If the soldier who sent it survived the war, then perhaps it was little more than a talking point. If the soldier never returned home, then perhaps it became a poignant memento for the bereaved wife or mother – almost a substitute for the dead husband or son. And at what point did it lose its emotional value, and become a virtually anonymous piece of Grandad's war junk packed away in an attic or garage? Answering these difficult questions amounts to an anthropology or perhaps a social archaeology of the First World War and its material culture in the home, rather than on the battlefield.

The power of seemingly humble artefacts becomes increasingly evident the more they are investigated. Quite apart from their postwar life in somebody's home, similar objects can be dug up by archaeologists or by looters, and can travel by a variety of different routes to a private collection, a museum, or an Internet auction site. If enough interesting items are recovered from the ground

A car-boot sale of miscellaneous and anonymous war memories during the late 1990s. (© Author's collection)

they can become the centrepiece of a new museum exhibition that in turn becomes a 'must-see' stop on a battlefield tour, and at which, on occasion, other battlefield souvenirs (real and fake) are sold. In this way, it can be seen how war artefacts can become caught in a spider's web of war history, war heritage and tourism, and are further entangled with issues about their authenticity and the ethics of collecting and exhibiting them (see Belk 2001). In these situations, an anthropological approach to the study of the material culture of war is arguably the best way to investigate the various different meanings that individual items may possess.

Why do we need an archaeology of the First World War? What can it tell us that we do not already know? These are questions that are heard less often today than even just a few years ago. A cynical answer might be that until recently the First World War was all about military history, collectors of memorabilia, and enthusiasts walking the battlefields, and that these individuals saw no point in scientifically excavating war sites. Professional archaeologists, too, considered that the First World War was far too recent to be investigated.

Attitudes have changed rapidly, however, driven partly by a huge increase in battlefield tourism and its financial incentives, and partly by developments in mainstream archaeology and the influence of anthropology. Great War archaeology is not simply the excavating of battlefields, but a way of connecting with our own recent ancestors, of finding and identifying the fallen, of understanding the war from the individual soldier's (and civilian's) perspective, of making physical (and emotional) contact with the landscapes in which they fought, and with the objects they carried, touched and lost. Great War archaeology connects with an extraordinarily wide range of issues that reach out into many aspects of family history, personal memory and national identity, as well as to the wider cultural worlds of history, art, museums and heritage.

As Great War archaeology matures, it seems likely that it will transform our knowledge and understanding of that conflict, and offer new insights into many later twentieth-century wars. It has the potential to connect in powerful new ways with younger generations of students, scholars and battlefield visitors, and those who are interested in understanding the human cost of creating the modern world in which we live.

CHAPTER 2

Bodies of Metal, Shells of Memory

Modern archaeology is shaped by anthropology, particularly in the investigation of material culture and landscape – two aspects that dominate Great War archaeology, and that are linked by issues of memory, commemoration and imagination. Perhaps no other kind of archaeology is so deeply and poignantly anthropological as Great War archaeology, and the archaeology of twentieth-century conflict more widely. This chapter focuses on the first of these anthropological aspects of Great War archaeology – material culture – and attempts to unlock some of the meanings embedded in war objects, souvenirs, personal belongings, books, films, architecture, museums and memorials.

A distinctive feature of Great War archaeology is its focus on the living aspects of material culture, appropriately for a war that produced and left behind more artefacts (from landscapes to bullets) than any other conflict in history. Unlike other kinds of archaeology, a unique aspect of this new kind of investigation is that objects dug up on battlefields can be identical to others kept in a museum for eighty years, displayed on a living-room mantelpiece as a family heirloom, or traded on the vigorous international market for war memorabilia at militaria fairs (Isyanova 2009) and on the Internet (Fabiansson 2004: 171–2). Few if any other kinds of archaeology are so democratic in the way their artefacts are scattered around the world.

It is clear that the archaeology of the First World War goes beyond the excavation of battlezones. In Chapters 4–6, we shall explore the battlefield dimension, but in order to sensitise ourselves to the unusual nature of the conflict's physical legacy, we must look more closely at the tales that objects can tell. To borrow an evocative phrase from anthropology, we shall explore the 'social world of objects' to consider how seemingly random and unpromising artefacts can open our eyes to a different view of the war and its aftermath.

Until recently, most knowledge about and interest in the First World War have been based on the many books published by military historians, or those who adopted a military history approach. These have comprehensively documented the main events of the war, pored over tactics and strategy, and put into context the global nature of the conflict. They have made impressive and acute contributions to our understading of the conduct and consequences of the war (e.g. Ferguson 1998; Gilbert 1994; Keegan 1991; Sheffield 2002; Strachan 2003; Terraine 1992). Mainly during the last decade, cultural historians have added a unique depth and breadth of knowledge and perceptive insight in work which has transcended the boundaries of their discipline and become of central interest and value to other investigators (Audoin-Rouzeau and Becker 2002; Becker 1998; Bourke 1996; Das 2005; Eksteins 1990; Fussell 1977; Leeds 1979; Mosse 1990; Winter 1995).

Given this weight of scholarship, it is hardly surprising that, until the late 1990s, virtually all radio and television coverage of the war was historical, not archaeological or anthropological. The military history (and to a lesser extent the cultural history) approach to the First World War had become a tradition – the only way to investigate and understand this most tragic and iconic of wars. The extraordinary remains that lay beneath the Western Front's battlefields, and the equally insightful stories that were sealed within the material culture of war, were, for the most part, ignored, unsuspected or simply not recognised.

Today, as the old soldiers and their immediate families have all but passed away, not only does history become archaeology, but we enter a new realm, a world where memories and experiences of war are locked up in objects that are investigated and interpreted by those who had no part in their production or original wartime purpose. One consequence of this is that archaeologists and others often ponder on the use of items that were commonplace to the soldiers of the trenches less than a century ago. In other words, we have entered a world of objects – items that military specialists may be able to identify, but that hardly a single living person can relate to the war through their own experience. Before we can understand the new archaeology of war, we must become familiar with some of its artefacts, and attune ourselves to the different voices with which they speak.

War can be seen as the transformation of matter by the processes of damage and destruction. War creates as well as destroys. This point is both obvious and subtle, and offers many opportunities to investigate the ambiguous meanings of the artefacts of conflict and its aftermath. These objects can be small, for example a bullet or an identity disc, medium-sized, such as a tank, aeroplane or bunker, or as large as a trench system or a whole battlefield landscape. All share one thing – they are produced by human beings at war rather than by natural processes. In this way, the Western Front of the Great War of 1914–18 is as much an artefact as a Second World War V2 rocket, Blitz-damaged buildings, war memorials, wartime photographs and diaries, souvenirs and the battlefield tourism phenomenon now under way (Walter 1993). By understanding the material culture of war, we can begin to explore an artefact's social life by investigating the changing values and attitudes attached to it by different people over time.

The objects of war represent memories, ideas and emotions for the people who created them, for those family members or museums who inherited them, and for archaeologists who excavate them. These objects recall the First World War in different ways – they are inescapably real, and can be touched, handled and sometimes smelt. They can transport us back some ninety years in an instant, and in a more personal way than any amount of books about the war that we may read. These objects are three-dimensional memories of the war, fragments of a world long gone, yet from which our modern world is built. Once we begin to appreciate these objects for their true value, we can understand more about ourselves, our families and our history, as well as about the conflict that gave birth to them, for these objects contain part of the lives of their makers and inheritors in different ways than do those from ancient Rome or Egypt. More than any other kind of archaeology, Great War archaeology is the archaeology of us. As we explore these objects, we create a personal and emotional link between the past and the present, but also between our own recent ancestors and ourselves.

We live in a world of objects, and interact every day with countless things that we, and others, make and sell, wear, use and throw away. Each of these objects, however humble or expensive, allows us to relate to (and in a sense create) the world around us. But, as time passes, ideas and fashions change, and the objects that we once cherished are discarded and forgotten, belonging, as they do, to a different time, and the way we were then. Years later, if we stumble across one of these items, we are carried back to our youth, to a different world. The objects once so desirable, then cast off, are suddenly revalued, and can become memory-objects of our lives. If this is true of everyday life, how much more so must it be with the artefacts of war, which carry within them the life and death experiences of countless young men and their families, not just between 1914 and 1918, but for the long aftermath of the twentieth century. The secret life of the material culture of the First World War lies not only in the objects themselves, but also in the experiences of everyone through whose hands they have passed.

It often seems that few items could be as humble as a war-related object, but few things are as powerful in unleashing our emotions, shaping our attitudes, and conjuring images in our imaginations. A roll of rusty barbed wire from

Original barbed-wire entanglements (*chevaux-de-frise*) frame the war memorial at the site of the French town of Vauquois, blasted out of existence by mine warfare in 1916 and 1917. *(© Author's collection)*

a Great War trench, for example, can lead us to investigate the century-long cultural history of what has been called the 'Devil's Rope' (Krell 2002). Equally, the study of wartime silk postcards can lead to the unfolding of intense personal recollections of the war, as well as the social relations involved in their production (Huss 2000; Tomczyszyn 2004). By understanding the material culture of the First World War – whether it has survived in a home or been excavated from a battlefield – we can gain new ways of exploring the meanings of conflict for soldiers and civilians alike, and for all those (including ourselves) who came after.

OBJECTS OF WAR

The objects of war, the artefacts of conflict, come in many shapes and sizes, and all share a fundamental relationship with the people who made, used and discarded them. Many of these items, despite their different purposes, became revalued during the war as souvenirs, obtained by purchase, exchange or opportunism. The First World War was, as many soldiers observed at the time, a 'war of souvenirs'.

> The moment we landed in France we started collecting and giving away souvenirs. For your cap-badge you obtained, perhaps, a little tricolour rose, and for your button a kiss, smile, or a wave of the hand. Then we moved up the line and started collecting sterner stuff; one carried a six-inch shell on one's pack for a week or so, and then discarded it for something a trifle more portable. (Gwinell 1919: 45)

So common was the hunt for souvenirs that the term 'souveneering' became a thinly veiled euphemism for looting. The war experience was so extreme that it had the power to revalue almost any object, from a lump of chalk to a splinter of coloured glass from a stained-glass window, a fragment of shrapnel, live bullets, empty artillery-shell cases, and the military equipment and personal possessions of a dead soldier. Acquiring such items was both lucrative and dangerous: it allowed soldiers to make extra money and permitted those who were not front-line troops to acquire items that suggested they were, and around which many a tall story was spun. Such was the soldiers' passion for collecting the miscellaneous objects of war that 'There were times when No Man's Land on a misty morning resembled nothing so much as Margate sands in August, only instead of happy children building castles there were men digging for [artillery-shell] nose-caps' (Gwinell 1919: 46).

The Australian John (Barney) Hines – the 'Souvenir King'. Hines was branded a barbarian and a price put on his head when Kaiser Wilhelm saw this photograph. *(Courtesy and © Australian War Memorial, Canberra)*

Acquiring these items could be a dangerous and gruesome undertaking. Dead soldiers lay contorted in ghastly death throes, putrefying, and covered in flies or rats, and yet the living were gripped by a strange fascination as they scavenged one corpse after another, seemingly oblivious to the dangers and nauseating sights. Photographs and diaries show just how far men had been changed by war, and how the everyday objects they sought had become worth risking their lives for. The dead lay with pockets turned inside out, stripped of socks and boots, helmets, weapons, wallets and finger rings. Even tunic buttons were cut off and sent home to families as souvenirs. And it was not only the enemy dead who were at risk. One British soldier was wounded by his own side's shellfire, whereupon half a dozen of his comrades fought to retrieve the piece of shell that had wounded him.

Many soldiers survived artillery barrages that rained high-explosive shells on their positions, only to be killed by enemy snipers when they attempted to retrieve shell fragments and others items from No Man's Land. The objects designed to kill them had failed at the first attempt, but succeeded at the second. So commonplace was it for a soldier to be killed or wounded while 'souveneering' that it could be reported almost nonchalantly. One officer who was sniped and killed while looking for souvenirs was described simply as 'a lovely young fellow' (Winter 1979: 62), and of another it was said, 'Napper was found dead, bayoneted in several places; he was a great souvenir hunter' (Dunn 1997 [1938]: 527).

Those wounded soldiers who had been evacuated from the front line to the relative safety of the rear areas were not exempt from these curious and deadly experiences – this new world of objects and meanings. The hospice at Locre near Mount Kemmel in Belgian Flanders had been converted into a wartime orphanage, and was run by nuns. On 17 July 1916, shell shrapnel crashed through the roof of a building onto a bed vacated just minutes before. Nobody was hurt, and in gratitude to God, Mother Claudia allowed soldiers to collect up the shell fragments not as personal souvenirs, but to work them into a flower vase for the chapel (Franky Bostyn, pers. comm.).

Religious feelings also were changed by the war, particularly in the way that Protestant British soldiers felt about that definitively Catholic icon, the crucifix. Newly arrived on the Western Front, British soldiers were sceptical about the crucifix's protective powers. Typical of these initial reactions was the statement by one British soldier that 'What I don't like about this 'ere Bloody Europe is all these Bloody pictures of Jesus Christ an' 'is Relatives, be'ind Bloody bits of glawss' (Rupert Brooke, quoted in Fussell 1977: 118). Yet even hundreds of

A rosary made of ivory by a British soldier on the Somme, and donated to the Basilica at Albert in 1992 by a French family who had acquired it. Note the small Stanhope lens in the cross – held to the light this reveals a miniature photographic image of a battlefield scene. (© Author's collection)

years of proud British Protestantism fell victim to the intensities of modern industrialised war, as soldiers soon began buying crucifixes and amulets from Catholic churches and local shops, and even fashioning them from the bullets they found on the battlefield.

The extent to which war changed the attitudes of these men to these religious objects can be seen from the story of Private John Scollen of 27th Battalion, 4th Tyneside Irish. On 27 June 1916, he wrote a heartbreaking letter to his wife just days before he went into battle on 1 July on the Somme. He entreats his wife to be of good heart and hopes that he can do his duty, and then adds:

Dearest wife Christina, accept this little souvenir of France, a cross made from a French bullet which I enclose for you. . . . GOODBYE GOODBYE and think of me in your prayers.

From your faithful soldier
Husband and father
John Scollen B Coy 27th SB NF
Goodbye my loved ones DON'T cry
I made the cross myself

(James Brazier, pers. comm.)

John Scollen died on the first day of the battle of the Somme. He evidently regarded his bullet-crucifix as an eloquent testament to his experiences, emotions, and perhaps also to a sense of impending death. This little object had lost its purely Catholic overtones and become a simple yet powerful and poignant symbol of loss for a soldier, his wife and his children. Because it had been fashioned and last touched by the still-living husband/father, the family's handling of the crucifix would have been a direct and painful connection between the living and the dead. By sending it to his wife, Scollen was giving away an intimate part of himself, an embodiment of the time he had spent making it while thinking about his loved ones.

For British Catholic soldiers, the meanings of such miniature talismanic crosses were even more powerful, as they recalled the imagery of Christ's sacrifice as well as their own suffering. Vincent Sabini of 18th London, 47th Division, went over the top at Messines in Belgium in 1917, and was almost immediately hit in the leg by a German bullet. After the bullet was removed, Sabini made it into a crucifix, which he wore around his neck until his death in 1981, aged 90 (Saunders 2003a: 14–16) For Sabini, this bullet-crucifix was more than a souvenir of war – it represented his survival, and was a constant reminder of the conflict in the permanent limp that he had until death. The German bullet had become a part of his life.

Vincent Sabini's crucifix made from the German bullet that maimed him on 7 June 1917 at Messines, Belgium. (© *Author's collection*)

Rifleman Vincent Sabini with his walking stick. *(Courtesy and © Tony Spagnoly)*

Equally remarkable was the fact that the crucifix was inherited and worn by his nephew Tony Spagnoly, a First World War historian and battlefield tour guide. Spagnoly would stand with his group on the spot of his uncle's wounding, recount the story, and show the crucifix in an act that often produced an emotional response from the tour group. Here we can plainly see how a single bullet (one of millions) was transformed into a crucifix, moved through time and space, and affected generations of people for the best part of a century. The crucifixes belonging to John Scollen and Vincent Sabini were small and commonplace objects of war, but they are packed with meaning and emotion for the two soldiers who made them and the families who inherited them.

The intensity of the war affected civilians as well as soldiers in strange ways, by changing their relationships with the objects of war. As early as 1914, *The War Illustrated* magazine published photographs showing Belgian civilians searching for German bullets in the long grass of late summer. The caption included the prophetic comment that

Souvenir hunting has become quite an industry where the fire of battle has raged, and it is certain that the traffic in war souvenirs will flourish in the years to come when battlefields are the haunt of summer tourists. (Quoted in Lloyd 1994: 30)

These examples illustrate the way in which the First World War redefined the relationships between men and women and the objects of war. Yet these items were not just souvenirs, talismans and memory objects: many of them belonged to a much wider category of war-related objects – a phenomenon known as trench art.

Trench art

The war affected the relationships between people and apparently mundane items in a host of ways. This is an important point for archaeologists to consider when they excavate battlefields, and encounter seemingly meaningless objects among the debris of industrialised war. Epitomising the strange transformations that war artefacts underwent are items known as trench art, three-dimensional objects made by soldiers, prisoners of war and civilians from the scrap of war, or from ordinary materials – such as embroidery, carved wood, and stone – made under the duress of conflict.

Trench art is an evocative but misleading name applied to a dazzling array of artefacts, for which there are as many definitions and alternative terms as there are collectors and museum curators. One useful way of defining trench art is that it is 'any item made by soldiers, prisoners of war and civilians, from war materiel, or any other material, as long as the object and its maker are associated in time and/or in space with armed conflict or its consequences'. While trench art takes its name from the First World War, it is in fact more a concept than a collection of objects, and examples exist from many pre-1914 conflicts and later twentieth-century wars.

Trench art of the First World War and its aftermath includes obvious instances of items made from recycled war materiel such as artillery-shell cases, detonators, bullets, grenades, shrapnel, ship and aircraft parts, as well as a host of miscellaneous scrap. These items were fashioned into a variety of objects, such as matchbox covers, bullet–pens, inkwells and writing sets, cigarette-lighters, ashtrays, identity tags, letter-openers and crucifixes, and are often best preserved in extraordinary private collections (e.g. Warin 2001, 2005). The most famous and frequently encountered kind of trench art is that made from the definitive and iconic weapon of the First World War – the artillery shell (Saunders 2002c). Once the shell had been fired, the empty shell case could be picked up and transformed, more or less artistically, into a piece of trench art, either as a personal memento or, more likely, as an item to be sold or exchanged. Trench art also includes commercially made metal items that have been personalised with a name, service number, and sometimes the battlezone location where it was made. Personalised items include cigarette cases, weapons, writing materials and painted helmets.

Apart from metal, there are objects made from beads, embroidered and painted cloth, and innumerable items of carved wood, bone, stone, and such unlikely materials as army-issue biscuits (used as photograph frames). In the chalk and limestone country of the Somme and Champagne, large-scale images were produced in vast underground tunnel systems and galleries mainly by Allied soldiers. These range from simple pencil sketches of men and women to elaborate painted carvings of army insignia, patriotic (French) images of the Cockerel and Marianne, various animals, and even complete subterranean religious altars used by the Catholic French infantry before going over the top. Each of these different kinds of artefact is a trace of humanity, saying something about the person who made it, and those who bought it, inherited it or came into contact with it.

Trench-art objects could embody experiences of war that are not obvious at first glance today. For some soldiers, trench-art items could be amulets – symbols of divine protection, or of luck and relief at having survived life-and-death struggles. Some objects were sent home to sweethearts and families almost as trophies of the war, while other were made as a medium of exchange, to earn money or gain favours. Refugees who made trench art for sale to the soldiers during the war were understandably motivated by the terrible circumstances in which they found themselves. Far from being the anonymous junk of war, trench art is revealed as a rich source of information and insight into how individuals coped with their very different experiences of the war. Trench art could evoke feelings of love, hate, fear, grief and boredom, as well as display extraordinary inventiveness, and be motivated by profit.

The stories and insights that trench-art objects contain cannot be gained simply by looking at the mass of objects that were produced. Millions of items all speaking at once confuse and disorientate the archaeologist and anthropologist alike. It is only through a classification of these endlessly varied artefacts that their information can be unlocked, a process which simultaneously transforms them from the 'junk of war' into meaningful items that throw light on the relationships between people and objects during and after the conflict.

It is possible to identify different categories of trench art, each with its own features and associations, and sometimes also with a string of extraordinary stories attached. Trench art is best understood not by being organised by shape and function – i.e. all artillery-shell 'vases', or all bullet–pens – but rather by who made what, when, where and why. In this way, we can identify different types, date them, describe their processes of manufacture, track them as they move from the battlefield to the home or museum, and sometimes identify those who created them or for whom they were made.

The metal matchbox cover illustrates this point. They were made by front-line soldiers, auxiliary personnel in (safer) rear areas, prisoners of war, internees and civilians both during and after the conflict. All examples served to protect the matchbox, and thus appear the same. Yet the item meant different things (and had different values) according to who made it and where it was made. A soldier might create one simply to protect his own matches, a prisoner of war could be motivated by the desire to exchange one for food from his guards, and a refugee would be mainly interested in the money made by selling it to others. We soon realise how powerful these items were, and often remain. A war orphan would regard 'Daddy's shell' in quite a different way than would a surviving soldier, a war widow, or the returning refugees who made them in vast quantities along the old Western Front and elsewhere after 1918. The brief overview that follows of how trench art can be organised into categories shows how these objects can reveal their human, spiritual and cultural meanings and associations.

Category 1: Soldiers, 1914–30

Trench art made by soldiers in the front line, behind the lines, in prisoner-of-war camps or recuperating in hospitals displays the greatest variety of shape, size and decoration. Because of the many different situations in which soldiers found themselves, this category is sub-divided into 1a, 1b, 1c and 1d. Generally speaking, this category contains such items as cigarette-lighters made from

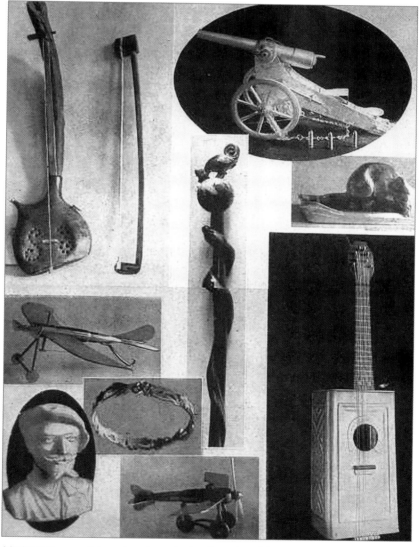

Various items of trench art made by French soldiers and displayed in Paris during the war. (© *Author's collection*)

bullets, matchbox covers commonly made from brass or steel scrap and often simply inscribed and decorated, ashtrays (made from cut-down artillery shells), letter-openers made from bullets and scrap metal, pens/pencils made from defused bullets and cartridges, artillery-shell cases that were simply decorated near the front lines or more elaborately shaped and decorated by service personnel behind the lines, finger rings made mainly from aluminium, steel or brass, lockets and brooches made from scrap metal and sometimes incorporating defused bullets or cartridges, bracelets and wristbands often made from the ridged copper drivebands of artillery shells, miniature tanks and aeroplanes made from scrap metals, military caps made from the base of a brass shell case, walking sticks and photograph frames, ships made from wood, carved pieces of bone, stone and chalk, beaded items, and embroidered postcards and handkerchiefs and painted textiles.

Items made by soldiers on active service between 1914 and 1918 (sub-category 1a) reflected the harsh conditions of the war. A favourite was the finger ring made by French and Belgian soldiers in the trenches, and fashioned from the aluminium fuses taken from incoming German shells or crashed Zeppelin airships. These were melted down and poured into a mould, engraved and polished, and then sold or bartered to other soldiers or sent home to loved ones.

Aluminium trench-art ring just before it is separated from its German fuse. (© *Author's collection*)

French soldiers making artillery-shell case flower vases. (© *Author's collection*)

Other soldiers, including the British, also in the front line, made and decorated trench-art 'vases' from artillery-shell cases. One example was made by a British soldier who purchased a paper template from a Belgian for five cigarettes and then transferred the design to a shell with a bent nail. In this way he decorated two British 18-pounder shell cases with art nouveau style female figures and flowers, inscribing one 'Souvenir of Loos', the other 'Souvenir of Ypres'. When he returned home, he polished and lacquered them, keeping both on his mantelpiece for sixty years.

An unusually well-documented example was made by Sapper Stanley Pearl of the Australian 5th Field Company Engineers, and which he called a 'Chrysanthemum Vase'. This object was a virtual three-dimensional record of some of his wartime and early Armistice-period experiences. It was, he recalled,

Made at Thy-le-Cateau from a French 75-mm shell-case and embellished with the Royal Artillery badge and a French artillery button. The shell-case was souvenired from a French battery south of Villers-Bretonneux, while the handles are 1-inch copper steampipes split down and flattened out. The latter

French soldiers removing the copper driveband from an artillery shell. (© *Author's collection*)

were purloined from a German locomotive which formed part of the Armistice indemnity and were removed at night with a hacksaw in spite of a guard. (AWM 14161)

Such battlezone activities were not, of course, without their dangers, as the German stormtrooper Ernst Jünger observed: 'Even when the men were only chipping off the copper rings from the shells to work them into paperknives or bracelets, there were incidents' (Jünger 2003: 61). These incidents were sometimes fatal, as the wartime diary of Achiel Van Walleghem recalled:

On the farm of Cyriel Lammerant, a terrible accident has happened. Three Belgian soldiers . . . were working on a fusée [shell fuse], which they wanted to open *to sculpture the aluminium*. Unfortunately, there was still powder in [it], and while they were busy, there was at once a terrible explosion. The adjutant lost his fingers and was much injured in his face, the arm of the chief lay open in three places and the soldier was horribly injured in chest and belly. All three were transported to Poperinge hospital, where the soldier died the other day. (Van Walleghem 1965: 70–1. Translated by F. Bostyn, adapted by N.J. Saunders)

In the safer areas behind the front lines, the Royal Engineers and Belgian metalsmiths who had joined the Belgian army in 1914 made more elaborate pieces, such as shaped and fluted shell-case vases, officers' swagger sticks artfully made from bullet cartridges fitted one inside another, and miniature biplanes produced from bullet cartridges and metal scrap. Many items were made 'on spec' while others were made to order, sometimes engraved with a man's name, service number, regiment, and a date or place name.

Prisoners of war also made trench art between 1914 and 1919, when they were released (sub-category 1b). These items, however, were not produced in life-and-death circumstances, and tended to be made partly to alleviate boredom, but mainly to earn extra money, food and favours from their guards. In prisoner-of-war camps, trench-art objects were made primarily of wood, bone and textiles. Battlefield debris was usually not available, though bully-beef tins sometimes substituted for the metals of war. With different raw materials, and under different circumstances, prisoner-of-war trench art had quite different meanings than those items made by soldiers still engaged in fighting.

Apart from carved-wood items such as cigarette boxes, prisoners of war made a range of objects depending on their nationality and where they were imprisoned. Turkish prisoners, for example, made striking 'beadwork snakes', sometimes with lettering picked out in black beads reading 'Turkish Prisoner 1915'. German prisoners, by contrast, made letter-openers and matchbox covers, engraved with the names and places of their imprisonment.

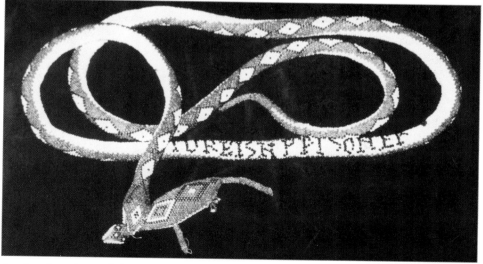

Beadwork snake made by a Turkish prisoner of war. (© *Author's collection*)

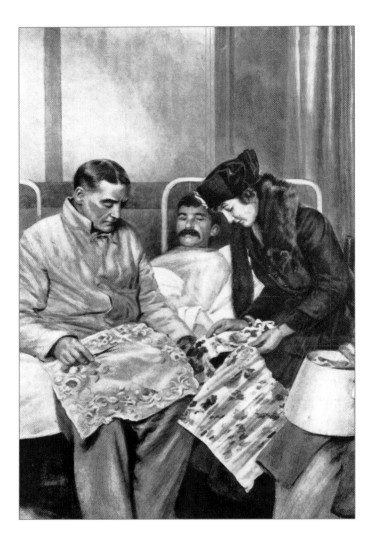

Wounded soldier
making embroidery
as part of his
recuperation.
(© Author's collection)

Another kind of trench art (sub-category 1c) was made by the wounded and maimed. Doctors sometimes arranged for recuperating soldiers to make objects as part of their physical or psychological recuperation (Reznick 2005; Saunders 2003b: 114). Depending on their injuries, the wounded made wooden picture frames and boxes, or a variety of embroideries and textiles, of which the most striking (though somewhat sentimental to modern eyes) was the embroidered heart-shaped cushion.

The final kind of soldier trench art (sub-category 1d) was made by new recruits who, too young to fight during the war, joined up after 1918 and were part of the Allied forces that occupied the German Rhineland between 1918 and 1930. Metal objects and wooden carvings were made during this time, and painted wooden plaques were a favourite, sometimes having a dated inscription, such as 'Souvenir from Germany, December 1918–20'. These items of course were only ever souvenirs of routine military activities in a foreign land, rather than of fighting.

Category 2: Civilians, 1914–39

The wide range of mainly wartime trench art made by soldiers had a parallel in items made by civilians, although the meanings and associations were usually quite different. The First World War had a devastating effect on civilian life, through deprivation, starvation and the destruction of towns, farms and homes. Yet the conditions and debris of war also produced a thriving civilian industry in trench art and general war memorabilia, which lasted for twenty-five years from 1914 to 1939, and which forms the basis of many private collections to this day (although such artefacts are not always recognised as made by civilians).

As with category 1, category 2 can be also be sub-divided (2a, 2b and 2c). The differences between sub-categories 2a and 2b are important and poignant, yet difficult to pin down. In both cases, almost identical items could be made by the same individuals, working the same raw materials, and with the same tools and techniques. Except where an object was dated, or had an inscription which indicated that the war was over, the difference between the two sub-categories was not in their materials or shapes, but in the changing circumstances of their production and use associated with the shift from war to peace.

Sub-category 2a items were sold mainly to soldiers during the war, whereas 2b objects were sold to war widows, pilgrims and battlefield tourists between 1919 and 1939 (see next section). Sub-category 2c items were made by civilians who were living in the enemy's country when war broke out, and were imprisoned in internee camps. This range of situations gave diverse meanings to these objects of war.

Many examples of civilian trench art can only be distinguished from soldier-made types by their dates and inscriptions. Artillery-shell vases, bullet–pens, letter-openers, metal crucifixes, wooden carvings and textiles made by civilians during the war can appear identical to those made by wartime soldiers, or civilians after the war. The easiest examples to identify are those made after 1918, and that carry such inscriptions as 'Souvenir of the Great War 1914–1918', or an artistic image of a postwar battlefield memorial. While the war lasted only four years, and produced a large amount

Civilians selling souvenirs to British soldiers on the Western Front during the war. *(Courtesy and © Imperial War Museum, HU 74884)*

of trench art, the interwar period was twenty years long, and so it is not surprising that the greatest quantity of surviving trench art belongs to the peacetime aftermath rather than to the conflict itself. The greatest quantity of apparently war-related objects was the product of civilians in peacetime – an ironic comment on the nature of war and its material legacies.

During the war, civilians made trench-art souvenirs for the captive market comprising the two contending armies (sub-category 2a). French and Belgian civilians found themselves caught on different sides of the front line, but this did not adversely affect their trench-art-making activities. Local embroideries, carved-wood items and metal objects were made and sold to all soldiers irrespective of nationality. In Liège, war widows and the wives of Belgian soldiers made toy guns, miniature bayonets, and trench-art letter-openers with characteristic crescent blades.

After the war, refugees returned home to their devastated villages and farms and continued making trench art between 1919 and 1939 (sub-category 2b). Around the Belgian town of Ypres, up to five unexploded artillery shells could be found in one square metre, and some 5,000 kilograms of shrapnel

Three crescent-bladed souvenir trench-art letter-openers, with bullet handles and inscriptions. (© *Author's collection*)

per hectare. All had to be cleared before resettlement could begin, a process that yielded vast quantities of raw materials for the making of trench-art and associated war souvenirs. Returning refugees scoured the battlefields to collect this scrap as a way of earning money for their families, who sold it on or used it to make trench-art souvenirs for the battlefield pilgrims and tourists who were arriving in ever greater numbers.

Between 1919 and 1939, it was the battlefield visitors who replaced the soldiers as a market for trench-art items. The meanings and associations of such objects

French civilians clearing the battlefields by collecting unfired artillery shells. (© *Author's collection*)

for the makers and the buyers were quite different to those held during the war itself. The hidden cost of sourcing the raw materials was borne by the civilians who sent their children out into the battlefields; some children were injured or never returned. For the purchasers, however, this was an invisible tragedy, and such objects recalled only the memories of their own loved ones who never came back.

Away from the battlefields, civilians trapped in enemy territory in August 1914 were interned in special camps, where, again because of boredom, depression and the desire to make extra money for food, they too would make trench-art objects between 1914 and 1919 (sub-category 2c). These objects were not from the spoils of war and/or weaponry, but they were associated with war, and similarly represented ideas of isolation, captivity, loneliness and alienation for their makers.

The best-documented internee camps were those established on the Isle of Man, where internees (Germans, British citizens with German names, Turks and Austrians) used their time and ingenuity to make inlaid wooden boxes, furniture, and trinkets for barter and sale (Cresswell 1994: 23–7). Most famously, they recycled the bones of animals consumed in the camps to make ashtrays, brooches and countless leg-bone 'vases' carved with art nouveau floral designs – an interesting parallel to the decorated artillery-shell vases made by soldiers and civilians in the battlezones.

Belgian poster of the 1920s,
warning children not to pick up
war objects on the battlefields.
*(Courtesy and © In Flanders
Fields Museum, Ypres, Belgium)*

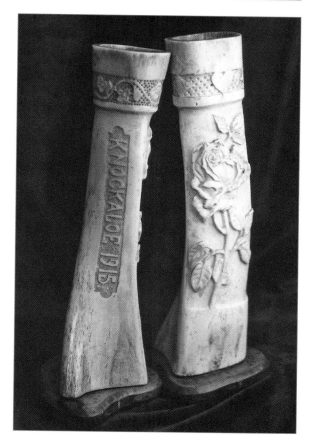

Two ox-bone 'flower vases'
carved by wartime inmates at
the Knockaloe Internment Camp
on the Isle of Man. *(© Author's
collection)*

Category 3: Commercial production, *c.* 1918–*c.* 1939

The great public interest and obsession with Great War memorabilia was not lost on commercial companies in Britain, France, Germany, Austria, Italy and elsewhere. British companies made so-called heraldic china (miniature aeroplanes, tanks and memorials) (Pugh 1972), while the French produced patriotic images (paintings and postcards) as well as trench-art look-alike metal cigarette-lighters, and the Italians created painted ceramics in the shape of artillery shells.

Many category 3 items were made from the raw, unworked and often randomly collected materials of war brought back as souvenirs by returning soldiers, and from available war-surplus materiel. The transformation of these 'found objects' of war into cultural items was undertaken by large and small firms. Some of these, such as the Army and Navy Store in Britain, and Francis Bannerman and Sons in the United States, advertised their services and their ready-made items. They offered to mount a piece of shrapnel or a bullet, adapt an artillery-shell case for use as an electric table lamp, clock or dinner gong, and create cutlery from bullets and shrapnel. Artillery-shell fuses and grenades were made into paperweights and inkwells, and scrap metal into writing sets and cups with elaborate handles. Some of these items were (and still are) called 'mounted war trophies'. Considered together, these commercially made trench-art items are an easily identifiable category, even though they represent an ironic civilising of some of the war's deadliest weapons.

These items tended to tame the experiences of war, to soften harsh memories, and to embody the 'swords into ploughshares' philosophy – a phrase frequently engraved on them. Many, perhaps most, of these items were to be found in homes where the men had survived and simply paid for their mementoes to be made into items suitable for the house. Their associations were quite different from trench-art souvenirs bought by bereaved widows on battlefield tours to the Somme or Belgian Flanders.

At first sight, much trench art can appear crude and uninteresting, and sometimes little more than tasteless kitsch souvenirs. As this brief overview shows, however, it is in fact rich in symbolism and irony, a powerful connection between soldiers and civilians, men and women, and between individuals and industrialised society. Trench-art objects are also a powerful link between the living and the dead in acts of commemoration, and, most recently, have been found in archaeological excavations.

The memory bridge (1919–39)

The power of the artefacts of war was not limited to the conflict itself, or to those who fought in it. As civilian categories of trench art show, such objects had a long, poignant and sometimes painful afterlife for the families affected by the conflict. The war ended with the Armistice signed on 11 November 1918, but it changed the relationships between people and war-related artefacts long after the formal conclusion of hostilities. At a deeper, almost philosophical level, the scale and intensity of a war that pitched millions of frail human beings against industrial quantities of iron, steel and high explosives had highlighted difficult moral and cultural issues. What was civilisation? What was the relationship between technology and humanity? What was art? And what was an artefact?

The First World War defined the twentieth century, transforming technologies, national boundaries, and social, political and cultural attitudes. In many respects, our modern world is an artefact forged in the crucible of the Great War, and, later, modified by the Second World War, and then the cold war (and, currently, the 'war on terror'). One way of tracking and investigating what might be called the social archaeology of Great War objects in peacetime – i.e. between 1919 and 1939 – is what I have called the 'memory bridge' (Saunders 2001b).

The memory bridge is one way of thinking about and understanding the effects of the artefacts of the First World War on those who lived during the interwar years. Great War objects, ideas, experiences and attitudes linked the two world wars during a period of dramatic social, economic and cultural change, forming a bridge composed of material culture, emotion and memory. In the physical and symbolic space spanned by this bridge was a world which not only shaped people's everyday lives, but also their perceptions of the past (i.e. the First World War as the 'war to end all wars') and of a hoped-for future. These views became increasingly ironic as a second conflict loomed in Europe during the 1930s, tarnishing if not corroding the sacrifices made by so many families.

In Britain, the physical nature of the postwar world was everywhere apparent in different kinds of material culture that intentionally or by accident provoked commemorative feelings. The obvious and well-documented objects and attitude-shaping events – such as Sir Edwin Lutyens's Cenotaph in London's Whitehall, the tomb of the Unknown Warrior in Westminster Abbey, and the grand annual Armistice Day events – were restricted mainly to those who lived in or visited the capital. More significant on an everyday basis were other artefacts and occasions that intersected the lives of the wider population.

Perhaps the most obvious, and poignant, physical aspect of everyday life was the absence on the nation's streets of large numbers of young men, together with the inescapable presence of many damaged and impoverished men – the war-maimed. As one observer recalled,

> there was a Mr Jordan who'd lost his right arm, my old man who'd been gassed, and the man at the top of the street who was so badly shell-shocked he couldn't walk without help. And there were lots of one-armed and one-legged old sweats begging in the streets. (Jim Wolveridge, quoted in Bourke 1996: 35)

These men, broken by war, were in a very real sense also the artefacts of conflict.

Such powerful visual reminders of the war were joined by large numbers of widows, single women, fatherless children and incomplete families. Statistically, the numbers of the dead and wounded were perhaps less significant demographically than might at first appear, but nevertheless it was true that many of the social structures of pre-war British society had been greatly altered. It was undeniable that the physical and psychological features of a civilian population reduced by four years of war were an integral part of postwar social realities and interactions. In the interwar years, people were missing from the country's byways, and the war-maimed and war-affected were ever present.

These new social conditions were played out against a changing physical background of architecture and objects that altered perceptions of space and tugged at the emotions. Vivid reminders of the war appeared in many cities, towns and villages in the form of tanks and cannon placed in central locations. Nearby, so-called street shrines were a constant reminder of the conflict. Begun during the war, these shrines associated the Christian cross with ideas of military self-sacrifice and patriotism. Flags, flowers, embroideries, photographs of the king and his generals, and of Tommies smoking in their shirtsleeves were all used in such spontaneous displays. The power of these ephemeral but highly visual examples of material culture to affect people's attitudes and behaviour is seen by the fact that local people made and maintained these shrines, and they were widely held in respect. The shrines were often aimed especially at women, and were seen by the Anglican Church as a way of presenting the idea that the sufferings of citizens in arms were achievements of public significance (King 1998: 55).

Captured German guns on display in the Mall, London. *(Courtesy and © Imperial War Museum, Q 31244)*

Other physical traces of the war in peacetime civilian locations were the 'rolls of honour' that had also first appeared during the war. These were lists of the dead prominently displayed in public places, and could not but be a constant reminder of the human cost of the war. In the years after 1918, villages, towns and cities also erected their own war memorials to act as a focus for the Remembrance Day ceremonies on 11 November. Some memorials were grand and expensive, others of more humble proportions, and many were raised by local public funds as a sign of the community's gratitude for and pride in the sacrifices their men (and they themselves) had made. The issues of design, location, who should be on the organising committees and who should inaugurate (and sometimes pay for) these memorials was often a focus for civic dispute (Black 2004: 135, 137; King 1998: 86–103). Nevertheless, it remains a fact that Britain's urban and rural landscape was reshaped by this process of memorialisation.

War memorials were also closely associated with technology in a more fundamental transformation of the British landscape. In the postwar years, there was an increase in motoring and road construction. This development shaped and perpetuated memories of the war by virtue of the belief that local war

The Royal Artillery Memorial at Hyde Park, London. Designed and sculpted by Charles Sargeant Jagger, it was unveiled in October 1925. (© *Author's collection*)

memorials were expected to be of interest and accessible to the rising number of leisure motorists. This idea is well expressed by the view of Ian Hay that 'every English highway is now one continuous memorial avenue. The cumulative effect upon the traveller's mind is almost unendurable in its poignancy' (quoted in King 1998: 23).

The transformation of public space into miniature commemorative landscapes by the unveiling of war memorials was further advanced by larger architectural projects. These included the founding of memorial hospitals, public halls, libraries, playing fields and, in places such as Stockport, Aberdeen and Hereford, museums that were themselves (or that combined elements of) war memorials (Kavanagh 1994: 155–6). A new kind of institution appeared, the regimental museum, large numbers of which were opened during the interwar years. The most famous of all British museums was the Imperial War Museum, which was opened on 9 June 1920 by King George V and Queen Mary at Crystal Palace in London, and acted as a national focus for the commemorative display of war-related objects (Cornish 2004; Kavanagh 1994: 155–6).

Even places of worship were not immune from the presence of the war's material culture. At the parish church at Burgate in Suffolk was a shrine of trench-art objects made by wounded soldiers in Belgium in 1917. Artillery-shell cases were used as altarpieces, German aluminium had been recycled into several crosses, and a larger cross was fashioned by a local blacksmith after the war from the debris of a crashed 1917 aeroplane that had thoughtfully been brought back to England.

The wartime manufacture of all but the last item was made possible by B. Appleyard, the army chaplain at the casualty clearing station where the wounded men had recuperated. Appleyard scoured the Belgian and French countryside, collecting the waste metals of war from military dumps, and encouraged the men to make the items that became known as the 'Padre's Souvenirs'. After the war, he became rector of Burgate church, where he assembled his trench-art collection around the altar. One of Appleyard's trench-art souvenirs invoked a very personal memory, as it had been damaged by a piece of shrapnel during a German bombing raid on the casualty clearing station's tented encampment. Appleyard observed that if the trench-art shell had not been placed exactly where it was, then the shrapnel would have ended up in his own body (Appleyard 1929).

Postwar street life was changing rapidly, but so was the domestic landscape of the home. During and after the war, soldiers sent and brought home large quantites of battlefield souvenirs with which to decorate their living rooms

The trench-art altar display at St Mary's Church, Burgate, Suffolk.
(*Courtesy and © www.suffolkchurches.co.uk*)

and hallways. Sometimes these were unaltered mementoes of war, such as the rifles, helmets, bullets and lumps of shrapnel that they had somehow acquired. Sometimes, as we have seen, they were more elaborate souvenirs, such as trench-art shell cases, bullet–lighters, carved-wood or carved-bone implements, and a miscellany of embroidered items and scrap metal made into artefacts. These objects, saturated with the memories of conflict, now became an integral part of the world of the home – artefacts of war in the surroundings of peaceful family life (see Allison 1999, Cieraard 1999 and Radley 1994 for anthropological approaches to the study of the home).

The ability of these objects to embody and stimulate memories of the war was not confined to the men and (occasionally) women who brought them back. *Auntie Mabel's War* is an account of a nurse who served with the Scottish Women's Hospital in northern France and the Balkans during the First World War, and who brought back several decorated artillery-shell cases as souvenirs of her experiences. Some sixty years later, her niece, Mrs Turner, was asked about one of the shells – a question that released a memory sealed inside the shell case for over half a century.

'Auntie Mabel's Shell' – a French 75 mm artillery-shell case elaborately decorated in art nouveau style. It was bought by Mabel Jeffrey as a memento of her wartime service as a nurse on the Western Front. *(© Author's collection)*

Yes, that thing by the fireplace with the flowers on it is really a shell case. . . . She brought that back from France for her parents; I thought it was an awfully morbid thing. . . . It got to Granny's house and then it came here. . . . I often look at it and wonder how many men its shell killed. (Wenzel and Cornish 1980: 8)

Great War objects in the home altered physical space, changed the emotional atmosphere, and were constant reminders of absent loved ones. A pair of decorated shells on a mantelpiece, a bullet letter-opener on a desk, or a shell dinner-gong sounded at mealtimes, was an ever-present memory-object, and only a glance away. Sometimes, such items were the only material reminders of the dead, whether sent home by a soldier who was subsequently killed, or bought by a widow on a visit to the battlefields.

The social archaeology of such objects overlaps with the anthropology of the senses in investigating these artefacts. Many of these poignant souvenirs were made of brass, a metal that tarnishes quickly. This led the bereaved wife or mother to develop a routine of cleaning and polishing that may have had a therapeutic effect. The smell of brass polish, the sound of the dinner-gong, and the feel of carved-wood photograph frames or embroidered textiles all produced sensations that added texture to the memories of these war-related objects. The sense of touch evoked a different world – a pre-war life – that heightened the sense of loss in the home. In its own peculiar way, the tragic legacy of the First World War involved a reorientation of the senses for civilians, just as it had (albeit in different circumstances) for soldiers during the war.

In and around the home during the interwar years, a wide variety of items kept alive the memories of the dead. Trench-art souvenirs, war trophies, heraldic china and campaign medals in Britain and its empire were joined by ex-voto paintings (often with a photograph and a man's name) placed in churches and cathedrals in France, thanking saints for their intercession in saving a soldier's life (Becker 1996: 60–1). In Germany, miniature memorial shrines to dead husbands were set up in the home, and across Europe, so-called mourning (or sweetheart) jewellery was worn by many women (Maas and Dietrich 1994).

An integral part of the memory bridge was also what might be called 'background cultural noise' – everyday items such as books, magazines and films about the war. Many now-famous publications, such as Robert Graves's *Goodbye to All That* (1928), Edmund Blunden's *Undertones of War* (1928) and Erich Maria Remarque's *All Quiet on the Western Front* (1929), and films such as *Dawn Patrol* (1930), *Westfront 1918* (1930) and the cinematic version of Remarque's novel (1930) contributed in equally powerful ways to the memory of, and feelings about, the war. Whatever their literary or artistic merit today, these creations were material culture that owed their inspiration to the war, and were available to all who were interested, either to challenge or to reinforce personal views of what the war had been about. They often had a powerful effect on emotions, and could shape attitudes accordingly. In the case of books, they crossed the boundary between public and private domains, existing in bookshops and libraries, from where they moved into the home to be discussed and argued about by family and friends.

A different kind of material memory was that which saw the spirit world take on physical form. For some individuals, the trauma of loss was so deeply felt that they felt drawn to believe that the dead could reappear in this world and visit the living, or, at the very least, speak to their loved ones through a medium during a seance. As Jay Winter has shown, the First World War triggered an avalanche of interest in spiritualism during the 1920s, and reached a peak – in terms of a material culture bridge between worlds – in the 'psychic photographs' of Mrs Ada Emma Deane (Winter 1995: 54, 75–6). These obviously altered images purported to show the faces of the dead hovering above the living at the London Armistice ceremonies during that decade. On such occasions, the individual's willingness to believe in spirits created a need for physical proof in the form of photographs, where the invisible were made visible, and the spirits of the dead lived once again in the material world.

In this chapter, we have explored some of the unexpected and more obvious meanings of war objects, both during the conflict and afterwards. All in their own way are products of the war. Some are similar or identical to artefacts discovered during archaeological excavations of Great War sites, while others only ever existed in the postwar civilian world. Many still survive in museums, private collections, and for sale on the international market in military memorabilia. Each carries a story, a biography of itself as it travelled down through the decades from the war or the interwar years to today, passing through the hands of individuals and generations whose lives it affected in some way. Having opened the door to a different way of looking at the material culture of the First World War, it is time to explore the physical and symbolic places where such objects came from or arrived at – the landscapes of conflict.

CHAPTER 3

Landscapes of Memory

The Western Front is a symbolic landscape for our time, standing in many ways as a metaphor for the defining human activity of the twentieth century – industrialised war. Its old battlefields are arguably the most expensive real estate in the world in terms of their cost in human lives and suffering. The human experiences of these landscapes between 1914 and 1918 were deeply formative, engraving vivid imagery into the minds of those who lived and fought in them. Even today, we still talk of going 'over the top', of being 'in the trenches', suffering shell shock, and being caught in 'No Man's Land'.

In this chapter, we look at these killing fields in an anthropological way, to show and explore the difficult issues and troubling emotions that are raised by their archaeological investigation, and the ways in which they are developing under the pressures of tourism. In the same physical space and at the same time, these battlefields are 'industrialised slaughter houses', vast tombs for 'the missing', places for returning refugees and bitterly argued reconstruction, popular tourist destinations, locations of memorials and pilgrimage, sites for archaeological research and cultural heritage development, and still dangerous places full of unexploded shells and bombs. In other words, Great War landscapes are not single entities, but palimpsests – layer upon layer of different meanings and values – whose archaeological excavation raises deeply problematic and poignant moral issues as well as offering unique perspectives on the war itself.

Archaeologists and anthropologists see landscapes in different ways than do the military historians whose accounts of them have dominated our understanding of the Western Front for the past eight decades. Military history sees battlefield landscapes as places of stasis and attrition, of human misery, tactics, strategy, victory and defeat – an almost empty backdrop to military action. Modern archaeology has a broader perspective that draws on anthropology, geography, art history and other disciplines to analyse and understand landscapes over time, not just during conflict.

This different approach sees the Western Front not just as a series of battlefields, but as a layering of superimposed landscapes, each of which speaks to us with a different voice. Each of these landscapes belongs to a different group of people who regard it, value it and interact with it in often quite different ways. Their experience of being in what they regard as *their* landscape produces a distinctive sense of place and belonging: the soldiers of 1914–18, the returning refugees after the war, bereaved widows, First World War enthusiasts, modern tourists, and archaeologists and cultural heritage professionals all see something different in a landscape that to all intents and purposes appears to be one place.

It is clear that the Western Front is not a series of fossilised battlefields, or 'dead places', but rather an example of what have been called 'socially constructed' landscapes – 'living places', whose development is ongoing, and whose different meanings have affected the lives of untold numbers of people since 1914, and continues to do so today.

The First World War brought cataclysm and chaos to large areas of northern France and Belgium. It banished the idea of a prosperous, mainly pastoral past, and replaced it with a new and momentous reality – total war. There is little doubt of the scale of devastation that took place along the Western Front – a 'zone of death, 500 km long and 10–25 km broad' (Demangeon, quoted in Clout 1996: 3–4), in whose worst-affected areas more than 1,000 shells fell in each square metre. In the area around the French city of Verdun, there were so many unexploded artillery shells that in November 1918 the French government closed off some 16,000,000 acres (Webster 1998: 12–13). It was estimated that some 330,000,000 cubic metres of trenches scarred the French landscape alone, as did some 375,000,000 square metres of barbed wire, with an estimated 794,040 buildings damaged or destroyed (Clout 1996: 46, 49).

The destruction of land and life forged new landscapes infused with new meanings – a reshaping of everyday experience whose memories and associations came into conflict with changed priorities and other realities after 1918. Great War landscapes still provoke fierce arguments, as different groups confront each other and champion their own views of what the battlefields should mean, and how they should be treated. This legacy of the war reveals that the Western Front is neither a single place nor a solely historical entity, but a concept inextricably tied to a kaleidoscope of cultural images. Like Stonehenge, Great Zimbabwe, the Soviet Gulags or Gaza, the Western Front is 'something political, dynamic, and contested, something constantly open to renegotiation' (Bender 1993: 276). For these (and other) reasons, Great War landscapes are arguably some of the most complex places ever to be considered for archaeological investigation.

War-shattered Ypres, a shell of its former medieval glory.
(Courtesy and © In Flanders Fields Museum)

French military artillery-shell dump. *(© Author's collection)*

DESTRUCTION AND CREATION

While the war on the Western Front was dominated by the static nature of opposing trenches, the battlefields themselves were often spiritually troubling and metaphysically unstable places. Once-rich arable land had been 'drenched with hot metal', the earth shattered, and pastoral idylls transformed into lunar landscapes of endless craters, swathed in barbed wire, and populated by devastated buildings and blasted trees. The countryside of Pas-de-Calais, Artois, Picardy and Flanders had been industrialised by force, transformed from rural haven to hellish wasteland. Where pre-war life had been regulated by the primordial rhythms of nature and the medieval peal of innumerable church bells, there was now a terrifyingly new environment of the senses, an

> otherworldly landscape, [where] the bizarre mixture of putrefaction and ammunition, the presence of the dead among the living, literally holding up trench walls from Ypres to Verdun, suggested that the demonic and satanic realms were indeed here on earth. (Winter 1995: 68–9)

Living and fighting in such places, soldiers transformed these landscapes through their own woundings and deaths – experiences and events that, for the survivors, made them into different people. It was ironic and tragic that British and French artillery shells fired in endless barrages at the enemy more often than not served only to churn the ground over which their own men had to advance, making progress a slow and deadly affair, if not impossible. Tactics and technology combined to forge new identities for the soldiers who practised and used them. The many personal accounts of this process of landscape formation are vivid.

> Showers of lead flying about & big big shells its an unearthy [sic] sight to see them drop in amongst human beings. The cries are terrible . . . (Papers of Miss Dorothy Scoles, quoted in Bourke 1996: 76)

When an attack ended, the landscape had been changed as if by giant hammer-blows. Trenches, dugouts, No Man's Land and rear areas were strewn with the detritus of industrialised war – spent shells, cooling shrapnel, smashed tanks, dead horses, lingering gas and unexploded bombs. Interspersed with these were the fragmented remains of the soldiers themselves. Through memoirs, newspaper reports and official accounts, we find a complex layering of language describing such events. The desolation of landscape is described with words such as 'skeleton', 'gaunt' and 'broken', in such a way that the imagery they evoke moves backwards and forwards between landscape, village and human corpse. The result, as the French cultural historian Stéphane Audoin-Rouzeau perceptively saw, was 'a close connection, an osmosis between the death of men, of objects, of places' (Audoin-Rouzeau 1992: 81).

The effects of these bombardments in creating new landscapes at the same time as destroying old ones were vividly captured in Belgian Flanders by Major John Lyne of the 64th Brigade, Royal Field Artillery, who observed

> The conditions are awful, beyond description, . . . a desolate wilderness of water filled with shell craters, . . . Dante would never have condemned lost souls to wander in so terrible a purgatory. Here a shattered wagon, there a gun mired to the muzzle in mud which grips like glue, even the birds and rats have forsaken so unnatural a spot. Mile after mile of the same unending dreariness, landmarks are gone, of whole villages hardly a pile of bricks amongst the mud marks the site. You see it best under a leaden sky with a chill drizzle falling, each hour an eternity, each dragging step a nightmare. How weirdly it recalls some half formed horror of childish nightmare. . . . Surely the God of Battles has deserted a spot where only devils can reign. (Steel and Hart 2000: 269)

The physical and psychological intensities of these experiences produced a different view of the world, if not a new world entirely, for many soldiers. In this universe of mud, trenches, dugouts, deafening artillery bombardments, night raids, choking gas, and blind advances across No Man's Land, it was often impossible to see anything at all, and so sight was replaced by other kinds of sensory experience, such as smell and touch (e.g. Howes 1991: 3–5; Eksteins 1990: 146, 150–1; Classen 2005). Industrialised war had created a new landscape of the senses that was captured time and again in diaries, memoirs and war poetry (e.g. Blunden [1928] 1982; Sassoon [1930] 1997). As one soldier put it, he had quickly to acquire

> An expert knowledge of all the strange sounds and smells of warfare, ignorance of which may mean death . . . My hearing was attuned to every kind of explosion . . . My nostrils were quick to detect a whiff of gas or to diagnose the menace of a corpse disinterred at an interval of months. (Paterson 1997: 239)

In his acclaimed 1917 war novel, *Under Fire*, the French soldier-author Henri Barbusse drew on his own experiences of this new world of the senses in describing an infantry attack: 'There is no whistling through the air. Amid the huge pounding of the guns, one can clearly perceive the extraordinary absence of the noise of bullets around us' (Barbusse 2003: 225). The English war poet Wilfred Owen had a darker experience. After just three weeks in the trenches, he wrote to his mother, 'I have not seen any dead. I have done worse. In the dank air, I have perceived it, and in the darkness, felt' (Wilfred Owen, quoted in Das 2005: 7).

The human body is the way we understand and relate to the world around us, although in normal times it is our eyes that we depend on most. On the battlefields of the First World War, and for the first time in human history, the literal fragmentation of human bodies and the earth (by artillery barrages and machine-gun fire) was on such a vast scale that reality itself was pulverised. The result was a surreal world – a landscape of darkness, sound, touch and smell. As the Great War poet Siegfried Sassoon later wrote in commenting on the poem 'Break of Day in the Trenches' by fellow poet Isaac Rosenberg, 'Sensuous frontline existence is there, hateful and repellent, unforgettable and inescapable' (quoted in Das 2005: 5).

In a world of trenches, dugouts, bomb craters and No Man's Land, where seeing was impossible or lethal, soldiers were often reduced to crawling and slithering, feeling and smelling their way around. In other words, their knowledge of the world came not from sight, but through tactile sensations – the so-called 'haptic' way of knowing the immediate environment. It is perhaps for this reason that soldiers' experiences (and writings) of Great War battlefields were often less concerned with what they could see than with what they could feel – a kind of haptic landscape (Das 2005: 23). Given this, it is hardly surprising that the fear of mud (with its metal splinters, diseases, effluents and fragments of other men) sucking the body down to a suffocating death was one of the most common nightmares suffered by soldiers (*ibid.*: 37).

It was also no surprise that soldiers' experiences of these strange, horrifying and disorienting landscapes led many to reassess their spiritual lives, take solace in their religious beliefs, or perhaps hedge their bets by adopting elements of different faiths (or by denying God altogether). By the intense alchemy of the war, new religious landscapes also came into being, and were, unexpectedly, blended with pagan prehistory and mainstream Christian symbolism.

Across northern France and Belgium, wayside calvaries were a feature of what was, in many respects, still a medieval agricultural landscape. Located at the

Battlefield calvary on the site of Maltz Horn Farm near Guillemont in the middle of the Somme battlefield. *(© Author's collection)*

junctions of roads and tracks, they served as navigational devices and objects of veneration, fixing the landscape at the same time as symbolically acquiring it for the Christian faith. These monumental images of the crucified Christ were revitalised by the war as they resonated increasingly with soldiers who saw themselves as being sacrificed on the battlefields. The wayside calvary now commemorated not only Christ's sacrifice, but the sacrifice through woundings and deaths of countless soldiers as well. Wherever men died, 'that spot must be for ever sacred, for it is a true calvary, and there is again repeated the infinite tragedy of the Cross' (Brittain 1917: xv).

For the French soldiers especially, many of whom had come from a rural peasant background, the Somme battlefields dotted with calvaries sometimes recalled far older historical landscapes. Soldiers from Brittany often came from communities where Neolithic and Bronze Age megaliths had been Christianised during medieval times by having scenes from Christ's Passion engraved on them, as at St Duzec, or had a cross carved on top, such as La Pierre de Lande-Ros (Burl 1985: 42–4). Folklore beliefs still clung to these monuments, in the healing properties of the stone and associated rivers and wells. For men such as these, the experience of war landscapes could be an intensely spiritual affair, a curious and deadly mix of prehistory, medieval Christianity and modernity.

On these ancient landscapes, now transformed into industrialised battlefields, the image of the crucified Christ was reconfigured for the new world of experience. Many of these calvary locations trapped experiences, fixed memories and, with a quasi-spiritual irony, were renamed 'Crucifix Corner' by the soldiers. Captain J.C. Dunn recalled meeting two old school friends for the first time in twenty years at the calvary near Jaulzy in France in 1914 (Dunn 1997: 38–9). Eighteen-year-old B. Neyland was a sapper in the Royal Engineers Wireless section near Arras in 1917, and remembered having to climb a crucifix under enemy fire to attach an aerial (GODA 2001). The Crucifix Corner near Ovillers on the Somme was the place where British troops entered the communication trenches on 1 July 1916 at the start of the battle of the Somme – in retrospect at least a commemorative monument to the sacrifice that so many would make that day.

This unusual kind of landscape endured beyond the war, as, for example, Brittany's prehistoric megaliths were recycled as war memorials after 1918. Their already ambiguous religious nature was enhanced by their new role as commemorative monuments, as at Plozévet, where a menhir (standing stone) was incorporated into a war memorial (Burl 1985: 72). Arguably the most striking example of this is the Breton memorial known as the 'Carrefour de la Rose' near the Belgian town of Boezinge just north of Ypres. On 22 April 1915, the French 45th and 87th Divisions – whose soldiers were ageing Breton reservists – suffered a devastating German gas attack.

After the war, this area became a place of regular pilgrimage for Breton families, and a typically Breton landscape was created by the planting of pine trees, broom and heather, and augmented by an authentic sixteenth-century calvary made of pink granite and decorated with figures of Jesus, Mary and Mary Magdalene brought from the Breton village of Louargat (Baccarne and Steen 1975: 76–81). In front of the calvary, a memorial was built from prehistoric megaliths and an 8,000 kilogram dolmen also transplanted from Brittany. Here was (and remains) a curious mix of prehistoric and medieval

The Breton Memorial, Carrefour de la Rose, at Boezinge, near Ypres, Belgium. The sixteenth-century calvary and prehistoric megaliths were transplanted from Brittany during the 1920s. (© *Author's collection*)

monuments in a geologically and geographically alien region, and a unique intermingling of the most ancient and the most modern landscapes forged by the war and its aftermath (Saunders 2003a: 9–10).

So powerful was the religious impulse under the pressures of war in reshaping these battlefield landscapes that the monumental calvary image revitalised the popularity of the miniature crucifix worn around the neck as a protective amulet. Soldiers observed the apparently miraculous survival of calvaries during the endless barrages, and it occurred to many that these monuments were protected by the sacred image of a crucified Christ. A famous example was Crucifix Corner at the crossroads near Bazentin-le-Grand in the middle of the Somme battlefield, which was named after the metal wayside cross that survived intact and still stands today scarred by shellfire (Middlebrook and Middlebrook 1994: 164).

In the minds of Protestant and Catholic soldiers alike, seeing such things created an imaginary connection of form and belief between landscape and human body through large and small cruciform objects. Many men came to believe that the protection that the calvaries enjoyed could be transferred to themselves if they carried or wore small amulet crosses or crucifixes. The human

Watercolour of a photography and souvenir shop in Ypres during the 1920s by the Belgian artist Octave Grimonprez. (© *Author's collection, and acknowledgement to Patrik Indevuyst*)

experience of battle-torn landscapes and religious belief was never so clearly shown. Large and small examples of crucifixes were made from bullets and scrap metal and sometimes adorned with (commercially made) figures of Christ.

Christ images, as a distinctive kind of trench art, embodied wartime experiences for the soldiers who made and bought them, but similar (if not identical) examples also helped to create feelings of connectedness between battlefield pilgrims and the landscapes of commemoration after the war. Battlefield visitors bought souvenirs of their visit for many reasons: as 'acts of worship' to the deceased's memory, to express solidarity and empathy with local people for whom their loved ones had died, and, above all, perhaps, to become spiritually reunited with the dead through the acquisition of such obviously war-related items.

Bullet-crucifixes, stripped of their wartime protective qualities, now became more elaborate, and were often mounted on tripods of bullet cartridges or circular bases, and sometimes adorned with small memorial plaques decorated with images of postwar memorials, such as the Menin Gate at Ypres, or nearby 'Hill 60'. In other words, they carried miniature landscape scenes – not of the war, but rather of its commemorative aftermath. These objects, embodying aspects of the devastated landscapes from which their raw materials came (and,

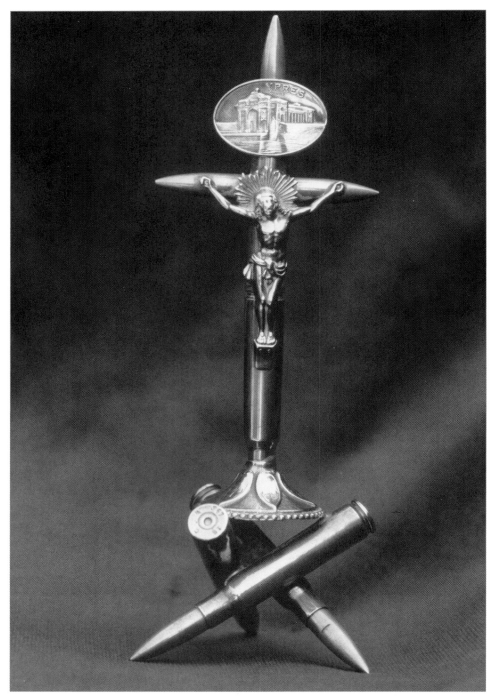

Bullet-crucifix on a tripod of German bullets. The memorial plaque shows the Menin Gate memorial to the missing at Ypres, and dates the piece to 1927 onwards, indicating this was a souvenir for battlefield pilgrims. (© *Author's collection*)

of course, helped create), were, as we have seen, most often destined for a quite different environment – that of the home. As commemorative ornaments they brought the battlefields into the house, where they served not only as souvenirs of a wife's or mother's pilgrimage around the battlefields, but also (and more painfully) became the centre of private attention by embodying the absence of the missing father, brother or son.

For soldiers during the war, and for bereaved battlefield pilgrims during the 1920s and 1930s, crucifixes, calvaries and crosses merged with devastated countryside, broken human bodies and 'the missing' to create an experience of 'being in' a landscape – of simultaneously creating and living 'the commemorative act', and thereby acknowledging the sacrifices made by the living as well as the dead.

In this world dominated by industrialised death, it is not surprising that the 'sense of place' – the mix of geographical and meteorological features, sounds, smells and knowledge of what happened – has taken on a heavy burden of sensibilities for soldiers, pilgrims and modern visitors. It is also no surprise that almost any kind of physical matter associated with such locations – from a piece of earth, stone, or wood, to 'found objects' of battle, and commercially made souvenirs – possesses meanings that are emphasised by the tension between their associations with death and their continued life as memory-evoking objects for the living.

An example of the way in which landscapes of destruction could create new meanings is the Butte de Warlencourt on the Somme battlefield. The butte was an ancient hill some 20 metres high, and was said to have been the burial mound of a Gallic chieftain during Roman times (Charles Carrington, quoted in Davidson 1990: 26). It reportedly played a prominent role during the Franco-Prussian War in 1871 and, by 1916, was already riddled with tunnels before the German troops reinforced it. As the battle of the Somme unfolded, the butte's height enabled it to dominate this sector of the battlefield, and consequently it became a principal objective of British attacks. It saw bitter fighting, and terrible and ultimately futile losses by the attackers as it was never taken and held by the Allies until the German retreat of 1917.

The effect of the Butte de Warlencourt on the minds of its attackers reveals deeply ambiguous, other-wordly sensations that seemed to fuse the physical place and the imagination. Charles Carrington remembered

That ghastly hill, never free from the smoke of bursting shells, became fabulous. It shone white in the night and seemed to leer at you like an ogre in a fairy tale . . . it haunted your dreams. (Quoted in Davidson 1990: 27)

Covered with crosses. The Butte de Warlencourt on the Somme battlefield in September 1917, during the visit of the British minister Sir Edward Carson. Within months, the butte would be recaptured by the Germans. *(Courtesy and © Imperial War Museum, Q.11,633)*

The butte was subsequently covered with memorial crosses, first by the British, then by the Germans when they recaptured it during their March 1918 offensive. The German cross disappeared after August 1918, when the butte was taken for the last time by the British. During the interwar years, this now sacred eminence became the focus of pilgrimages, during which time it was, once again, adorned with memorial crosses by Allied soldiers and the bereaved. In 1944, a German cross was once again placed on its summit, this time by Hitler's invading Wehrmacht soldiers (Coombs 1994: 101). Today, all these crosses have disappeared. Although it was an integral part of the prehistoric and historic patrimony of the Somme (and France), the butte was sold in 1990 to The Western Front Association of the United Kingdom, and now bears their official memorial (Davidson 1990: 18).

The Butte de Warlencourt on the Somme battlefield in May 2006. The photograph shows the low-lying land beyond the butte, and The Western Front Association's memorial. *(© Author's collection)*

The Butte de Warlencourt shows how a single feature of one battlefield landscape can possess many different layers of meaning. Prehistoric aspects were transformed and overlain by layers of industrialised war, and the mound then symbolically acquired, lost, then regained through the appearance, disappearance and reappearance of memorial crosses up to the last decade of the twentieth century, when all these destroyed and rejuvenated pasts were figuratively bundled together, and sold as a 'job lot' to an organisation whose interests were in commemorating – and in a sense recreating – only one of the butte's many different pasts.

Representing landscape

All landscapes are cultural images as well as physical places. Between 1914 and 1918, the landscapes of war were presented to the British public in a variety of ways, from official drawings to paintings, from photographs to films and maps.

Many painters struggled to show what they saw in the traditional pre-war manner of romanticised heroics and pastoral landscapes. Such images stood in stark contrast to the works of others, such as Paul Nash and Wyndham Lewis, who grasped the change in perceptions of reality produced by the war (e.g. Gough 1997: 417–20; Cork 1994).

For Nash, Lewis and others, the war seemed a valueless, formless experience, which could not be represented by the artistic conventions of the day (Hynes 1990: 108; Nash 1998: 29–30). It was as if the Western tradition of landscape art had broken down, and had been replaced by something nearer to the non-Western art of indigenous peoples, where landscape was about memory and experience. 'In a land where Nature was dead, paintings were more like elegies for the death of landscape' (Hynes 1990: 199).

New technologies also contributed different, and often highly contentious, perspectives on battlefield landscapes. Photography, in particular, offered a new world of images, some of which were highly distinctive, such as panoramic views of battlezones (Barton 2005), while others were clearly faked to make a particular point (Decoodt 2002). The ways in which different nations used photographs of war landscapes in their popular presses also differed over time according to the message they wished to convey (Beurier 2004).

Carrying a camera (for those who could afford one) and taking photographs was prohibited by several military authorities, especially the British, who sought to conceal the dreadful scenes of carnage. Even official photographers were constrained by agreeing not to show British dead in exchange for being given access to the battlefield. These restrictions produced a sanitised (and highly unlikely) view of the war – landscapes of terrible destruction peppered with enemy dead but few if any Allied casualties. For the bereaved, the vast numbers of 'the missing' (in battle) were strangely prefigured by even larger numbers of 'the invisible' (in photographs). Civilian knowledge of and ideas about Western Front battlefields consequently bore little resemblance to those of soldiers – a fact that contributed to the (sometimes bitter) alienation felt by many servicemen returning home on leave (see Hynes 1990: 116).

Photography itself developed under the pressures of war. As aircraft became more reliable and stable, so aerial photography became more widespread and useful, producing a highly symbolic vertical perspective. Aerial photographs revealed vital military information, but also produced new and unusual views of landscape. For the first time in history, battlefield images showed clearly the shapes and sizes of natural and man-made features in relation to each other, and the ant-like proportions of human beings themselves. The initial strangeness of

The propaganda landscape. A French postcard from the beginning of the war, showing the Allies of the Triple Entente (France, Britain and Russia) ranged against the Germans. All the technologies of modern war are here, but note Russia represented by an already anachronistic cavalryman. (© Author's collection)

these photographs was reinforced by the fact that the landscapes they revealed often seemed more like images of the moon's surface than of the earth – both kinds appearing as other-worldly, and both equally hostile to human life.

Maps, too, gave competing versions of what battlefield landscapes looked like, and, more importantly, how they should be understood (see Chasseaud 1999, 2002 for an assessment of wartime maps and surveying). While generals calculated seemingly minimal distances of hoped-for advances, soldiers in the front line had a quite different appreciation of the task ahead. The more detailed scale of their trench maps revealed a topography of death measured in feet and yards, an unnerving calibration of the terrible cost of minuscule territorial gains. The same battlefield landscape was represented and understood quite differently on the two different scales of maps.

Apart from being represented on the trench maps that soldiers used, the landscapes of war were also shown on or near the battlefields in a quite different three-dimensional fashion. In a very personal way, the soldiers' (and civilians') experiences of landscapes were captured as artistic decoration on various kinds of trench art, particularly artillery-shell cases. The irony of such objects is clear, as shells were the definitive weapons of industrialised war, destroyed and created the iconic landscapes of the conflict, and inflicted terrible suffering and death on the soldiers themselves. Yet it was these same objects that soldiers engraved, hammered and painted with images of the battlefields. It was as if the essence of a landscape had passed through a man, changing him as it went, and emerged as art on the very object that had wrought such damage to earth and flesh (see Saunders 2004a for the relationship between art and trench art).

These metallic landscapes could be large-scale vistas, famous landmarks or more personal excerpts from life, such as a soldier in a greatcoat standing on guard duty in a trench. Some are almost dreamlike in what they portray, such as wading birds strolling through sand dunes, or springtime rural idylls. Others show the landscapes of war, such as the famous leaning Madonna and child atop the basilica at Albert on the Somme – a well-known sight to thousands of soldiers who passed through the town, and glanced up at the two figures damaged by shellfire.

Before-and-after scenes are also known on pairs of shells, though many have become separated. On one of two Russian shells from the Eastern Front is depicted a peaceful and bucolic farmhouse, while the other shows a destroyed building with a biplane flying above. Both have the identical painted inscription '1917. Osmihowicze. Russl.' (PTA 2002: 172, 0/1, 182, 1/4). Another example, from the Western Front, and perhaps originally one of a pair,

German 77mm artillery-shell case painted with an idealised summer landscape. (© *Author's collection*)

is an unusual enamelled shell case, whose blue-on-white painting portrays a snowy wintertime landscape with a bomb-shattered house, and with a black painted inscription, 'Yser 1914–1918' and signed 'H.J.' (Saunders 2005: colour plate 6).

One particularly illuminating example engraved onto a 1917 British 18-pounder shell case, shows stylised biplanes flying over the French town of St Omer. What is interesting is that the shallowness of the original engraving combined with subsequent polishing has rendered the design difficult to see. Only when the image is traced as a drawing can the scene be appreciated in its entirety (Saunders 2003b: 135).

Roll-out drawing of a wartime landscape, showing biplanes flying over St Omer on the Western Front. The scene was originally engraved on a 1917 British 18-pounder artillery-shell case, but had been polished almost to the point of invisibility. *(Courtesy and © P.A. Stringfellow)*

Artistic depictions of Great War landscapes and their features are not confined to artillery-shell cases. Some are painted on helmets, others etched onto matchbox covers, and some painted or engraved onto wood. German soldiers especially were keen on making wooden plaques from thin cross-sections of tree trunk fringed with their original bark – onto which they drew and painted views of French towns that they had overrun. One such example shows the French town of Montfaucon in 1917 (the town was held by the Germans for virtually the entire war), with the unambiguous 'Frankreich 1917 Montfaucon' as an accompanying inscription.

Soldiers' inventiveness at representing and using the landscape artistically also extended to using objects taken directly from the environment. One

British helmet painted with a scene of the war-torn French town of Péronne on the Somme. *(Courtesy and © Historial de la Grande Guerre)*

example is a miniature model of a trench, just 12.5 centimetres long and 5 centimetres wide, carved out of chalk by a German soldier, Hans Schloß, and inscribed and dated to September 1916. This may well have been a fragment of chalk debris left over from digging a real trench in the chalklands of the Somme or Champagne, and is similar to more common chalk square plaques that were outlined in black paint, adorned with a black-painted Iron Cross, and the inevitable 'Gott mit uns' (God with us) inscription. Small and robust, these chalk items could easily be slipped into a pocket or backpack, and are an eloquent testament to the intimate relationships soldiers had with their

Piece of painted wood bark showing the wartime devastation of Albert on the Somme. Note especially the leaning Madonna of the Basilica damaged by shellfire. (© *Author's collection*)

landscapes and trenches (PTA 2002: 188, figure II/3). Far more fragile were several oak leaves, delicately made into photograph frames by François Gournay, a French soldier, for a Belgian comrade (Saunders and Dendooven 2004: 26).

New landscapes

In the immediate aftermath of the war, Western Front landscapes did not become, as had so many previous battlefields, empty places where once battle had raged. Instead, a new layer of meaning was superimposed on the ravaged land (Saunders 2001a). From 1919, battlezone landscapes were assessed, graded, and, in France, mapped in blue, yellow and red, to designate areas of increasing devastation. The worst-affected areas, the *zones rouges*, had between 80 and 100 per cent of the land destroyed, and were considered too dangerous ever to rebuild or reoccupy. This multi-coloured paper landscape created a new tension between villagers and farmers who wanted to return to their land, and the French government that used the maps to try and stop them (see Starling 1998).

Between 1919 and 1939, the First World War's battlezone landscapes took on a host of new and complex meanings. These were focused on the issues of the ownership of the physical landscape itself, and of the collective memories associated with it after four years of war. In one sense, the question was whose memories of what past should be given precedence now that the war was over.

Oak leaves embroidered into photograph frames by the French soldier François Gournay. (© *Author's collection*)

Should these war-torn landscapes be left as memorials to German aggression and those who had died in them, or should they be rebuilt for their original pre-war owners? In the years following the war, the French farming peasantry repeatedly challenged the official assessments, and their petitions led to ever-downward revisions of the *zones rouges* (Clout 1996: 28–9).

Many examples of the disputed future shape of these landscapes can be found. At the huge Lochnagar Crater at La Boiselle, outside Albert on the Somme, the local farmer's desire to fill in the crater to increase his productivity was opposed by those who preferred to keep it intact as a memorial to all who had fought during the battle of the Somme in 1916 (the crater was one of several blown up by the British in advance of their 1 July attack). The impasse was only resolved in 1978, when the site was bought by an Englishman, after other nearby craters had been filled in, and the landscape of 1 July 1916 looked as if it would disappear for ever. Until recently, the Lochnagar Crater attracted a handful of

Lochnagar Crater, at La Boisselle, resulted from a British mine blown at 7.28 am on 1 July 1916 to begin the Battle of the Somme. It is the largest surviving crater on the Western Front, and attracts thousands to the annual remembrance ceremony held there. Note the poppies in the centre, and the memorialising cross at the crater's edge. *(© Author's collection)*

visitors every 1 July, but today thousands come to pay their respects, and the yawning gap on the Somme has become a 'new' place of remembrance in a landscape that is becoming increasingly memorialised.

Even more bitterly contested were the events surrounding the reconstruction of the medieval Belgian town of Ypres (now Ieper) in the centre of the infamous Ypres Salient battlefield. During the 1920s, the Belgian architect Eugène Dhuicque said, 'leave the ruins as they are. Why should the 13th or 14th centuries be of more value than the four years of the World War?' (Vermeulen 1999: 10). Similar views were expressed by the British military authorities and veterans' associations, who believed the ruins should be holy ground held in memoriam for soldiers who had died in the area (Willson 1920).

Yet the shape of postwar Ypres was not decided by the voices and memories of those soldiers who had lived in, passed through, and fought around the city from 1915 to 1918, nor by those citizens of Ypres who argued that they believed in looking forward rather than backward. 'Instead of modern town-planning there was much pre-war town-scaping . . . [which produced] an ersatsz replica of what was lost forever' (Derez 1997: 450). The debate continues today: 'Ieper is a lie, a missed opportunity. [It could have been] . . . the first modern city of this century, a symbol of regrowth, forgiveness and inventiveness.' Instead, 'people prefer the sheltering past to the present and future' (Vermeulen 1999: 9–10). One consequence of the decision to rebuild Ypres as a facsimile of its glorious medieval self is that today the city has become an astonishingly energetic focus of commercial activities related to the war. For some, it is ironic that, by erasing virtually all traces of the war's destruction, the anachronistic medieval replica that is modern Ypres has become a centre of battlefield tourism.

The interwar years saw the Western Front's landscapes being revalued and added to by many competing interests – returning refugees, government authorities, veterans' associations and visitors. At the same time as arguments raged over what areas should be reconstructed, and how, battlefields were also becoming landscapes of remembrance for tens of thousands of battlefield pilgrims and tourists (Lloyd 1998). Their connections were less with the physical landscape than with a symbolic one full of memories of loved ones – and which they felt they knew through letters, postcards, souvenirs sent home, and (sometimes) home-leave conversations (Huss 2000; Tomczyszyn 2004).

Armed with a copy of the Pickfords or Michelin battlefield guides, whose illustrations portrayed devastated villages and countryside, visitors tramped across the landscape looking for places associated with their fathers, brothers and sons (Eksteins 1994). As they sought to identify their guidebook images in the real world, visitors encountered discrepancies (and suffered disappointments) as Nature and reconstruction began changing the face of the land yet again.

Battlefields were being cleared, villages rebuilt, and new war cemeteries and memorials began to shift the focus of visits away from land and towards architecture. For many pilgrims, there was disappointment, fulfilment and irony in varying measures. The reconstruction that so changed the landscapes of war and disoriented so many was partly funded with money raised by British towns. After sacrificing their menfolk, many British visitors now donated money for rebuilding, and formalised the process by twinning themselves with French towns, such as Birmingham and Albert, and Ipswich and Fricourt. In France and Belgium, the money brought in by battlefield tourism contributed to local economies and strengthened the financial basis of reconstruction, which in turn added another layer to the landscape.

The process of creating a new memorialised layer to these landscapes continued throughout the interwar years, and was only brought to an end by the advent of the Second World War in 1939. This war added its own very different battlefields to parts of the old Western Front that in turn became memorialised after 1945 – a process beyond the scope of this book. During the 1950s and early 1960s, Great War battlefields experienced a low point of public interest, and the Western Front became a virtually forgotten landscape, at least in the minds of British visitors.

Everything changed in 1964, with the commemorations of the fiftieth anniversary of the start of the First World War, and especially with the broadcasting of the BBC's monumental series, *The Great War*. The screening of this epic brought the 1914–18 conflict into countless homes, newly equipped with a television set – and, appropriately, in black and white. Public awareness of the events of the First World War was possibly deeper and more widespread during the mid-1960s than at any time since the war itself. The Great War became, in one sense, the first 'television war', preceding daily news coverage of the Vietnam conflict. The impact was immediate. The First World War was rebranded as 'cultural memory', and television images stimulated the public's desire to visit the battlefields and memorials of the Western Front. A new landscape of battlefield tourism and itineraries was about to be born.

At the beginning of the 1970s, around 50,000 visitors per year were travelling to the Western Front, and by 1974 this had increased to 250,000 (Lloyd 1994: 289). This interest was paralleled by increases in personal enquiries to the Commonwealth War Graves Commission (CWGC) concerning the whereabouts of the graves of family members who had died in the war. During the mid-1960s, the CWGC received about 1,500 enquiries per year, but by 1980 this had risen to 8,000 per year, and to an astonishing 28,000 per year in 1990 (Walter 1993: 63). The number of battlefield visitors grew steadily during the 1990s, inevitably changing the physical landscape, and creating new tourist places where battlefield features were preserved, reconstructed (and sometimes created) and included in visitors' itineraries (Iles 2008).

To cater for the rising tide of tourists, new tour companies appeared, especially from the mid-1990s onward, and larger companies began to include battlefield tours in their brochures. Visitor numbers swelled again with the inclusion of the First World War in the national curriculum of British schools. Each and every tour needed an itinerary – a selection of sites to visit – and these in one sense became their own landscapes of the war, created less by what was historically important to see than by what was commercially possible to visit by coach in a limited time. In other words, battlefield tour itineraries are landscapes within landscapes – a time-sensitive schedule that typically includes 'preserved battlefields', impressive or newly erected memorials, café-museums, a token CWGC cemetery, and the major museum of the area – the In Flanders Fields museum at Ypres, and L'Historial de la Grande Guerre at Péronne on the Somme.

As the twenty-first century began, the 'Western Front Experience' on the Somme became part of an integrated tourist circuit as conceived and promoted by the official tourist office at Amiens, and Great War battlefields became 'of a piece' with the nearby attractions of Euro-Disney, Parc Astérix and the archaeological theme park at Samara (Dieudonné 1999). At Ypres, in Belgian Flanders, a similar integration of Great War sites with other local attractions has developed.

What we see here, and what is continuing apace today, is the ongoing creation of new layers of landscape and meaning. The physical and symbolic landscapes of 1914–18, and the social worlds of those who lived through the war, have been, and are still being integrated within an ever-changing economic reality. New kinds of tourists now visit the Western Front. In their efforts to peel back the layers of landscape that have accumulated since 1914, they struggle to imagine the verdant woods and fields as monochrome images of the Hell that guidebooks and television tell them were here – exactly where they are standing – but that are now almost invisible.

The Western Front has become a symbolic landscape of remembrance, a place where personal and cultural identities are constantly being explored and created (Tilley 1994: 15, 26), not least by personal experiences of simply walking the ground (O'Shea 1998). Yet here, despite the numbers of visitors, and the commercialisation, the landscape is still dominated by 'the missing', both as a spiritual presence, and in the huge memorials such as Thiepval on the Somme (where more than 100,000 men of both sides remain unfound), Tyne Cot near Passchendaele, and the Menin Gate at Ypres (Dendooven 2001).

The battlefield landscapes of the First World War are different from all previous places of conflict in another important way. Until the twentieth century, and the advent of industrialised war, battlefields were physical places, most of whose symbolic dimensions endured only as long as the memories of individuals involved (and those of their families) allowed. These battlefields did not on their own create new associations, nor did they have the capacity to kill and maim once the battle was finished. From Megiddo (Armageddon) to Canae, Agincourt to Waterloo, such landscapes were deadly only to those who were present at the battle itself.

This atmospheric image shows sunlight breaking through storm clouds and shining on the small CWGC cemetery known as Track X, adjacent to the Cross Roads archaeological site, near Wieltje in the Ypres Salient. (© *Author's collection*)

The First World War changed this for ever. Battlefield landscapes were now 'live' and proactive because of the vast quantities of unexploded ordnance left in the ground. These landscapes could now kill and maim indiscriminately, long after conflict had been resolved, and long after the original protagonists had passed away and direct memory of events had faded.

Today, unexploded ordnance is a defining feature of the Western Front. More than 28,000,000 artillery shells, bombs and grenades from both world wars have been collected in France alone. In 1991, a total of 36 French farmers were killed when their machinery hit unexploded shells, and between 1946 and 1994, 630 French bomb disposal experts died during attempts to retrieve and defuse ordnance (Webster 1998: 28–9).

During the late 1990s, the Somme yielded an average of 90 tonnes of dangerously volatile munitions a year – the so-called 'iron harvest' – and throughout France some 900 tonnes of shells, of which 30 tonnes are toxic, are recovered annually (*ibid.*: 24). Until recently, at Le Crotoy on northern France's Opal Coast, unexploded ordnance was buried in the sand at low tide and exploded at high tide at the rate of 6 tonnes per day, 5 days per week,

The Thiepval memorial to the missing on the Somme. *(© Author's collection)*

The Menin Gate memorial to the missing, at Ypres. *(© Author's collection)*

for 1 week per month (*ibid.*: 56). In Belgium, around Ypres, up to 250,000 kilograms of such materials can be recovered in a year – disposed of by the Belgian army in two or three controlled explosions a day (Lt. Col. L. Deprez-Wouts, pers. comm.; Derez 1997: 443).

The presence of such volatile munitions has in turn given rise to two other kinds of Great War-related landscapes, both of which have restricted public access. The first contains the *villages détruits* (destroyed villages) such as Louvemont near Verdun, and the remains of five villages that lie within the French army training area of Camp de Suippes in Champagne (Fair 1998). Accessible only with special permission, these are truly fossilised landscapes that preserve the untouched ruins of the war, with very few added layers that are so characteristic of the Western Front battlefields in general.

The second kind of landscape includes places that exhibit a strange arrangement of death and leisure. In the midst of some prohibited regions are areas that have been cleared of unexploded ordnance and that now have signs announcing their suitability for picnicking. Mount Kemmel, near Ypres, was devastated by German bombardment in April 1918. Today it is a popular weekend leisure spot. Belgian and French families picnic and walk along narrow paths on its forested slopes separated by flimsy wire fences from thousands of volatile unexploded shells and bombs lying just inches away. After eighty-eight years, as the French bomb disposal expert Remy Deleuze says, 'Any dreams France [or Belgium] has of feeling completely safe from the First War . . . are exactly that: dreams' (quoted in Webster 1994: 30).

It is clear from this that a Great War battlefield landscape is a complex artefact, and not simply the physical remains of a terrible conflict between 1914 and 1918. It is into this kind of landscape, with all its personal, political, cultural, physical and symbolic layerings, that archaeologists have recently begun to dig. It is hardly surprising that archaeological excavations of such landscapes is a difficult, dangerous and emotional undertaking that can have unexpected consequences almost unknown to traditional archaeology. As we have seen in Chapter 1, these landscapes are sensitive places, and the digging activities of looters, enthusiastic amateurs and professional archaeologists are all entangled in identifying, creating or emphasising 'new' places on the landscape for Great War heritage.

Adding a further complicating layer of meaning to the already overloaded landscapes of war are the linked issues of preservation, conservation, reconstruction and presentation of the battlezones to the public as more (or less) emotionally charged features of cultural heritage. What places should be

The reconstructed trenches at Vimy Ridge north of Arras. *(© Author's collection)*

preserved and conserved, and how? Should archaeologists dig, and, if so, where? To what extent should some landscape features be rebuilt in order to appeal to (and educate) the hundreds of thousands of visitors who annually flock to the Western Front, and who, along with developers, are increasingly threatening the integrity and appearance of the very sites they visit?

These issues affect many places along the old Western Front (and elsewhere), and are particularly serious at popular tourist stops. One such place is Vimy Ridge, north of Arras, where, after the war, the Canadian government purchased 250 acres of battle-scarred landscape, then proceeded to selectively reconstruct it by clearing bombs and shells, grading the land, filling in some trenches and dugouts while cleaning and reconstructing others, and making safe and then opening one (of the many) underground galleries – the Grange Tunnel. Once this had been done, the surface was planted with a variety of trees and shrubs, and the whole area was ready to receive its visitors. The question today is the same as it has been since the 1920s – what is Vimy Ridge? Is it an authentic battlefield landscape? A neatly landscaped site of memory and commemoration? A tomb for 'the missing'? A Great War heritage site? A resource for education and perhaps future archaeological investigation? Perhaps it is all of these, and more.

Another example is Newfoundland Memorial Park at Beaumont-Hamel on the Somme, a 16.5-hectare section of battlefield whose purchase by the Newfoundland government after the war involved negotiations with 250 local French landowners (Gough 2006). The impulse for this purchase was to commemorate the heroic attack by the Royal Newfoundland Regiment between 9.15 a.m. and 9.45 a.m. on 1 July 1916 – a tragic and costly failure that left the regiment with 90 per cent casualties (only 68 of the original 801 officers and men were unwounded). The smashed and cratered land was cordoned off with seedlings and trees, but mainly left as it was in 1918, so that Newfoundlanders and others could walk and pay their respects at the exact spot – the sacred soil itself – where so many had suffered and died. The park was opened by Sir Douglas Haig in 1925.

In 1960, in order to preserve this memorial landscape against the ravages of time, several 1916 trenches relating to the 1 July attack were re-excavated and reconstructed – a process of remodelling that erased (or ignored) traces of two further battles fought over the same land, one by the 51st Highland Division in November 1916, and another in 1918. In other words, despite the importance of this ground to the soldiers who had preceded the Newfoundlanders on 1 July 1916 (the South Wales Borders and the Border Regiment), the later

The preserved trenches and battlefield landscape at Newfoundland Memorial Park, Beaumont-Hamel on the Somme. (© *Author's collection*)

51st Highland Division, and others (including Germans) in 1918, only the landscape of 30 minutes' fighting by the Royal Newfoundland Regiment on 1 July 1916 has been preserved (Gough 2006: 18).

As at the Butte de Warlencourt, only one (very brief) past out of many has been chosen for preservation. As most of the 250,000 annual visitors to the Newfoundland Memorial Park cannot be expected to know these details, and presumably assume that they are witnessing a 'real' battlefield landscape somehow frozen in time – 09.45 on 1 July 1916 – the issues of accuracy and authenticity in Great War heritage become ever more difficult to resolve.

The vastly rising numbers of battlefield tourists increasingly demand new and informative places to visit on the Somme and in Belgian Flanders, and the hotel, café and restaurant infrastructure that goes with this. They desire key locations to visit where they can experience an apparently authentic battleground – trench systems, dugouts, bunkers, and craters – and large and small museums where they can see weapons, uniforms and material culture of war. All of these demands place more pressure on the battlefields and on those whose job it is to investigate and preserve them. Tourism, more than any other factor, drives the creation of new kinds of landscape, adding yet more layers to

A First World War tree, whose battle-scarred stump is decorated with commemorative poppy-crosses. *(© Author's collection)*

The French ossuary and war cemetery at Douaumont, Verdun. The ossuary contains the remains of 130,000 French and German soldiers, and was opened on 7 August 1932. It was a centre of French battlefield pilgrimages during the interwar years. (© *Author's collection*)

the palimpsest, more meanings, and ever more ways for people to experience what, for them, the war represented. In this situation, it is easy to see how there is no longer one single battlefield landscape – but rather as many different kinds as there are different visitors with widely different interests and motivations. Archaeologists must take all these layers of meaning into consideration as they dig into the earth.

The Western Front is a complex series of landscapes, made poignant by the vast quantities of dead it produced (and in large part still conceals), the memories of the bereaved who visited it during the interwar years, and modern tourists and investigators who seek to experience and understand it. These landscapes are not only the remains of war, but are ongoing, ever-changing, and are constantly being rejuvenated and reinvented in the long afterlife of four years of war between 1914 and 1918. They are landscapes of memory as well as of the earth, and so demand a new kind of archaeology.

CHAPTER 4

Bones of the Somme

The Somme is a byword for British tragedy. The 57,000 dead, wounded and missing of 1 July 1916 have come to symbolise incompetent generals and the futility of the war in the public imagination. Military historians continue to debate and revise their assessments of the tactics, strategy and significance of this battle that ended only in November 1916, after five months of terrible suffering and losses on both sides. The human cost was staggering – altogether, 150,000 Commonwealth servicemen lied buried in 400 separate cemeteries (military and civilian) on the Somme, of whom 50,000 remain unidentified. A further 100,000 are still on the battlefields, and are commemorated on six more memorials to the missing (Dyer 1995).

Across the Somme battlefield – below ground and above – are the remains of the landscapes these men knew. Trenches, bunkers, unexploded bombs, bullets and military equipment lie interspersed with countless bodies (more usually their fragments) that rise to the surface every year, as they do along the entire Western Front. They are joined by the remains excavated by professional archaeologists and those uncovered by developers building motorways and industrial estates. This chapter explores the extraordinary and sometimes contentious discoveries made over the past seventeen years, and the distinctive contribution they have all made to Great War archaeology.

As we have seen in Chapter 1, the archaeology of the First World War in France developed along a different course than in Belgium, mainly because the French system of Direction régionale des affaires culturelles (DRAC) required and authorised its archaeologists to investigate and record Great War sites as just another part of France's archaeological heritage. While French archaeologists do not seek out these sites, they have built a unique expertise by virtue of having to investigate (and in some cases developing a particular interest in) them, particularly in northern France, in Nord-Pas-de-Calais, and in and around the city of Arras.

French archaeology's remit to engage with the First World War, reinforced by the legal requirements for conducting excavations, meant that there never developed in France a strong amateur tradition of battlefield digging, as happened in Belgium. In France, there was no obvious gap to be filled in this respect. There may also have been less obvious, perhaps cultural, differences between French and Belgian attitudes towards digging up Great War remains.

Although the boundary between postwar battlefield clearance and looting and opportunist digging (for military memorabilia) is a notoriously grey area for both countries, the French attitude to the land itself (and perhaps the bodies it contains) may partly explain the absence of any quasi-formal associations of battlefield diggers. This attitude, a strong sense of *patrie*, was certainly influenced by the Franco-Prussian war (1870–1) and the German occupation of Alsace-Lorraine (memories of which were still fresh in 1914), and may have contributed in a political and religious sense to notions of the sacredness and inviolability of French soil. Whatever the explanation, Great War archaeology in France involved professionals at one level or another from the beginning.

The only notable (and albeit partial) exceptions to this, and perhaps the nearest French equivalent to the Belgian tradition of organised groups, are the Association Souvenir Bataille de Fromelles (ASBF; see Chapter 1), and the Durand Group. ASBF includes Belgian and French members, and investigates the battlefield that was the small French town of Fromelles, some 12 miles west of Lille, and halfway between the well-known Great War towns of Laventie and La Bassée.

From 1914 to 1918, Fromelles was a town divided, one half occupied by the Germans, the other by the Allies. Between 19 and 20 July 1916, British and Australian forces launched an attack that was supposed to be a diversion from their activities further south on the Somme. The Battle of Fromelles (as it was called) was a disaster for the Allies, who suffered 8,500 casualties in twenty-four hours for no obvious gain.

ASBF works with the town authorities, the local museum staff and French archaeologists, and has several overlapping projects: archaeological excavation, museum displays, and the creation of a document and resource centre on the First World War at Fromelles. Located in the town hall, the museum was opened in 1990, and displays uniforms, military equipment and objects found in local excavations as part of dioramas of trench life. To date, ASBF has excavated a British dugout at Cellar Farm Avenue, a German trench mortar (*Minenwerfer*) position, and a shaft leading to a 1915 Australian tunnel system called Cordonnerie Post.

The Durand Group, by contrast, is composed of expert military and civilian volunteers, and has been investigating underground tunnels, particularly at

Vimy Ridge since 1997. Some of its members specialise in the identification and handling of unexploded munitions, but their work also includes photographic surveying and mapping, and the pioneering of non-destructive geophysical prospection of battlefields. In recent years, they have been involved with ground-penetrating radar investigations of tunnels at the Newfoundland Memorial Park at Beaumont-Hamel, and excavation in advance of building the new visitor centre at Thiepval Memorial to the Missing (Dolamore 2000; Watkins 1998).

THE BEGINNINGS OF ARCHAEOLOGY

In France, as elsewhere, traditional and academic archaeology has not until recently been particularly interested in the physical remains of the First World War. The main issue appears to have been what role archaeology could play in a war that apparently was so well known already from military history – the sole exception being finding, perhaps identifying, and reburying Great War soldiers. The fact that there has, again until recently, been little communication between military historians and archaeologists compounded the problems facing Great War archaeology.

The wind of change first blew across the battlefields of the First World War between 1987 and 1989, when the professional archaeologist Yves Desfossés and his colleagues became involved in archaeological reconnaissance along that part of the TGV rail link that passed through Artois – from the Somme town of Bapaume north to the city of Lille (Desfossés 1999). Preliminary test trenches were dug along this north–south route that followed the British–German front line as it was in 1917. For the first time, these archaeologists were confronted with bullets, artillery shells, grenades, mortars, dugouts, trenches and abandoned war materiel of the First World War. The construction schedule for the TGV was such that it was impossible to investigate the many remains that were identified during this reconnaissance; it was only possible to highlight the problems presented by unexploded bombs and the remains of soldiers.

Ten years later, in 1997, archaeologists were asked to assess the archaeological potential of the A29 motorway on an east–west line between St Quentin and Amiens. Three areas received special attention as they represented different experiences of the war: the area around Villers-Bretonneux, which saw the rapid German advance of spring 1918 (and the equally rapid British response); the area around Vermandovillers and Ablaincourt, which had been a stable French-controlled area between 1915 and July 1916; and the area around

Francilly-Selency, which had the first constructions of the German Hindenburg Line of 1917 (Desfossés 1999: 44–5). Altogether, some forty sites were located, ranging from Palaeolithic times to the present.

In the 80 kilometers of trenches dug, human remains of the Great War period were also found, and it was possible to identify those who had been intentionally buried, and those whose bodies had been covered over by an explosion. It was also sometimes possible to establish names and nationality by their locations and the personal effects that were retrieved. At Les Fiermonts, the remains of an 18-year-old British soldier were found in a shell hole and identified as those of a member of the 52nd battalion Northamptonshire Regiment, who possibly met his death during fighting in the area on 3 April 1918.

Other excavations in 1997, at the site of an industrial estate in the village of Braine, uncovered three burials within each of which was the skeleton of an adult horse (Desfossés 1999: 41–3). The presence of artillery shells in one burial, and the location of Braine in relation to the presence of cavalry in the area, suggested that these horses had been killed by German artillery fire during the British pursuit of the Germans at the end of the Allied counter-offensive on the Marne around 13 September 1914.

Arguably the most publicised archaeological investigation to date (and certainly one of the earliest) was the 1991 excavation of the bodies of twenty-one French soldiers at Saint-Rémy-la-Calonne (Meuse) (Adam 1991, 2006). The excavation was significant and contentious for several reasons, not least the presence among the dead of the French novelist Alain-Fournier, author of *Le Grand Meaulnes*. Lieutenant Fournier was one of a group of soldiers of the French 288th Infantry Regiment of Mirande that had gone missing in a wood on 22 September 1914.

As with so many other actions at the beginning of the war, this event had attracted a sinister legend – namely that all of these men had been executed by the Germans rather than been killed in battle. This rumour fitted well with other German war crimes reported during the early years of the war – it transformed Alain-Fournier into a hero, and added to the mystery of his inexplicable disappearance. Later research in German military archives indicated that, for unknown reasons, Alain-Fournier and his men might have attacked a German Red Cross ambulance before their deaths.

As an early example of Great War archaeology in France, it is notable that the excavation was surrounded with controversy even before it began. Searching for and excavating the remains of Alain-Fournier was not a priority for French professional archaeologists at a time when archaeology's potential for investigating the First World War had only just begun to be realised in the wake of the preliminary excavations along the TGV route just a couple of years before. In fact, in 1990, a request to investigate the area believed to contain the remains of Alain-Fournier and his men had been denied.

Yet, only six months later, permission to dig and exhume the bodies was granted. New evidence had come to light – part of a French army boot and fragments of red material had been found at a spot that suggested a communal grave from the early part of the war. This second request to excavate was not made by an archaeologist, but by Michel Algrain, an admirer of Alain-Fournier who had been obsessed for years with finding the author's grave. Together with a German colleague, and two local men equally fascinated by Alain-Fournier's disappearance, Algrain appealed directly to Jack Lang, the French Minister of Culture.

The normal channels for archaeological research were circumvented, and permission was granted for a rapid exhumation of the bodies by the local Lorraine Archaeological Service under the leadership of Frédéric Adam, a contract archaeologist, and with the active collaboration of the official body known as the 'Anciens Combattants et Victimes de Guerre'. The first scientific excavation of a Great War site in France was the result of individual motivation and political interest, and was anything but a straightforward archaeological project. From the beginning, all who promoted the venture saw it not as an archaeological investigation, but rather as a (physical) anthropological undertaking, designed explicitly to identify the remains of a famous personality.

Seventy-seven years after their death, Alain-Fournier and his fellow soldiers were recovered during a month-long excavation in November 1991. Initially, the excavation proceeded without any undue public attention, but, within days, the publication of an article in the Parisian press produced a media circus, and an influx of reporters and the public. Alain-Fournier's fame, and the mystery of his disappearance, fanned the flames of public interest, and the possibility of obtaining war mementoes and relics lifted the excavation into a media event that required the placing of an armed guard round the clock at the excavation site. Even at this early stage of development, Great War archaeology demonstrated its ability to transform in unexpected ways, to connect with all kinds of interests, and to take on a life of its own.

The excavation itself revealed a strict adherence to military hierarchy, in that the bodies were laid head to toe, with the captain buried at one end of the communal grave, followed by the lieutenant and sub-lieutenant, the NCOs, and finally the ordinary soldiers (Adam 1999: 32). Among the equipment and

The mass grave of twenty-one French soldiers, including Alain Fournier, at Saint-Rémy-la-Calonne in 1991. *(Courtesy of and © Frédéric Adam)*

personal effects were cartridges, water bottles, dentures, tent rivets, a pipe, fork, belt buckles, religious medallions, well-preserved boots, and sixteen identity discs (*ibid.*). Despite this apparent wealth of items, other objects were noticeable by their absence. There were no weapons and no kepis (caps), and some identity tags were missing – perhaps these items had been lost during the burial, or kept as souvenirs by the Germans who had buried the bodies.

One consequence of the focus on detailed physical anthropological evidence (rather than broader archaeological concerns) was to establish that the average height of the ordinary soldiers (mainly farmers and artisans) was 1.60 metres, whereas that of the three officers was 1.78 metres (Boura 1999: 81). This gave an insight into the social and economic background (and the dietary consequences) of men from different classes in French society.

These measurements were compared to the French Army's official list of soldiers missing in action in this sector, and their physical characteristics and ranks. These, in turn, were supplemented by the more personal evidence of family records and photographs. This information, combined with the evidence of fragments of coloured uniforms, buttons, and pieces of braid attached to the foreams and epaulettes that still adhered to the skeletons, identified them beyond doubt as belonging to the 288th regiment. Altogether, archaeological, forensic and archival evidence allowed for nineteen of the twenty-one bodies to be identified (Adam 1999: 34).

Careful examination of the wounds inflicted on these men allowed for an accurate assessment of how they had met their death. Far from indicating a systematic mass execution, as had long been rumoured, forensic examination revealed that the bodies had random wounds. This was consistent with the soldiers meeting their death in combat, most probably by being surrounded and shot at from all directions and angles by German troops (*ibid.*: 35). This aspect of the investigation seemed to explode the myth of a German war crime that had endured for almost a century in the minds of many people.

The excavation at Saint-Rémy-la-Calonne raised many important issues, not least because of the celebrity status of Alain-Fournier, and the press attention his discovery and exhumation attracted. It was also significant because the mystery of his fate in 1914 had embedded itself deep in the French psyche concerning the war, and was connected to the shaping of national identity in the postwar years. It was important, too, because it highlighted the issue of the relevance of archaeology to investigate the (comparatively recent) events of the First World War. More far-reaching, perhaps, was the fact that while the events that surrounded Alain-Fournier's death took place on French soil, they were by definition part of an international, not solely French, war heritage.

Although the excavation at Saint-Rémy-la-Calonne was an important milestone for Great War archaeology in France, its main impetus, focused on identifying an important French literary figure, meant that it was an unusual and isolated event. More influential for the archaeology of the war, in France and internationally, would be a series of discoveries (and subsequent rescue excavations) of British soldiers further north, on the later battlefields of the period 1916–18.

A MODERN ARCHAEOLOGY OF BATTLEFIELDS

In December 1996, during the excavation of the Artoipole industrial estate at Monchy-le-Preux just east of Arras, archaeologists discovered a battlefield cemetery containing twenty-seven British soldiers, laid out in several communal graves. One of these was a shell crater that had been extended so as to contain six individuals; two other rectangular graves contained six and five bodies respectively; a fourth grave revealed the remains of four NCOs; and yet another (also originally a shell hole) nearby contained the incomplete remains of perhaps another six individuals (Girardet *et al.* 2003: 103).

The British Commonwealth War Graves Commision requested that the bodies be handed over within twenty-four hours, which precluded the forensic study (and perhaps identification) of at least some of the bodies. The men appeared to have been buried fully clothed, but the acidity of the soil meant that almost nothing of these materials survived. Nevertheless, with the exception of several steel helmets too badly damaged to be reused, the bodies had evidently been stripped of their weapons, much of their military equipment, regimental badges, and perhaps also their identity discs, by those who had buried them. What little remained, however, was enough to identify at least some of the men as belonging to 13th Battalion, Royal Fusiliers, part of the British Third Army, which had been fighting here between 9 and 14 April 1917. This regiment had attacked and taken the small village of Monchy-le-Preux held by the Germans, but sustained heavy losses.

The majority of the bodies were incomplete, with arms or legs missing, indicating a brutal death by artillery-shell fire. Several bodies still had embedded in them the remains of high-explosive shrapnel. It is known that British soldiers in this area belonged to the Third Army, and that heavy losses occurred during a particularly fierce German bombardment on 11 April 1917. As the burials were near to where an advanced medical station was known to have been located, it is possible that some of the men may have survived briefly and then been buried alongside their comrades by the medical staff. It proved impossible to identify twenty-four of the twenty-seven bodies found, and these men were reburied in 1997. But the British Ministry of Defence (MOD) believed that the other three could be identified.

On 15 April 1998, another aspect of the archaeology of the war became apparent when the three remaining Royal Fusiliers were buried in the small CWGC cemetery at Monchy-le-Preux. One was still unknown, but two others had been identified. Private Frank King was 23 years old when he died, and George Anderson was aged 31. It had taken more than a year to track down relatives of the two men, some of whom had known nothing about their long-lost family members. Not only had archaeology given these men back their names and identities, but it had rewritten family genealogies as well. In the case of Private King, one relative watched the burial holding perhaps the last letter the young soldier had written home to his mother. Great War archaeology was revealing its unique ability to have an almost unbearably poignant emotional impact on the living, who, only a short time before, were totally unsuspecting of any such links to the First World War.

While the recovery and reburial of the war dead was understandably becoming a focus of Great War archaeology, at least from a media perspective, more typical kinds of excavation were also occurring. At the Newfoundland Memorial Park at Beaumont-Hamel, dominated by its caribou sculpture and memorial to Newfoundland's 800 missing servicemen, a team from Parks Canada and the French Association pour les fouilles archéologiques nationales (AFAN) began excavations in 1998 (Piédalue 1998).

The site had been designated a Canadian National Heritage site in 1997, and the need to manage and redesign parts of the site for the growing numbers of visitors led to archaeological investigations in advance of building a visitor centre and car park. Excavations of the modest car park area revealed part of what on wartime trench maps was called Uxbridge Road trench. The archaeologists traced a portion of the trench's zigzag course towards the front line, and discovered two distinct phases – one associated with the Battle of the Somme in 1916 (the area saw much fierce fighting, and the blowing of the mine on Hawthorn Ridge that always features on television programmes), and the other with the German advance in March 1918. Butchered cow bones (the remain of soldiers' meals), bottles and live grenades were found, a report written, and the car park laid.

In the same year as the bodies from Monchy-le-Preux were reburied, and the Beaumont-Hamel car park site was excavated, a quite different discovery was made, but one that was to have a profound effect on the development of Great War archaeology in France. At the small village of Flesquières, near Cambrai, a British tank was discovered and excavated, and attracted international media coverage.

Apart from the publicity, the only similarity to the excavation of Alain-Fournier and his comrades was that at Flesquières the impetus for discovery was the obsessive enthusiasm and energy of a single person. Philippe Gorczynski, a member of the French Association 1914–1918, possessed an intimate knowledge of the area, and a special interest in the British tanks that took part in the famous tank battle of Cambrai in November 1917. Gorczynski followed up local rumours that a tank was buried in the area, and finally located it on the outskirts of the village. The tank's upper entrance hatch was only 1 metre below the surface, and a first look inside revealed it to be virtually intact.

Excavating the British tank *Deborah* at Flesquières near Cambrai, France, in 1998. *(Courtesy of and ©
Philippe Gorczynski)*

When Gorczynski and others excavated the tank in November 1998
(Desfossés and Gorczynski 2002), it was immediately apparent that it was a
Mark IV ('female') tank, with heavy damage to its front right side, including the
destruction of the tank commander's seat. However, the left side had survived far
better, and the caterpillar tracks, Daimler engine and exhaust pipe were intact.
The rear section was especially well preserved, and its crew door was still open.

What struck everyone as unusual was that the tank had evidently been
dragged into a hole, not left abandoned on the battlefield, and that there was a
large quantity of German war materiel scattered around, including poor-quality
steel shells typical of the final months of the war. In addition, everything that
was recovered from inside the tank was German, not British. It seemed to
Gorczynski that the tank had been knocked out during the Cambrai battle and
had then been moved, buried and reused as an armoured German dugout; hence
the presence of German war materiel. The tank's British machine guns had
been removed, presumably because the Germans had no suitable ammunition,
and these had been replaced with their German equivalent. Several early
identifications were made of the tank, but research in military archives, a study

of trench maps and a contemporary photograph of a tank with identical damage ultimately convinced Gorczynski that the tank was D51 (called '*Deborah*'), that had belonged to D Battalion of the British Tank Corps in 1917.

What was inexplicable was, if the tank had been used as a shelter by the Germans, why had it not been stripped of its valuable workable items (especially the caterpillar tracks) for reuse as spares in their recycling of tanks to be used against the British? Only a few miles away, at Bourlon, the Germans salvaged many damaged (and sometimes only broken-down) British tanks for reuse against their former owners – might *Deborah* have been one of these?

While the excavation of *Deborah* was an important event in its own right, and particularly as it related to the great tank attack at Cambrai, it was equally significant for the effect it had on Great War archaeology more widely. The tank became a dramatic icon of Great War heritage, a kind of historical monument that excited great interest in France and around the wider English-speaking world. It represented the disappearing international heritage of the war, and demonstrated the need for, and power of, archaeology to rescue important objects from the conflict.

Soon after the discovery of *Deborah*, archaeologists found and excavated another battlefield mass burial at Gavrelle, a small village just a few kilometres northeast of Arras. It contained twelve German soldiers hastily buried by their comrades in an improvised shell-crater grave. Many of their personal effects had been removed, though pipes and a fountain pen (with a phial of ink) were found. Sections of their aluminium identification tags had been removed before burial, but enough remained to identify the men as belonging to 6th and 7th companies of the 152nd Infantry Regiments, 48th Division (Desfossés and Jacques 2000: 35). These men had evidently been killed during the great German spring offensive of March 1918. Their hasty and improvised burial presented a startling image to the excavators – a huddled mass of skeletons wearing only damaged steel helmets and boots.

In October 2000, beneath the streets of Arras, the city's archaeologist Alain Jacques discovered and investigated the only complete subterranean British field hospital ever found on the Western Front. Less than 800 metres from the front-line trenches, a large underground quarry had been transformed into a casualty clearing station between Rue St Quentin and Rue du Temple in February 1917 (Girardet *et al.* 2003: 92–3). The realisation of this project was due to the energetic Colonel A.G. Thompson of the Royal Army Medical Corps (RAMC), who calculated correctly that a large hospital so near to the battlezone would save many soldiers' lives. Today, the site is known as Thompson's Cave (*ibid.*).

Mass German battlefield grave at Gavrelle, Arras, France. *(Courtesy of and © Alain Jacques – Service Archéologique d'Arras)*

Alain Jacques and his team surveyed the vast undergound cavern, which is about 120 metres long at its longest point. They identified, among other things, a waiting room, dressing room, operating theatre, kitchen, officers' ward, mortuary, toilets and a well, and painted signs on the walls indicating not only the hospital facilities, but the direction of the front line as well. It has been calculated that the RAMC could treat around 700 men in these safe and electrically lit surroundings.

Above ground, and just a stone's throw away from Thompson's Cave, is another and quite distinctive kind of archaeological record inscribed on wartime dwellings along the streets that the soldiers of the First World War knew well. Just visible on the walls of several houses are black-painted signs, announcing 'DCLI' (Duke of Cornwall's Light Infantry) and 'Hair Cutting Saloon', which have survived for almost a century despite having no preservation order to protect them. Even more remarkable, and intensely personal, are the inscriptions that can be seen if one looks closely at some of the bricks in

Brick engraved 'Thomas [unreadable] C. Coy. 11 Platoon. 1st DCLI. B.E. Force' in street near Thompson's Cave, Arras. (© *Author's collection*)

the doorways. Here are names, dates and regiments, scratched by young men waiting in line for a military haircut, such as 'Thomas [unreadable] C. Coy 11 Platoon 1st DCLI B.E. Force', and (upside down and obviously refitted at some time), 'R.D. Oliver 26 M.G.C, B.E.F.'. These artefacts form a particularly social kind of archaeology, an intimate landscape of soldierly experience, capturing time, inscribed into the pre-war topography of Arras, and today almost invisible, although in plain view, to those who hurry past.

The ZAC Actiparc excavations

In 2001, the year after the discovery of Thompson's Cave, the truly multi-period nature of Great War archaeology became apparent, when Yves Desfossés from the Regional Archaeological Service (DRAC) Gilles Prilaux of the Institut National de Recherches Archéologiques Préventives (INRAP) of Nord-Pas-de-Calais joined forces with Alain Jacques and his colleagues from the Municipal Archaeological Service of Arras to investigate 63 hectares (out of a total area of 300 hectares) of the ZAC Actiparc site at Le Point du Jour, some 6 kilometres north-east of Arras, and on which a BMW car factory was to be built. Between April and July 2001,

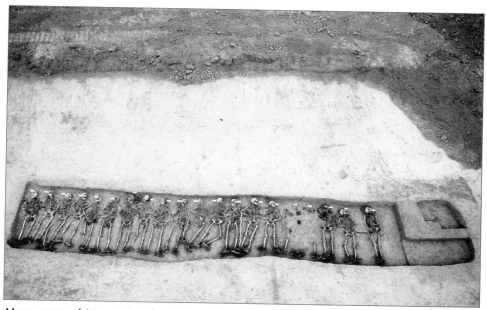

Mass grave of twenty British soldiers discovered during excavations at the ZAC Actiparc site at Le Point du Jour, near Arras, in 2001. They belong to 10th Battalion, Lincolnshire Regiment – the Grimsby Chums. *(Courtesy of and © Alain Jacques – Service Archéologique d'Arras, and Gilles Prilaux, INRAP)*

and again between January and September 2002, a total of some 120 kilometres of trenches was excavated, further areas evaluated, and five major occupations were found. There were significant remains from the prehistoric (Bronze and Iron Age) and also from the Gallo-Roman period, including a burial ground, and a small fort from the time of Augustus (Desfossés *et al.* 2002 and 2003).

These traditional kinds of remains had been cut into by some 6,000 structures associated with the First World War, highlighting again the complex relationship between the most ancient and most recent kinds of archaeology. Between October 1914 and April 1917 this sector of the Arras front had been fortified by two lines of German trenches (the intermediate and rear trenches). Constructions that were found included defensive and communication trenches, dugout shelters and observation posts; also found were the remains of thirty-one British soldiers, who seem to have been casualties of the British attack on 9 April 1917.

Twenty of these men were buried together, almost certainly by their comrades, in a shallow mass grave. They were laid out in a row, seemingly arm in arm, perhaps as a last poignant show in death of the comradeship they had shared in life. They were all still wearing their boots, though there were no weapons, equipment or helmets (except one) that, presumably, had been removed by those who had buried them. While none of the men could be identified – no identity discs were found – the presence of several regimental badges on some of the bodies indicated that they were from the 10th Battalion, Lincolnshire Regiment – the Grimsby Chums.

A grim reminder of the nature of industrialised war was evident where two men had been laid next to each other but all that remained of both men was a single arm, and four boots – in two of which was the lower half of a leg bone. Every other trace of the two men was missing, presumably blown to pieces by devastating artillery shellfire. In what must have been a gut-wrenching act, the survivors had collected these scattered pieces of their comrades and laid them out in exactly the same position as the other complete bodies. At the far end of the burial was a soldier slightly separated from the others, whose arms were laid out along his sides.

Apart from this poignant and well-publicised find, another, more unexpected – and so far unique – discovery was made. As we saw in Chapter 2, soldiers spent considerable time and effort in making objects from the debris of war (see Gygi 2004). These items, known collectively as trench art, were also made by prisoners of war on both sides, and after as well as during the war. While hundreds of thousands of such objects were made by soldiers, the preference of modern collectors for objects in perfect condition has meant that few half-finished pieces, rejects or manufacturing scrap have ever been found, published or offered for sale.

The excavators at Actiparc not only uncovered a treasure trove of such incomplete pieces and manufacturing debris, but were also the first to discover and investigate the remains of a trench-art workshop or *atelier*. Equally interesting was the fact that this was a postwar workshop, and the makers were German prisoners of war (POWs) engaged in repairing the railway from Arras to Lens in 1919 (hence this date inscribed on some of the pieces). Some items had the names of their makers engraved on them, while others were adorned with such incriptions as 'Weltkrieg' (World War), 'POW', and 'Arras–Lens'. One of the matchbox covers was inscribed 'Andenken', German for 'souvenir' (Desfossés *et al.* 2005). The range of items included crescent-bladed letter-openers, fuse-cap inkwells, imitation belt buckles, and the ubiquitous matchbox covers, and made from such raw materials as empty artillery-shell cases, and brass and aluminium scrap.

What was especially valuable about this discovery was that among the items recovered were numerous cut-outs of scrap metal in the shape of these

Finished and unfinished items from the trench-art workshop excavated at the ZAC Actiparc site at Le Point du Jour, near Arras. *(Courtesy of and © Alain Jacques – Service Archéologique d'Arras)*

trench-art objects, half-completed (as well as finished) items, and even several small improvised hammers used (with a chisel) for decorating and inscribing the different kinds of trench art. This was a significant find from the point of view both of Great War archaeology and the anthropological study of trench art. It demonstrated how a modern archaeology of the war could uncover and make sense of a trench-art workshop, and fill in the gaps in knowledge concerning the (hitherto almost invisible) processes of manufacture of objects that are otherwise so well known as artistic souvenirs of the war. For once, it was the scrap and debris associated with trench art that was more interesting than the finished object.

While the ZAC Actiparc excavations were on a large scale, and revealed many different aspects of Great War archaeology, smaller discoveries continued to be made. In 2003, the remains of three German soldiers killed in 1915 were found at Thélus near Arras. 'Soldier 2', who belonged to the 12th Grenadier Regiment, yielded well-preserved personal effects, including a pipe, matchbox, pencils, a small crucifix, and a purse containing German and French coins. His corroded identity tag revealed a name beginning with 'SPO . . .', and showed his Berlin address as '144 Köpenickerstr.'. But there was also an intriguing paradox, as his possessions included a gold chain and a silver medal that was in effect a swastika surrounded by a twelve-rayed sun.

Here was a First World War German soldier carrying the emblem of the postwar Nazi Party at a time when Adolf Hitler himself was still a lowly corporal fighting in Belgium. The paradox was resolved when it was found that on the reverse of the swastika was the name 'CARLSBERG', referring to the Danish beer company. At their brewery in Copenhagen, Carlsberg had adopted the swastika (an ancient good-luck sign) along with the twelve-rayed sun and elephant as corporate symbols around 1880, possibly because of their commercial involvement with the British in India. They abandoned it in 1920, when the Nazis adopted and for ever changed its significance (Alain Jacques pers. comm.; Desfossés *et al.* 2004). It is interesting to ponder what battlefield looters would have made of such a find.

The Ocean Villas Project

One of the most sustained and innovative excavations on the Somme has been the 'Ocean Villas Project', an archaeological investigation of Great War features located on the property of Avril Williams, owner of the Ocean Villas guest house and tearooms in the village of Auchonvillers on the Somme.

In 1996, the site had originally been investigated by a British group of Great War re-enactors, known as the 'Khaki Chums'. A year later, in 1997, the excavation was taken over by a team that included a museum professional from the National Army Museum in London, a professional archaeologist and a historian, supported by volunteers. The aim of the investigation was now to explore the communication trenches leading to a cellar used by troops during the war, and to reconstruct everything as a commemorative tourist feature.

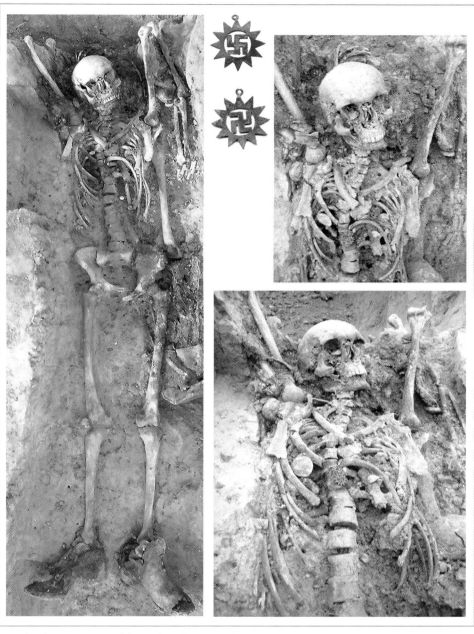

Burial of a German soldier of 12th Grenadier Regiment killed in 1915, and discovered at Thélus near Arras in 2003. His personal effects were well preserved, and included a Swastika medallion, a symbol used by the Danish beer company Carlsberg in the pre-Nazi era. *(Courtesy of and © Alain Jacques – Service Archéologique d'Arras)*

Excavation of a trench at the Ocean Villas tearoom and guest house at Auchonvillers on the Somme in 1999. (© Author's collection)

The motivation for the Ocean Villas Project is typical of the complex nature of Great War archaeology – neither obvious nor straightforward, and full of fascinating and difficult issues. The Ocean Villas tearoom is adorned with locally discovered Great War memorabilia in ways not dissimilar to the café-museums that have operated in the area since the 1920s. However, the owner's strong personal commitment to the commemoration and interpretation of the war prompted her interest in offering her own battlefield visitors a glimpse of a conserved and reconstructed part of the tearoom building they were visiting. An important aspect of this was the existence beneath the building of a cellar that had served as a dugout during the war, and that contains wartime graffiti carved by soldiers.

Jon Price, the archaeologist in charge of the excavations, has observed another aspect of this kind if archaeology in such a rural area. In a village with a shrinking and ageing population, the Ocean Villas tearooms (made more attractive by the results of the Ocean Villas Project) offers local employment and improves the local economy (Price 2004).

The primary intention of the excavation at Auchonvillers was to find the original wartime form of the trench, and to relate this to traditional archaeological stratigraphy, and subsequently to allow for an authentic trench to be reconstructed for visitors in a way that demonstrated the validity of scientific excavation. This would stand in contrast to previous Great War digs that had uncovered many artefacts, but which could not relate them in any meaningful way to different levels and periods of trench building.

This approach, which saw the excavation and subsequent presentation of a Great War site as an achievable and worthwhile effort in its own right, also differed from most other kinds of archaeology on the Somme, where, constrained by traditional archaeological concerns, excavations of Great War sites (with their bodies and volatile munitions) were sometimes viewed as a hindrance to excavating the 'real' archaeology of the prehistoric, Gallo-Roman, or medieval periods that lay beneath. Implicit in the Auchonvillers project was the understanding that Great War archaeology was a new kind of enterprise that was linked by the joint interests of the site owner and the excavators to public concerns and participation in terms of war remembrance rather than strictly academic issues.

The other major difference at Auchonvillers was the fact that this was not – as so many other 'battlefield archaeology' digs had been – an excavation of a battlefield per se, but rather of a rear area where soldiers spent more time than in the front line, and so would investigate a hitherto ignored aspect of soldiers' daily life. The composition of the excavation team reflected a recent development in archaeological thinking: there was not just one knowable past, but rather a diversity of pasts amenable to different interpretations and relevant to people with different motivations, different kinds of expertise, and different (sometimes emotional) ways of engaging with the First World War.

The original excavations by the Khaki Chums into the wind-blown loamy soil – with its liability to becoming waterlogged and to lose its features by weathering – had been such that the Auchonvillers team feared that archaeological signs of trench cutting, use and infilling might not be visible, and therefore would not produce the result that the team and the site owner wanted. Nevertheless, the Ocean Villas Project's first excavations in 1997 revealed a clear stratigraphy, in which it was possible to identify an original wartime trench cut, and subsequent layers of dumping and natural sedimentation. This key discovery allowed the archaeologists to identify a preliminary sequence of phases, and to incorporate additional archaeological and historical information in their interpretation.

In this first scientific excavation of a First World War trench, the potential of modern archaeology to add significantly to understanding the conflict at the level of individual features was dramatically illustrated. Phase 1 represented the original cutting of the trench (with its drainage features) and the laying of a brick floor; Phase 2 saw the trench in everyday use, with the brick floor being kept clean and sediment building up in the drainage area; Phase 3 had evidence of run-off from the sides of the trench; Phase 4 identified the accumulation of dirt on top of the run-off (suggesting the trench was not kept as clean as previously); Phase 5 saw the deliberate infilling of the trench; Phase 6 indicated that the trench was filled with wire debris and surface run-off; Phase 7 saw the slumping of soil into the trench; Phase 9 gave evidence of more wire debris and surface run-off in the trench; Phase 10 saw the more gradual slumping of the trench sides and accumulation of run-off sediment; Phase 11 revealed evidence of debris collected from the surrounding area being thrown into the trench; Phase 12 saw garden soil spread across the site; and Phase 13 revealed the non-scientific excavation and movement of excavated soil undertaken by the Khaki Chums in 1996.

In other words, the Ocean Villas Project had created the first life story of a Great War trench, from its wartime origins in 1915 to its investigation by amateur diggers in 1996, and has thus contributed significantly to the development of a specific methodology for the archaeology of the war.

In the wake of these investigations, the trench was consolidated and reconstructed so as to realise the original aim of creating an interpretative feature for visitors to the Ocean Villas tearooms. It is significant, also, that this work allows visitors to glimpse and understand a Great War site that is out of the ordinary, that is not a front-line battle scene, or a cemetery, but rather an everyday feature of soldier life, in a place so ordinary that it receives only a passing comment in the written sources of Great War military history. As Jon Price remarked, 'By approaching the excavation with the intention of delivering a product, rather than simply pursuing a research agenda, we have optimised the contextual synergy of the site, and have gone some way to establish the footings of a new and distinctively First World War kind of archaeological methodology' (Price 2004: 188).

The Serre excavations

During the excavations at Auchonvillers, the excavation team formally became No Man's Land, a group of professionals dedicated to bringing their own different specialisms to investigating First World War sites. It was as No Man's

Land that they were called upon to excavate several other Great War locations, one of which highlighted another distinctive feature of Great War archaeology – the investigation of sites associated with famous personalities from the war. While such a personalised agenda recalls John Laffin's typically 1980s call for battlefield archaeologists to dig in search of Victoria Cross winners, the results of digging First World War sites often bears little relation to the original intention.

Arguably the second most famous example of this kind of Great War archaeology in France (after the Alain-Fournier excavation) was also an example of the previously mentioned television archaeology of the war, where a television company set the agenda and funded the research. In this instance, No Man's Land were contracted by the BBC to investigate German trenches near Serre on the northern Somme battlefield that were captured and occupied by the British soldier and poet Wilfred Owen and his men in January 1917 (Brown 2005, 2009). Owen's patrol endured a heavy artillery barrage while in the trenches, and one of the soldiers was blinded – an event that inspired Owen's war poem 'The Sentry'. These events evidently appealed to the BBC, and instead of a straightforward programme on Owen and military history (as may have been the case just a few years previously), they decided to incorporate archaeology into the project.

No Man's Land excavated two trench sections at Serre, one of which had been filled in with chalk and other material (possibly as a result of German mine detonations designed to disrupt British attacks in 1916), and the second of which showed evidence of trench fighting, such as the empty magazines from a British Lewis machine gun, and a barricade known as a *chevaux-de-frise* (Brown 2005: 25–33). During the course of this main excavation, they also briefly investigated a nearby concrete observation post, the rear door to which preserved the impressions of hessian-weave sandbags, presumably laid there while the concrete was still soft. It may date to early 1918, a year or so later than the event that was the primary focus of the investigation.

The excavations of the Wilfred Owen dig recovered three skeletons, two German and one British. Both Germans have been identified, but the British soldier is still unknown. The recovery of his brass shoulder-titles indicated that he belonged to the King's Own Royal Lancaster Regiment, whose 1st Battalion had taken part in a British attack on the German salient at Serre known as the Heidenkopf on 1 July 1916 (the first day of the Battle of the Somme). He seems to have been killed by a shell burst, as numerous shell fragments were found in and around the skeleton, and his upper right arm had been shattered.

No Man's Land archaeologists excavate the unidentified remains of a British soldier of the 1st Battalion, the King's Own Royal Lancaster Regiment, at Serre on the Somme in 2003. *(Courtesy of and © Martin Brown).*

As he was discovered associated with chalk debris of the German mine explosion, and as some personal effects may have been missing and there was no trace of an identity disc, it is possible that his body was subsequently searched or looted, and these items removed. The position of the body also suggested that he may have been given a temporary battlefield burial, though the presence of rat burrows in the body itself indicates that, deliberate or not, the burial was not deep.

The personal effects that were recovered included a leather purse in which French and English coins were found, and, interestingly, a penny from Jersey (Channel Islands) that may relate in some way to the fact that the 1st Battalion were stationed there before the war. The penny was dated either 1913 or 1915, and the battalion had left Jersey in 1911, evidence that might suggest that the soldier was a native Jersey islander. Whatever the truth, he was reburied in nearby Serre Military Cemetery Number 2 by the Queen's Lancashire Regiment, successors to the King's Own.

As for the two German soldiers, 'skeleton 1' had been wearing (or perhaps was hastily wrapped in) a rain cape, and his ammunition pouches were full — furthermore, one pouch was open, evidently ready for immediate use. Several personal effects were also discovered, including a piece of a mirror, a manicure set and a comb — finds that suggested to Martin Brown, one of the excavators, that his personal appearance was one way of keeping hold of his humanity in the filth and chaos of the trenches.

The No Man's Land archaeologists also found a damaged identity disc, which, despite its corrosion, yielded a partial inscription that revealed he was number 2 on the company roll of 7 Kompanie. As 7 Kompanie of 121 Reserve Infanterie Regiment were at Serre between 10 and 13 June 1915, it is possible that he had been killed during the well-documented heavy fighting with the French at this time. As was often the case in the First World War, soldiers evidently felt the need to add some personal identification to their otherwise dehumanising military numbers, and scratched their names on the reverse of their identity discs.

Although heavily corroded, this man's disc retained a partly damaged engraving that read 'Mun . . .' on the top line, 'Hines' on the second, and 'Jak . . .' on the third. Other items gave a context to this fragmentary inscription. The cuff buttons were of a Swedish style worn by some Württemberg infantry regiments, of which one, the 26 Reserve Division, was in the Serre area between March 1915 and November 1916. In this division, only the 121 Reserve Infanterie Regiment wore these distinctive cuff buttons.

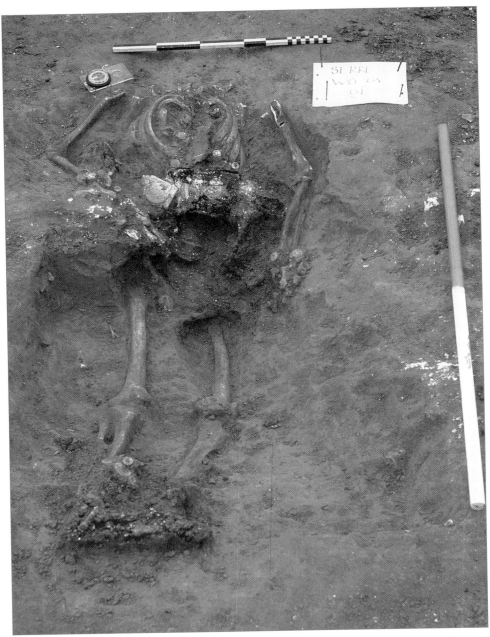

The remains of the German soldier Jakob Hönes, of 7 Kompanie, 121 Reserve Infanterie Regiment, found during excavations by No Man's Land archaeologists at Serre on the Somme in 2003. *(Courtesy of and © Martin Brown)*

Historical documents then came into play, and a search of regimental casualty lists for June 1915 showed that one Jakob Hönes, a labourer in a brickworks near Stuttgart whose family had fallen on hard times, had been lost in action. It seems as if the 'I' on his damaged identity disc was really an 'Ö'. The Hönes family, which included Jakob's only surviving son, was still living in the Stuttgart area, and, almost ninety years after Jakob died at Serre, he was reunited with his family, and buried in the German military cemetery near Metz (Brown 2009; Fraser 2004).

The second German soldier, known as 'skeleton 3', had also received no obvious burial, and he too still carried personal effects – a pocket watch, harmonica, penknife, razor and pipe, along with a bankbook from Halberstadt, in Sachsen Anhalt, eastern Germany. The presence of blowfly casts in the remains suggests that he also possessed perishable foods eaten by maggots, although such a discovery is also gruesomely typical of the decay of human soft-body tissue. Interestingly, he carried a prehistoric flint scraper of local Picardy flint, maybe found during his time in the trenches, and perhaps, as in other documented examples, suggesting an educated interest in the past. This artefact is also an indication, as we have seen in Chapter 1, that Great War archaeology involves a curious mixing of the oldest and newest kinds of material culture. Such discoveries reveal the intimate relationship between men and landscape that characterised the First World War, and led some individuals, evidently from both sides, to collect ancient archaeological objects which in turn became part of the modern archaeology of the war.

While no identity disc was found, archaeological and archival evidence indicates that skeleton 3 may belong to Albert Thielicke, an NCO in 7 Kompanie, 121 Reserve Infanterie Regiment (the same as Jakob Hönes), and who was killed in action on 11 June 1915. The NCO's buttons and other elements of the uniform can be connected only with one person in either 121 or 119 regiments known to have been in the area at the right time, and who had any association with Halberstadt. Thielecke's profession as an interior decorator, and his possession of a pocket watch, suggest that he may have been the kind of person who had a bank account. Whether or not this identification is correct, the circumstantial evidence convinced the German War Graves organisation – the VDK – that the body was Thielecke's, and this is the name on the headstone of his grave in the military cemetery at Metz (Brown 2009).

The cases of Jakob Hönes and Albert Thielicke demonstrated the uniqueness of Great War archaeology when conducted by professionals, upon whom, of course, there is a moral responsibility not encountered in, say, prehistoric and medieval archaeology. Painstaking attention to archaeological procedures and the smallest physical details was combined with expert military history research to achieve what was in effect an anthropological goal – the study of what it is that makes us human. Through the power of Great War objects, Jakob and Albert had been reclaimed from the list of the German 'missing' on the Somme, both were now recognisable men as well as numbers, and, most satisfying of all, in Jakob's case, he had been reunited with his son and family, bringing closure to everyone after almost a century.

The No Man's Land investigations at Serre were originally designed (and funded) to explore the war landscape of Wilfred Owen, but they found no trace of him. Instead, the project developed in a quite different way, and demonstrated the power of Great War archaeology to reconstitute men's humanity and identity through the objects associated with them, and to lift them for ever above the fields of 'the missing'. By searching for traces of a world-famous British war poet, three other 'unknown' men were reclaimed from the battlefields, and reburied in what amounted to acts of individual remembrance. Two of these men – the German soldiers – were reunited with their names (and in one case with his family) after almost ninety years. Few kinds of archaeology can match such a poignant and many-layered conclusion to their investigations.

While the excavations at Serre revealed no trace of Wilfred Owen, the idea of at least some instances of Great War archaeology being driven by associations with famous personalities will probably never lose its attraction. The First World War is not only a momentous period in world history, but seems full of iconic figures as well. While most of these individuals are understandably European, one stands out as a true American hero – now entwined in the developing archaeology of the war.

Sergeant Alvin C. York was a hillbilly from Tennessee, a troublemaker who had unsuccessfully made every effort to avoid being drafted in 1917, when the United States declared war on Germany. To everyone's surprise, York proved to be an excellent shot, and became a sharpshooter for G Company of the 328th Infantry Regiment, 82nd Division. He decided to fight in France rather than become a firearms instructor, and, on 8 October 1918, he advanced with sixteen men into an attack on German positions near Chatel-Chehery. After an initial skirmish, York silenced a German machine gun singlehanded, killed six charging Germans with only his service pistol, whereupon the surviving Germans surrendered. York and seven comrades then marched the 132 German prisoners back to their own lines. York became a hero, and was later awarded the Congressional Medal of Honor. He was immortalised by Gary Cooper in the 1941 Hollywood film *Sergeant York*.

In March 2006, despite the passage of almost ninety years, a team of military historians and a geographer announced that they had discovered the location of York's action. They said they had used a combination of trench maps, archival documents, Global Positioning System (GPS) and Geographical Information System (GIS) computer software to locate the spot, and had then verifed this on the ground by digging up spent bullet cases. While such evidence might be thought to be far from conclusive on a munitions-drenched Great War battlefield, more detailed investigations are planned, and final assessment awaits scholarly publication and scrutiny. It is interesting for ways in which different kinds of organisations can become involved with Great War archaeology that the expedition was supported and organised by a British battlefield tour company.

What emerges from many of these investigations is that Great War archaeology is more than the application of archaeological techniques to the battlefields of 1914–18 – it is fundamentally also about memory and commemoration, public participation and education, and tourism, in a far more complex and intimate way than more traditional kinds of archaeology. This aspect, albeit on a larger and more recognisably archaeological scale than the case of Sergeant York, has been highlighted by excavations of part of the battlefield associated with the opening of the Battle of the Somme on 1 July 1916.

Thiepval Wood, north of Albert, saw fierce fighting and terrible losses during the early stages of the Somme battle. From their trenches in the wood, the 36th Ulster Division attacked heavily defended German positions on 1 July, suffering around 5,000 fatalities altogether on the Somme battlefield. The 52-hectare wood had been owned by the same French family for more than a century, and was left virtually untouched since 1918, used to hunt wild boar and deer. In 2004, it was bought for £400,000 by the Somme Association – an organisation formed to commemorate the role of Ireland in the First World War.

An important aspect of the Somme Association's preparations for commemorating the 90th anniversary of the start of the Somme battle in 2006 was to commission a small excavation (and subsequent reconstruction) of part of the front-line trenches. No Man's Land archaeologists and soldiers from the Royal Irish Regiment found unexploded artillery shells, grenades, shaving equipment, bully-beef tins, and even a chocolate tin that had come from the cacao-growing Caribbean island of Trinidad. Evidence of the original construction and repair of trenches was used in the eventual reconstruction of the trenches as part of a guided battlefield walk for visitors (Kenyon 2005; Robertshaw and Kenyon 2008: 23).

Excavated and reconstructed British front-line trench in Thiepval Wood, as it would have appeared on 1 July 1916, at the beginning of the Battle of the Somme. *(© Author's collection)*

One especially valuable aspect of modern Great War archaeology is its role in shedding light on common myths that have grown up about the war in general, and the Battle of the Somme in particular. At Thiepval, one famous example concerns Rifleman William McFadzean of 14th Battalion, Royal Irish Rifles, who selflessly sacrificed his own life to save his comrades by throwing himself on top of two grenades (*ibid.*: 38) (Kenyon 2005; Robertshaw and Kenyon 2008: 159). The spot where this has long believed to have occurred is marked by three metal crosses, though in fact McFadzean's grave lies elsewhere in an as yet undiscovered location.

The Thiepval excavations are a truly cooperative venture – a community archaeology project, linked not only to Great War military history, but also to a wider network of related sites across the Somme battlezone, such as the nearby Ulster Tower, the newly opened Thiepval Visitor Centre, the Lochnagar Crater, the 'Somme 1916 Museum' at Albert, and the major museum of the area, the Historial de la Grande Guerre, at Péronne. Great War archaeology on the Somme is, as these varied developments illustrate, a complex and constantly evolving undertaking that raises (and cuts across) many different kinds of personal, political, economic, historical and ethical issues, and doubtless will continue to do so in the future (Saunders 2002b).

Subterranean worlds

Great War archaeology in France is nothing if not diverse, and, in this sense, reflects the increasingly wide definition of modern archaeology across the world. One of the most intriguing, if as yet undeveloped, kinds of archaeological investigation of the war concerns the underground caves and galleries carved into the limestone countryside of northern France. These caves are found in and around the city of Arras, and to the east, in the open country of the departments of the Aisne and Oise, at places that were once part of the front-line areas between 1914 and 1918.

Only a few of these sites have been investigated by archaeologists, and of the majority that have not, the best documented are known through work of Great War enthusiasts, military and cultural historians, and the landowners on whose property they are located. Similarly, although known mainly from wartime photographs and magazine articles, there are isolated outcrops, such as an exposed chalk cliff at Aveluy on the Somme. Here, a melange of images was carved probably by French soldiers before 1916, and included a reclining naked woman, the embodiment of patriotic French womanhood represented as the head of Marianne, a soldier firing his rifle, and caricature heads of *poilus* (French soldiers; Jones and Howells 1972: 54). Cave sites and large open-air examples of chalk carvings can, of course, be seen as monumental kinds of trench art, but, as a distinctive kind of Great War material culture, they also invite formal archaeological survey, excavation and intepretation.

Arras, situated to the north of the Somme battlefield, has a medieval secret. Unknown to the Allied armies of 1914 and 1915, the city had been riddled with underground quarries during the sixteenth and seventeenth centuries to obtain limestone as building material. Some of these long-forgotten caverns were huge, covering hundreds of metres in area, and sometimes up to 15 metres high, with giant limestone pillars left in place to support the roofs. This subterranean landscape has been memorably likened to a giant Gruyère cheese. A few of the smaller caverns to the south of the city were used by the French 33rd Infantry Division whose soldiers left their marks inscribed on the subterranean walls in 1914 and 1915, but the rest, it seems, had long since slipped from memory.

It was not until September 1916 that the true extent of Arras's underground city was realised, when officers of the New Zealand Tunnelling Company discovered a subterranean quarry that was part of a network of similar structures underlying the city's eastern suburbs of Ronville and Saint-Saveur (Girardet *et al.* 2003: 63–76). The New Zealanders' original purpose was to dig tunnels for mine warfare, but this was soon abandoned, and instead the cave systems were explored and adapted to shelter troops for the big Allied attack scheduled for April 1917 (the Battle of Arras).

The tunnellers had to learn to avoid areas where the limestone had vertical fissures that could lead to a roof collapse, and concentrate instead on locations with more stable horizontal stata. As they discovered and extended ever more caves, the New Zealanders gave them names from their homeland – such as Wellington, Auckland, Christchurch, Dunedin and Bluff. They also took over the enlargement of quarries and the digging of connecting tunnels first started by the British, which had been given names such as London, Manchester, Glasgow, Carlisle and Jersey. The main connecting tunnels had names such as Godley Avenue and King's Avenue.

The city's medieval quarries were first linked together by tunnels, and then extended out towards the German front lines. Electric lights were installed, telephone cables laid, and a narrow-gauge railway line put in. In early 1917, another large cave was discovered, and christened Blenheim. It became the headquarters of the 7th Shropshire Light Infantry, and was fully equipped with kitchens, toilets and medical facilities. Such was the disorienting vastness of this whole new underground world that the military authorities painted signs on the limestone to direct troops from one place to another, and the soldiers themselves carved inscriptions and left pencil graffiti on the walls. Beneath the city's central Grand Place, ancient limestone cellars were also connected (to each other and the wider network), and given their own water supply, toilets, cooking areas and medical quarters. Altogether, the whole subterranean landscape of Arras housed more than 24,000 troops on the eve of the Battle of Arras.

This vast system of subterranean tunnels, galleries and caverns – extending over 22 kilometres – was a testament to the skills and efforts of the men who explored, enlarged and extended them into a single huge interconnected network. After the war, they were not totally forgotten, and served to shelter the civilian population of Arras during the Second World War. After 1945 they mainly faded from public consciousness. However, this was not to be another centuries-long abandonment, as military records, plans, maps and diaries recorded the existence, location and use of the caverns, particularly in the run-up to the Battle of Arras. This historical fact combined with two other important developments to revitalise interest in the underground city. The rise of battlefield tourism from the 1960s onward saw visitors to Arras curious to inspect the small section of cellars open to the public beneath the *hôtel de ville* (town hall), and, from the 1990s especially, professional interest in the whole network of caves and tunnels was led by the city's own municipal archaeological service, and its chief archaeologist Alain Jacques.

Archaeological investigations of Great War heritage on the outskirts of Arras had already occurred (usually as rescue operations in advance of motorways and industrial estates) at such places as Actiparc (Le Point du Jour), Monchy-le-Preux and Gavrelle. Now, as at Auchonvillers, rising numbers of tourists were driving ever more commercially viable investigations into, and reconstructions of, Great War heritage. At Arras, one result of this was the archaeological investigation of the city's extensive underground caverns, known locally as 'les boves'.

Survey and prospection of many caves was undertaken by Alain Jacques and his colleagues, and produced, for example, a detailed map of all the caverns and tunnels in relation to the Allied and German front lines between 1916 and 1918. One such map showed the layout of Blenheim Cave, with its natural support pillars, and the locations of toilets, battalion headquarters, kitchen areas and medical quarters, access and exit points, and connecting tunnels to Nelson and Christchurch caves (Girardet *et al.* 2003: 69).

A photographic record of the caverns was also made, of both official and unofficial 'wall art'. Signs painted in black (and sometimes red), such as 'M.O. AND SICK', 'OFFs LATRINE' and 'To NELSON WELLINGTON' authorised by the military authorities were recorded, as were examples of soldiers' trench art, including pencil portraits of women, a mammoth (possibly elephant), and several small three-dimensional sculptures of human faces, one of which, uniquely, appears to be identified, as the name 'W. Thompson' is nearby. There are also several small crosses carved into the limestone, possibly as miniature altars – one has a rifle bullet still lodged on a ledge below it. The international nature of this aspect of French Great War heritage is vividly shown by the miniature carvings and inscriptions left by New Zealand Maoris, such as one that reads 'No. 20680 Toi. Karinini MANGATUNA Tologo Bay N.Z.' (Girardet *et al.* 2003: 67). What the Maoris, with their own traditional spiritual beliefs and worldview, thought about living in such a place is not recorded.

When first explored, the caves also yielded a wealth of everyday debris from their last soldier inhabitants of 1918. Cooking utensils, water bottles and cutlery lay rusted by the years, abandoned on the floors, alongside miscellaneous military equipment and the remains of telephone wires and electrical fittings. In Wellington Cave, high up in a niche of the limestone wall, were found two corroded coins (one French, the other British), which perhaps suggested that

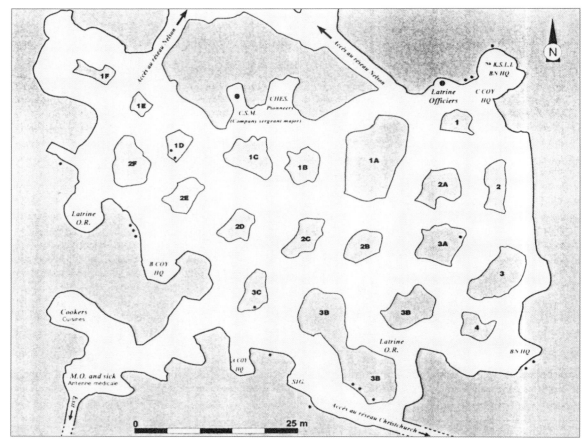

Plan of Blenheim Cave, beneath Arras, northern France. *(Courtesy and © Alain Jacques – Service Archéologique Arras)*

this was a kind of votive offering. The scientific investigation of these caves highlighted the information that could be gained from treating vestiges of the First World War as archaeological heritage – the latest use of what was, until 1916, a forgotten legacy of medieval town history. Equally important was the educational and commercial potential for opening up some of these sites to visitors. A project to open Wellington Cave as a kind of 'living museum' is under way, with a visitor centre, elevator and guided tours planned.

While Arras's underground Great War heritage has benefited from professional archaeological investigations, the same cannot yet be said for other subterranean vestiges of the war. At various locations around the Somme battlefield, but especially east of Arras, there is a similar array of caves,

Pencil drawing of woman's head on the wall of Wellington Cave, beneath Arras, northern France. (© *Author's collection*)

First World War debris (corroded cans and a fork) found in situ by archaeologists investigating Wellington Cave, Arras. (© *Author's collection*)

galleries, tunnels, rock shelters, and open-air sites that possess three- and two-dimensional decoration dating to 1914–18. Few, if any, of these places have received the level of archaeological attention that the caves in Arras have enjoyed, although their potential is equally significant. Among the best-known caves of the Aisne and Oise departments are the Carrière de Montigny, at Machemont, and the Carrière de Chauffour at Thiescourt – both in the area of Noyon–Confrécourt, and Bucy-le-Long in the Soissons area, and 'Dragon's Cave' on the infamous ridge of the Chemin des Dames.

These caves have a variety of carved images made by French, German, American and English troops, with such diverse images as portraits of an African Zouave (French colonial soldier), a French Joan of Arc and a Native American, and French cockerels, German and American eagles, and landscape scenes. A systematic survey and archaeological excavation would almost certainly yield new knowledge about even these well-known sites. It is certain also that many cave and tunnel systems remain to be identified and investigated, especially in more distant areas such as the Argonne.

Arguably the best-known and most accessible of these subterranean sites is the system of caves and tunnels at Confrécourt near Soissons (AIPS 1996; Becker 1999; Decock 1996). Carved deep into the local limestone, the caves here were occupied notably by the Zouaves, and part of the cave system served as a hospital. The walls of these galleries preserve a dazzling range of images produced mainly by French soldiers, and including military insignia, patriotic images such as Joan of Arc draped in the tricolour, and Marianne (symbols of the Republic and of French womanhood), patriotic landmarks such as the Arc de Triomphe, caricatures, and various kinds of religious iconography.

The French cultural historian Annette Becker has described a range of what she calls the psycho-sexual images of women, both clothed and naked, and carved in relief as fantasy figures with such titles as *The poilus's dream*. Perhaps, as Becker observes, these images represent the soldiers' need to leave a trace of their presence before a battle (and possible death) – an imprint of their life (Becker 1999: 124–5). In this sense, such artefacts are the definitive material culture of the First World War just as much as decorated artillery-shell cases, souvenirs and the more traditional archaeological traces of the conflict found on the battlefields.

Although professional archaeologists have hardly begun to investigate these caves, the work of the French Palaeolithic cave-art specialist, André Leroi-Gourhan, has been used to interpret them. It has been suggested that there is both order and disorder in the distribution of art in the Confrécourt caves, with profane images from the war (military insignia, caricatures, personal names and women) located in areas nearer to daylight, such as the entrance to 'la carrière du 1 Zouaves' (AIPS 1996: 14–15, figure 1), whereas more spiritual and religious imagery is found in the deeper and darker recesses (Decock 1996; Becker 1999: 18). However, the vast gulf in time, culture and context between these two eras, combined with the fact that military imagery appears throughout the cave, make this a rather idealised interpretation.

Far more convincing, and a view that connects the caves and their decoration to the specific conditions of 1914–18, is Becker's observation that the omnipresent names of individual soldiers, their regiments, armies, corps and commanders, seems focused on establishing a sense of identity and belonging, of presence and comradeship in the chaos of war (Becker 1999: 122–3). The frequency of personal and military names and numbers in this subterranean landscape contrasts with their absence on most other kinds of Great War material culture. Trench-art objects are only rarely signed, and soldiers' remains retrieved from battlefields are often impossible to identify. For Great War archaeologists, Confrécourt (and many other similar caves) is that rare thing – an archaeological landscape full of personal names and identifying inscriptions. Such places are a curious reversal of the official memorial landscapes of war cemeteries, where the bodies lie beneath, and the name above. At Confrécourt and elsewhere, the names are below, and the (often nameless) bodies somewhere above.

The underground limestone galleries of the area around Soissons and Noyon are also fertile ground for investigations that could be termed the archaeology of religion, not least because some had begun life as quarries for building materials to construct the medieval cathedrals and churches which dot the landscape of the departments of the Aisne and Oise. Archaeologically speaking, such locations were already places of deep time and ancient culture long before the First World War.

Appropriately (and ironically), the limestone that had been left behind in medieval times was itself now transformed into a new kind of religious architecture. Large three-dimensional altars were painstakingly cut into the limestone, and offered the (mainly French Catholic) soldiers a final spiritual moment before they shuffled up to the surface and into the trenches. The religious imagery of the altars is flanked by military insignia, regimental badges and numbers, and battle honours, as well with uplifting patriotic inscriptions such as 'Vive Le Christ Qui Aime Les Francs' in the cave at Pierre (Becker 1999: 120–1; 1996: 57), and 'Dieu Protège La France' in the so-called 'Chapel

Subterranean altar carved in the caves at Confrécourt, near Soissons. Known as the 'Chapel of Father Doncoeur', it is decorated with French army insignia, and the inscribed *'Dieu Protège La France'* (God Protects France). *(© Author's collection)*

of Father Doncoeur' at Confrécourt (AIPS 1996: 14–15, figure 2). What the African Zouaves, with their animistic and shamanistic religion, thought of such religious expressions – or indeed of their primordial life under ground – is not recorded, but perhaps might yield to archaeological and anthropological investigation.

A unique example of subterranean soldier-life in limestone caverns occurred at the 'Dragon's Cave' (*Drachenhöle*) on the bloody battleground of the Chemin des Dames. Here, almost unbelievably, the front line was extended and organised by mutual consent between the French and Germans among the underground quarries and galleries that had been used since medieval times. The walls of these linked caves have three- and two-dimensional images created by both sides during their long troglodyte conflict.

Material traces of the war in caves are also seen at the site of Les Cinq Piliers near Dreslincourt. The quarry and cave system was occupied by the

Three-dimensional Gallic cockerel on the wall of the cave at Les Cinq Piliers, near Dreslincourt. *(© Author's collection)*

Germans between 1914 and 1917, and was then taken by the French. There is a fascinating mix of imagery at this site, ranging from a monumental landscape scene painted directly onto a prepared chalk surface, a giant Imperial Prussian eagle sculpted onto a cliff face and (still today) painted red, and a smaller-scale but similarly three-dimensional multicoloured Gallic cockerel (Bonnard and Guénoff 1999: 15, 17, 31). This large site, part of which is open air, is a natural choice for a detailed archaeological survey and excavation.

Great War archaeology has not yet grasped the opportunities for research available in such unusual and challenging locations, despite modern archaeology's concern with nationality, ethnicity, religious belief, art, and the creation and organisation of living space – all of which are brought together at such places. Ironically, while subterranean wall carvings, sculptures and graffiti are fixed (though they could, of course, be removed), and never had a commercial value – as did so many other kinds of trench art – they are an unusual and visual (international) feature of France's Great War heritage, which will attract paying visitors in ever-greater numbers in years to come as they inevitably become integrated into battlefield tour itineraries.

Great War archaeology in France, while still in an early stage of development, has made many significant advances over the past two decades, due mainly to the expertise, professionalism and personal interest of the French archaeologists Alain Jacques, Yves Desfossés and Gilles Prilaux, and the British No Man's Land group. Unlike in Belgium (see Chapter 5), official involvement with the physical remains of the First World War has been an integral part of French professional archaeology for many years, and so there has been less incentive to incorporate foreign specialists or institutions into French excavations – although foreign projects, such as those at Auchonvillers, Newfoundland Memorial Park, Serre and Thiepval Wood, have coexisted.

In France, as in Belgium, however, Great War archaeology has only a nominal presence in the world of academic archaeology, although this will surely change as modern archaeology embraces the idea that Great War heritage is but one of 'the archaeologies of the contemporary past'. The approaching centenary of the start of the First World War in 2014 will surely stimulate public awareness of and interest in Great War heritage for a generation to whom the idea that the war is too recent for archaeology will itself be an anachronism.

Most Great War archaeology in France has taken the form of 'preventive' or 'rescue' excavations in advance of motorways, urban development, the building of industrial estates, and sometimes accidental discoveries that required professional attention. In many cases, also, Great War remnants have been found associated with prehistoric and/or Gallo-Roman remains, a fact that further required French archaeologists to investigate this overlapping or intrusive war heritage. By contrast, for example, the work of No Man's Land has been more proactively focused on sites yielding only Great War remains. By accident or design, the remains of the First World War have been regarded as part of France's wider archaeological heritage for far longer than has been the case in Belgium.

What emerges from the French experience of excavating Great War remains is, as in Belgium more recently, a realisation that modern archaeology can uncover and interpret a different view of a war hitherto known mainly from the historical sources of military history. Excavation – being down in the same soil as the soldiers of 1914–18 – gives a feel for the land, and the experiences of the men who fought in it. Subtle changes in soil colour, evidence of the recutting and repair of trenches, the identification of overlapping bomb craters, retrieving a man's identity from limbo through discovering his personal effects, and the discovery of concentrations of industrialised war debris – all yield a sense of the war that is impossible to gain from written documents alone.

Excavating Great War sites is an experience that deeply affects the body and mind of the excavator, rather than engaging the intellect alone. And it is also an experience that can, when interpreted and presented with sensitivity and accuracy, connect directly to present generations who perhaps react more readily to objects than printed words. Having said this, the wealth of historical documents on the war, and the skill of military historians in interpreting this material, means that Great War archaeology has to be a truly interdisciplinary endeavour. Both archaeology and military history can inform, test and correct the assumptions and interpretations of each other.

On the vast rolling landscapes of France's Great War battlefields, archaeology connects the ancient and recent pasts through the proximity of, for example, a Bronze Age enclosure, an Iron Age Gallic tomb and a First World War communal burial. Finding bodies and, more poignantly, dreadfully shattered pieces of bodies not only has an emotional force for excavator and audience, but also reveals the intensity and scale of the war at the most intimate level. Unlike the Ypres Salient in Belgium, French battlefields are vast, yet bodies are everywhere. And they are recent ancestors, not long-forgotten prehistoric forebears. Great War archaeology in France embraces landscape in a distinctive way – in depth and in breadth – testing assumptions, finding new truths, and breathing a different kind of life over the bones of the dead.

CHAPTER 5

Beneath Flanders Fields

In Belgian Flanders, the archaeology of the First World War has taken a different course than in France for many different reasons. Military actions in and around the Ypres Salient were of a different kind than those on the vast rolling chalklands of the Somme. The low-lying, waterlogged clays stretching from Steenstraete (10 kilometres north of Ypres) to Nieuwpoort on the coast made it impossible to dig trenches, and so sandbagged positions were built instead. The area south of Steenstraete (including the whole Ypres Salient) was silty loam, which did allow for trench digging, though the high water table caused endless problems even here. The geology of Belgian Flanders, therefore, presented severe difficulties for fighting soldiers at the time, and for archaeologists today (Doyle 1998). The geographical layout and geological structure of the Ypres Salient have created distinctive problems and opportunities for archaeology, as have the different cultural attitudes towards the physical remains of the war.

There exist, however, many similarities between these two important areas of the old Western Front. Whole battlefield landscapes survive just centimetres below the modern ground surface, with trenches, dugouts and subterranean galleries full of the detritus of war – and sometimes extremely well preserved because of the high water table in the region. As on the Somme, the soil of Belgian Flanders also contains thousands of 'the missing', their bodies, uniforms, weapons and equipment – sometimes even newspapers and blankets. Both regions also face the pressures of the modern age, as motorways and urban development threaten to disturb or destroy the battlefield heritage. As in France, so in Belgium, where the army is actively involved in clearing and disposing of unexploded and volatile Great War artillery shells. Yet, while many of the problems facing the developing field of Great War archaeology in France and Belgium are the same, there are also important differences that we shall explore here.

As we saw in Chapter 1, the local inhabitants of the Ypres area have engaged with the region's Great War remains very proactively, with local collectors, groups of amateur archaeologists and military history enthusiasts all paving the way for the recent arrival of a modern scientific archaeology of the war. What has been distinctive about the Belgian response in this respect has been the activities of quasi-formal groups or associations which have been actively digging Great War sites around Ypres, over the last decade especially. The two main amateur groups, already briefly mentioned, are The Diggers, and the Association for Battlefield Archaeology in Flanders (ABAF), to which a brief mention of the Association for Battlefield Archaeology and Conservation (ABAC) should be added. ABAF underwent personnel changes in 2001 (see below), and some of the original members split away to form ABAC, which investigated tunnels beneath Nieuwpoort, though it was the reconfigured ABAF that remained the major force.

The activities of these avocational archaeologists have, until recently, been almost the only kind of Great War-related archaeological activity in Flanders. This has been mostly due to the fact that Belgium's professional archaeologists have been concerned with the region's rich prehistoric, Gallo-Roman and medieval remains, with little time or resources to spend on such comparatively recent material whose status as valuable archaeological heritage was neither evident nor acknowledged.

Amateur battlefield excavations emerged out of a long tradition of clearing and digging the landscapes of war after 1918 in order to restore farmland and gather war debris (usually iron and copper) for sale, and for reworking into souvenirs for interwar pilgrims and tourists, on which the postwar economy of Ypres depended to a considerable extent. Consequently, as professional archaeologists have observed, while such amateur diggings can only be termed archaeology in a very general sense, these activities have a long tradition in the Ypres region.

THE BEGINNINGS OF ARCHAEOLOGY

The excavations of amateur groups such as The Diggers and ABAF have revealed many kinds of (often startling) information that had not previously been valued or investigated. Their work is not only an integral part of the historical development of Great War archaeology in Belgian Flanders (and therefore important in its own right), but is also significant from the perspective of what they found and where, and how their discoveries contributed to our understanding of the war itself.

The Diggers are a group of Great War enthusiasts and amateur archaeologists with a shifting membership who were formed during the 1980s to investigate

The Diggers excavating at 'Fortin 17', a German strongpoint at Boezinge. *(Courtesy and © Aurel Sercu)*

the old Ypres Salient battlefields. Their first digs were at Bayernwald (also called Croonaert Wood) near Wijtschate, and Polygon Wood between Hooge and Zonnebeke. During these early years, they also investigated a German bunker beneath the old Ypres–Roulers railway, where they uncovered the remains of six German soldiers.

Their largest and most famous dig began in 1992, near Boezinge, a small town just north of Ypres, in an area marked for an extension to the Yperlee industrial estate along the eastern bank of the Ypres canal. This area had been part of the battlefield that saw the first German gas attack on 22 April 1915, and had been left virtually untouched since 1918. The high water table in this area has led to remarkable preservation of all kinds of material culture, from whole systems of intact trenches to a tin packed with tobacco found on the body of a Royal Welch Fusilier.

One example of how The Diggers' investigations have contributed to the region's war heritage is Yorkshire Trench, part of the Boezinge site. The dugout was begun

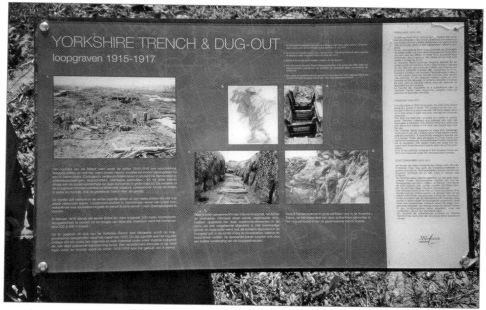

Visitor sign showing features of the reconstructed Yorkshire Trench at Boezinge, near Ypres.
(© Author's collection)

in early 1917 by the 173rd Tunnelling Company of the Royal Engineers, and it
served as a headquarters for the 13th and 16th Royal Welch Fusiliers at the start of
the Third Battle of Ypres (Passchendaele) later that same year.

The Diggers began their work in 1998, and soon revealed a zigzag line
of trenches footed with duckboards beneath which were drainage channels.
Investigations also uncovered two flights of steps leading down to a cluster of
eleven subterranean rooms and connecting galleries. On the surface, they found
a wealth of objects relating to the war, including the remains of a Decauville
light railway, unexploded artillery shells, bayonets, cartridge belts, telephone
cables, coils of barbed wire, rum jars, playing cards, pipes, iodine ampoules
(for soldiers' wounds), the remains of a stretcher, and even an English–French/
French–English dictionary. Although the area is now rebuilt with large
warehouses, Yorkshire Trench was reconstructed, and opened as a tourist
attraction in 2003, with new sandbag reinforcements and a visitors' information
board, along with an unusual display of British Livens projectors – a primitive
form of trench mortar.

Most poignant of all were the human remains that The Diggers found.
Between 1992 and 2000, they discovered 155 soldiers across the whole

Narrow-gauge (Decauville) railway excavated by The Diggers at Boezinge, near Ypres. *(Courtesy and © Aurel Sercu)*

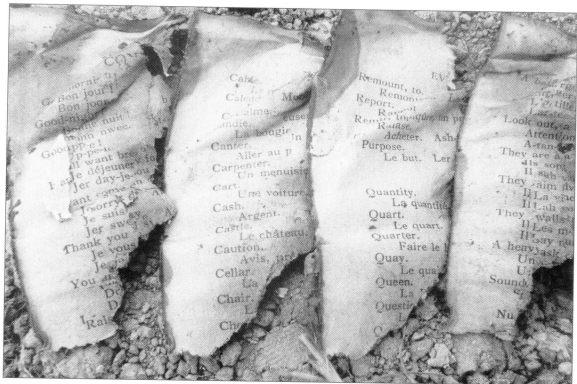

English–French dictionary found by The Diggers at Boezinge, near Ypres. *(Courtesy and © Aurel Sercu)*

Boezinge site, most of whom were found in No Man's Land, between the Allied and German trenches. These bodies belonged to the period of two great battles, Second Ypres (beginning on 22 April 1915) and Third Ypres/Passchendaele (starting on 31 July 1917). One was found with a miniature white porcelain crucifix, recalling soldiers' intimate associations with these images of religious belief. While identification was sometimes difficult because of the incomplete nature of the remains, roughly half appear to have been British, a third German, and the rest French.

In 2001, two more British soldiers were found, one of whom – designated Burial 124 – was carrying, among other things, a toothbrush, pocket knife, pencils and a small trench mirror, as well as (probably wearing) a gas mask. The second man had similar belongings, together with a spoon, an early form of hand grenade (called a Mills bomb), and a well-preserved purse, some of whose coins dated to 1917. The regimental badges associated with both men indicated they were Royal Welch Fusiliers. The evidence suggested that both men died between January and July 1917, when the regiment was stationed here, and that they had been found exactly where they had been killed.

It was one of these soldiers, Burial 124, who would become a virtual icon of Great War archaeology. This was due to his startlingly well-preserved remains – a complete skeleton wearing only his steel helmet and boots, and carrying his equipment – and the graphic position in which he was found, seemingly as he had fallen, on the very spot on which he had died. There were no obvious wounds on this man's remains, which led to speculation that he may have died (as did so many others) not from high-explosive shrapnel, but rather the invisible effects of a dramatic change of pressure in the body caused by a nearby shell blast. This soldier was reburied in a military cemetery, but, as no identifying items were found, he remains one of those men described so often in the Great War's cemeteries as 'known unto God'. His body has been found, but his identity is still with 'the missing'.

The Diggers have been criticised for their use of metal detectors, their lack of professional expertise, and their failure to publish technical reports of their work. Nevertheless, they did record and photograph the objects they recovered, held a local public exhibition of their finds, and donated the most significant items to the In Flanders Fields Museum in Ypres, which itself held several temporary exhibitions of the Boezinge discoveries (Chielens 2001). Another small exhibition of The Diggers' finds is on display at the Hooge Crater café-museum on the Menin road. The remains of the soldiers uncovered by The Diggers were reburied in nearby British, French and German war cemeteries.

While The Diggers, led by the indefatigable Patrick Van Wanzeele, never claimed to be professional archaeologists, there is little doubt that they added significantly to our knowledge of the area of the Yperlee industrial estate that would otherwise simply have been built over (The Diggers 2001). More widely, the publicity that surrounded their activities and discoveries, both good and bad, highlighted the interest of visitors in Great War archaeology, and the need for a change in official attitudes towards it. Throughout their work at Boezinge, the Diggers were licensed and to some extent monitored by the Institute for Archaeological Patrimony (IAP), now the Flemish Heritage Institute (VIOE).

ABAF, which had an earlier and a later formation, took a different approach to their investigations, though again, none of the earlier international team were professional archaeologists. They spent several years digging and filming at various locations in the Ypres Salient, though most of their work focused on subterranean features such as dugouts, tunnels and galleries – a particular interest of several group members. This was dangerous, painstaking and

Burial 124 – a British soldier of the Royal Welch Fusiliers – found by The Diggers at Boezinge, near Ypres. *(Courtesy and © Aurel Sercu)*

A German concrete bunker at Bayernwald, near Ypres. *(© Author's collection)*

systematic work that owed a great deal to the technical skill and ingenuity of Johan Vandewalle, a native of nearby Zonnebeke, and a carpenter and civil-engineer tunneller by training. This practical expertise was complemented by Franky Bostyn, a young battlefield historian with an encyclopaedic knowledge of the Ypres Salient. In the early days, ABAF also called on the expertise of the Peter Doyle, a British geologist with a special interest in the First World War, and Peter Barton, an independent film-maker.

In 1998, the original ABAF team began research on a mineshaft and bunkers at Bayernwald near Wijtschate, south of Ypres (Bostyn 1999; Doyle *et al.* 2001). The site was occupied by the Germans in 1914 – taking its name, Bayernwald (Bavarian Wood), from the Bavarian regiments stationed there – and was visited by Hitler in 1940, reportedly because he had served there in 1917. The area had been disturbed (in an archaeological sense) by battlefield clearance during the 1920s. This fact, combined with the damage wrought by tree growth, and the nature of the soil and water table meant that preservation of artefacts discovered during excavations was not as good as elsewhere.

Interestingly, from the perspective of Great War heritage, Bayernwald was a site that benefited from the 1960s upsurge of interest in visiting Great War battlefields. During the 1970s and 1980s, André Becquart, the landowner, ran a café-museum at the site, with trenches reconstructed, a mineshaft (used to tunnel beneath British lines) explored, and the museum building stacked full of the artefacts he had retrieved from his diggings – he even issued postcards of the private museum (Bostyn and Vancoillie 2000: 169–73). But Becquart's initiative was an individual obsession, and, after he died in 1986, the museum became derelict, and the wood overgrown. It remained in this state until the early explorations of The Diggers, and then ABAF's more systematic investigations.

ABAF underwent personnel changes in 2001, but under the direction of Bostyn, the work at Bayernwald continued and developed. Under the auspices of the European Union, and with the support of the Flemish government and local municipal authorities, as well as the Belgian Military Academy and the German Embassy in Brussels, the site was restored in 2003, and opened to the public a year later. The most startling feature of what is now a revamped (and more accurately reconstructed) Great War heritage site is the presence of wood panels that line the trenches, some 300,000 interwoven willow branches giving the site its distinctive appearance along a length of about 300 metres of restored German trench, which includes four restored German bunkers. It is a kind of living archaeology to see a photograph of two German soldiers in the summer of 1916, relaxing in their willow-panelled trench at Bayernwald, in an otherwise devastated landscape (Bostyn and Vancoillie 2000: 47), and to walk through the modern reconstructions today.

Bostyn's appointment as curator for the Memorial Museum Passchendaele 1917 (a total redesign of the old Streekmuseum), which opened in April 2004, enabled the new ABAF to conduct excavations and reconstructions at several other sites. In April 2005, a series of four bunkers – used as shelters and as a dressing station – was opened to the public at Letteburg, a hillside site near to Mount Kemmel, itself within sight of Bayernwald. On a more ambitious scale, a part of the old Ypres–Roulers railway running between Zonnebeke and Passchendaele (disused since 1952) was excavated in 2005, and has been reconstructed as a battlefield walk and cycle path between the Memorial Museum Passchendaele 1917 and the new visitor centre at the Tyne Cot war cemetery, which was opened in September 2006.

Several German bunkers and the well-preserved remains of a Lancashire Fusilier were discovered during these investigations. The presence of a silver cigarette case and a wristwatch has suggested to some that this may be the

The reconstruction of German trenches at Bayernwald, near Ypres. *(Courtesy and © Franky Bostyn, ABAF)*

The German trenches at Bayernwald, near Ypres, as they appear today. *(© Author's collection)*

remains of an officer. These activities were part of an ambitious programme of events across the Ypres Salient aimed at commemorating the 90th anniversary of the Third Battle of Ypres – or Passchendaele – in the summer of 2007, and clearly show how Great War archaeology in this region is now seen as an integral part of First World War history, local and international education and tourism, and more generally of the archaeological heritage of Belgian Flanders.

Despite these well-organised activities, the sheer number of dead in the Ypres Salient means that discoveries of human remains will occur far into the future. In September 2006, during the laying of a gas pipeline, the remains of five soldiers were found near the Frezenberg Ridge in the middle of the salient. Rescue excavations by 'Archeo 7' (the recently founded archaeological unit managing the archaeological heritage of this area) and ABAF required the digging up of part of a road, where the bodies were found seemingly intentionally buried in a shell hole. Early identification suggests they may have belonged to the 4th Australian Division. Preservation varied between

One of the reconstructed Letteberg shelters near Mount Kemmel, Belgian Flanders. Note the Red Cross sign, indicating a first aid post. *(© Author's collection)*

the remains, some of whom were interred in blankets, but one body was exceptionally well preserved, with fragments of corduroy still plainly visible.

Perhaps the best documented of ABAF's digs, however, was carried out mainly by the original team at Beecham Farm, located at the foot of the Passchendaele Ridge near to Tyne Cot cemetery. The site was discovered in 1999, when a farmer's wife fell into a hole that had suddenly opened up. Preliminary investigations showed that the farm had been built during the 1920s over the top of an underground structure that was later identified as a wartime dugout that had lain unsuspected since 1918.

ABAF carried out a thorough investigation of the site, stabilising the hole, surveying the dugout, plotting its artefacts, removing the whole wooden structure for later reassembling, and finally undertaking remedial work which saw compacted earth filling the yawning gap left by the dugout's removal, and aimed at stabilising the farmhouse above. Hand in hand with the physical work went a comprehensive investigation of the area in military history archives, in

View of the well-preserved interior of one of the Letteberg shelters. (© *Author's collection*)

order to better understand what the structure was, and who had built and used it (Barton *et al.* 2004: 279–88; Doyle *et al.* 2001). ABAF's work at Beecham Farm was detailed and meticulous, with attention paid to the geology of the area, and a wealth of drawn plans and photographs, as well as a film record made of the excavations. An inventory of artefacts was created, and special attention given to the dugout's architecture.

This research led to some interesting conclusions. As the depth of soil above the dugout was only about 2 metres, the structure itself was shallow and unsafe, and certainly not shell-proof. The shelter had originally had three entrances, and the lack of steel in its construction indicated a German origin, perhaps as early as 1915. Yet there was evidence of blankets being hung as protection from gas attacks, possibly put up by British Royal Engineers in the winter of 1917/18. Altogether, there were forty-two bunks inside the dugout, providing shelter for sixty-six men and three officers. While metal items such as buttons, belt buckles and an ammunition bandolier had, not surprisingly, survived well,

Excavations along the line of the old Ypres–Roulers railway, between Zonnebeke and Tyne Cot in the Ypres Salient. *(Courtesy and © Franky Bostyn, ABAF)*

preservation in the waterlogged conditions of other more fragile items was extraordinary. A greatcoat, a scarf, puttees and boots all looked as if they had been discarded only a few hours before. Even traces of black candle smoke could be seen on the walls.

ABAF's researches in the archives led to an insightful reconstruction of the history of the Beecham dugout. It is possible that it had originally been built by the Germans as a shelter for one of their artillery units, sometime between 1915 and 1916, when this was a quiet area some 3 miles behind the German front lines. By October 1917, as part of the battle for Passchendaele, the area was captured by the British, who in turn used the old German artillery positions for their own gun batteries, and occupied German dugouts, refurbishing them for their own use. This changing nature of the Ypres Salient battlefield as the war progressed seems to explain the structure of Beecham dugout, and the change of ownership, from German to British, explains why so many British objects were found in a German-built structure. ABAF's work at Beecham and its prompt publication was perhaps the best example of serious and in-depth research conducted by non-archaeologists, and has added greatly to our knowledge of the underground war in the old Ypres Salient.

Professional archaeology's engagement with the First World War before 2001 was not entirely absent. In 1989, during an excavation of the remains of the medieval abbey at Zonnebeke in the centre of the old Ypres Salient battlefield, the Institute for Archaeological Heritage (IAP), as it then was, discovered and investigated a deeply buried Great War dugout that was identified by Aleks Deseyne of the Zonnebeke Museum as having been built by the Australian Tunnelling Company by the end of 1917 (Dewilde 1991: 380). Nearby, a second dugout, known as the Bremen Redoubt, which had been discovered in 1983 at Zonnebeke's clay pits, was also investigated, photographed and drawn to scale by the IAP's archaeologists at the request of the town's municipal authorities. The German dugout at the Bremen Redoubt revealed remarkable preservation in its plank-lined galleries and double-plank beds, as well as miscellaneous items, from unexploded bombs to soldiers' spades. Nevertheless, these two excavations were the exceptions, and the majority of digging around Ypres was carried out by amateurs during these early years.

A MODERN ARCHAEOLOGY OF BATTLEZONES

In 2002, dramatic changes occurred, and Great War archaeology was incorporated for the first time into standard archaeological practice in Flanders.

The impetus for this development was political, and occurred when the Belgian minister Paul van Grembergen requested that the IAP, which had recently been renamed the Flemish Heritage Institute (VIOE), undertake an archaeological survey along the line of a projected extension to the A19 motorway across the old Ypres Salient, in order to evaluate its impact on the archaeological heritage of the First World War (de Meyer and Pype 2004: 3). In some ways, this was a Belgian parallel to the investigations by Yves Desfossés and his DRAC colleagues along the route of the A29 on the Somme in 1997.

While this request focused on one area and one project, its true significance lay in the fact that the physical remains of an event less than a century old were acknowledged as an integral part of Belgium's archaeological heritage – of equal worth to a Roman villa or a medieval abbey.

One consequence of the IAP's investigations was that a year later, in November 2003, van Grembergen was in Ypres announcing the formation of a Department of Great War Archaeology to the Belgian and international media. The department was a part of the VIOE, and was supported by the 'Flemish universities, the Belgian Army's Service for the Disposal and Demolition of Explosives (DOVO) and a wide range of international collaborators' (Dewilde et al. 2004). Later, some of the individuals concerned with the VIOE's excavations formed the Association for World War Archaeology (AWA) to publish and seek financial resources for Great War archaeological excavations (de Meyer and Pype 2004: 45, 47–8; www.a-w-a.be). These linked developments were a turning point. After some eighty-five years of ad hoc amateur digging and land clearance – and in the space of just over twelve months – a modern scientific archaeology of the Great War in Flanders had arrived in a legally constituted and academically and politically acceptable form.

Behind the scenes, professional archaeologists and other interested parties were engaging in a vigorous debate concerning the issues facing a modern archaeology of the Great War. Key questions were being asked, such as, are the remains of the First World War truly a part of Belgian national archaeological heritage? Are these remains old enough to be archaeologically important and valuable? How old does an object need to be in order to be considered appropriate for archaeological investigation? Should the archaeological record of the Great War be considered as equal to other, more traditional, kinds of archaeology? Is there an obligation to make an inventory of the remaining vestiges of the First World War and legally protect certain sites and their landscapes, as is the case with earlier archaeological remains?

Also, since there is a wealth of documentary evidence available for the First World War in general, and the Ypres Salient in particular (e.g. maps, aerial photographs, letters, civilian and military memoirs, and regimental histories), can archaeological survey and excavation, with its focus on three-dimensional material culture, add anything new and meaningful to our understanding of the conflict in Belgian Flanders? In other words, can archaeology cover the same ground as military history but bring distinctive new perspectives by virtue of testing the ground rather than simply relying on the printed word? Further, to what extent might acknowledging the war's archaeological heritage expand the scope and social impact of archaeology more generally in Flanders, in terms of the region's museums, tourism industry, and local attitudes to what had been evident but overlooked for decades?

These are important questions that had been waiting in the wings for generations, but that only now could be openly asked by professional archaeologists with any hope of a meaningful response. All these questions, and the issues they raised, were crystallised by the A19 project, albeit preceded and given momentum by the rising profile of amateur Great War archaeology that had occurred during the 1990s with the activities of The Diggers, ABAF and others.

The A19 Project

The Ypres Salient has a rich and complex military history, and the A19 area especially played a prominent role during the Battle of Second Ypres, between April and May 1915, and again in the Battle of Third Ypres (Passchendaele), which began on 31 July 1917. Nearby, the first use of gas occurred on 22 April 1915, when the Germans unleashed this new weapon against the Allied trenches. This was a significant technological and military development, whose invention and use influenced many later twentieth-century conflicts, and whose material traces from 1915 were found during the IAP's investigations of the area.

The reconnaissance of the route of the projected A19 motorway extension investigated the area from Wieltje, near Ypres, to Steenstraete at Langemark-Poelkapelle, a distance of some 7 kilometres across the old Ypres Salient battlefield. Several locations were identified for trial excavations to assess the potential impact on the war's archaeological heritage.

The investigations were designed to answer several important questions. What is the extent and state of preservation of the First World War's archaeological heritage in this area? How widespread is the presence of human remains on the battlefield? What damage would be caused to the material and human remains of the area's wartime archaeological record if the motorway was built along the projected route (Dewilde *et al.* 2004)?

Faced with an official request to conduct a professional archaeological investigation, the VIOE's archaeologists drew on their expertise of surveying and excavating the region's rich medieval heritage. At the time, there was no methodology specially tailored to investigating Great War sites, despite the extensive digging already carried out by The Diggers and ABAF. These groups were not trained archaeologists, and were motivated by enthusiasm and knowledge of Great War military history. Although ABAF published many of its results, overall these groups were not in any position to develop a scientific methodology for battlezone archaeology. The VIOE's approach was to undertake substantial preliminary research in order to narrow down the area to be investigated in depth. It was here that the distinctive newness of Great War archaeology became apparent.

There was a wealth of different kinds of documentary material that could be consulted, each providing a different view of the same area, and often overlapping in highly insightful ways. Regimental archives produced official views of the military actions of their regiments, war diaries provided personal and anecdotal accounts of individual actions, trench maps revealed how soldiers on the ground carried out the orders from above, how they were organised, and the sheer extent of the transformation of the landscape in the Ypres Salient. Further, contemporary and modern aerial photographs yielded extraordinary bird's-eye views of the changing battlefields that could be correlated with trench maps, and that gave detailed assessments of the effects of artillery barrages, advances and retreats. Traditional fieldwalking added further insights, especially in locating concentrations of metal scrap, concrete (from pillboxes), and traces of the Decauville narrow-gauge military railways that ferried men and supplies around the battlefield. All of these were powerful tools that enabled the VIOE to identify potentially valuable sites for excavation (de Meyer and Pype 2004: 9–18).

A significant innovation in this preliminary assessment, and an indication of the inescapably anthropological nature of Great War archaeology, was the creation of a 'battlefield ethnography', where contacts were made and interviews held with local residents (often landowners and farmers) to discover what they knew (or remembered) about Great War remains on their property. The VIOE saw this ethnographic approach as supplementing their archaeological prospecting, by helping them to identify vestiges of the war's physical remains.

In fact, this mainstream anthropological technique also had a wider application in terms of gathering information not just about actual places and events, but about changing local attitudes towards the battlefields, and concerning myths and stories about the war that sometimes owed more to imagination than to history. It also served to stimulate sometimes long-buried personal and family memories of experiences of the war and its interwar aftermath. This approach to Great War landscapes stood on its own as a powerful way of investigating the period 1914 to the present, quite apart from its value in locating the physical remnants of the war itself.

On the basis of the initial reconnaissance, several sites, known as 'Turco' and 'High Command Redoubt', were chosen for preliminary excavations. Investigations near Hindenburg Farm on the Mauser Ridge – an important observation post on the German front line – revealed traces of shell craters, rectangular wooden structures, a dump of abandoned German stick grenades, the concrete rubble from now-destroyed pillboxes, the remains of what may have been a gun emplacement, and also of typically German panels of interwoven branches that lined the German trenches. Despite their small scale, these test results showed plainly that archaeology could uncover significant traces of both British and German positions.

More significant, and on a larger scale, was the open-area excavation of the site known as 'Cross Roads', which was virtually in the shadow of the incomplete flyover section of the A19 motorway, and adjacent to the small CWGC war cemetery known as Track X.

Excavations at Cross Roads revealed sections of trenches, shelters, ammunition depots and gun emplacements (de Meyer and Pype 2004: 19–28). Importantly, these investigations shed light on the evolution of trench building in an area where the Allied front line had become stable between 1915 and 1917. Original straight-line trenches had developed into a zigzag system in order to protect the soldiers from shell blasts, and to provide shelter from direct rifle fire by any enemy who broke into the trenches. The changing methods of trench construction were also evident, with the introduction of different kinds of structures and materials, such as A-frames, corrugated iron, explosion-proof metal and sandbags – all of which gave soldiers greater safety and comfort.

Archaeology also revealed a clear distinction between British and German constructions, with German structures being more solidly built with thick beams, in contrast to the flimsy planks used by the British. The German preference for revetting trenches with wattlework rather than the corrugated iron or explosion-proof metal used by the British also proved to be much more

Aerial view of excavations at the Cross Roads site near Wieltje, Ypres. *(Courtesy and © Mathieu de Meyer and VIOE)*

stable, as well as archaeologically identifiable. Unlike the British and their allies, for whom trenches were temporary staging posts for the next attack, the defending Germans had the time and opportunity to choose and massively reinforce strategic positions that were built to last. They often protected their wooden shelters with concrete walls, whereas the British did not. Military history and contemporary photographs had long pointed out the different attitudes towards, and building techniques of, trenches by the German army – but here was first-hand archaeological verification.

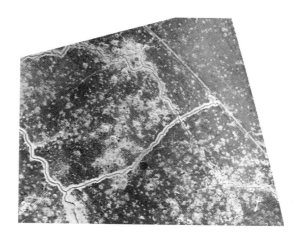

Wartime aerial photograph of the Cross Roads area, showing trenches and bomb craters. *(Courtesy and © Mathieu de Meyer and VIOE)*

Unlike the written sources of military history, archaeology adds often highly emotive texture to the everyday life of soldiers in the trenches by uncovering the military and personal items they carried with them. The A19 excavations uncovered numerous examples of such portable objects, including cap badges, buttons and boots, as well as weapons, ammunition, tools, rum jars, razors, wristwatches, combs and even the fragmentary remains of an early gas mask in the form of its mica eyepieces (de Meyer and Pype 2004: 28–42). The preservation of these items brought a personal element to the investigations in ways not usually experienced in more traditional kinds of archaeology, where such items either do not survive, or, if they do, they cannot produce the uncanny feelings that such implements could have belonged to the excavator's own relatives.

The regimental badges that were recovered indicated the presence of soldiers from the Royal King's Rifle Corps and the Dorsetshire Regiment, among others, and a standard-issue spoon engraved with a soldier's service number was tantalising evidence of the personalisation of belongings. Soldiers' habits of carving their names or identifying numbers onto their equipment connects the excavator to the person rather than simply to the object, and may also allow later research to track down the individual in question. Nevertheless, there is no guarantee that the item itself belonged to the individual with whose remains it was found. 'Souveneering', as we have seen, was a way of life during the war.

War, however, is fundamentally about the killing and wounding of soldiers, and, unlike most archaeologists, those who excavate Great War sites are almost certain to discover human remains. Moreover, these remains are often just

Part of an excavated trench at the Cross Roads site near Wieltje in the Ypres Salient. *(© Author's collection)*

scattered fragments of human beings who were killed by high explosive. While many were terribly mutilated, with their bodies blown across the landscape and into shell craters, others were virtually atomised into nothingness, and their remains little more than small pieces of bone. How to treat (and identify) such poignant remains is an ongoing challenge to Great War archaeologists.

The A19 excavations uncovered the remains of five British, five French, and three German soldiers. At one location at the Cross Roads site, three soldiers were found piled one on top of the other, suggesting to the excavators that they may have died during an attack. A Webley handgun, rather than the more usual Lee Enfield rifle, suggested that one individual may have been a machine-gunner (de Meyer and Pype 2004: 38). As the VIOE's archaeologists recovered these remains, there was a sense that with each discovery another personal history came into view, and the opportunity arose of identifying and reclaiming a soldier from the lists of 'the missing' engraved on the Menin Gate and Tyne Cot cemetery. There was a very anthropological dimension to what appeared to be a strictly archaeological investigation.

The excavations of the A19 Project clearly showed that the First World War possessed significant archaeological traces, and that this war's physical remains should be regarded as an important part of Belgian Flanders' cultural heritage. Equally significant, and a demonstration of the political dimension of archaeology, was the fact that on the basis of the VIOE's discoveries (as well as international media coverage of the investigations), the Flemish government announced in August 2005 that it would not to go through with the original plan for the A19 extension. Instead, the motorway would be diverted along a new course that avoided the front lines and the battlefields.

This was a victory for the fledgling archaeology of the Great War, and a public (and political) acknowledgement of the importance of Great War heritage in Flanders. It brought Great War archaeology centre stage, and showed that modern scientific investigations of the war's physical remains could provide new information for discussions about and evaluations of such developments as motorway construction, and the building of industrial estates and housing. Now, the traces of the First World War had to be regarded on the same basis as Belgium's better-known prehistoric and medieval heritage, and damage assessments would have to be made in advance of any urban renewal projects.

THE FUTURE OF GREAT WAR ARCHAEOLOGY

The breathtaking speed of Great War archaeology's development in Belgian Flanders does not disguise the fact that this new kind of archaeology possesses many unique and distinctive features that are only now beginning to be addressed. Not least of these is ensuring the safety of excavators in a landscape still saturated with volatile unexploded munitions. Constant contact has to be maintained with the bomb disposal team of the Belgian army based at Houthulst near Langemark, whose expertise in recognising and assessing the origin, type and stability of explosives provides archaeologists with important information as well as personal protection. Never far from the minds of Great War archaeologists in Belgium (and France) is the fact that what they are engaged in is, fundamentally, the 'archaeology of lethal behaviour'.

The A19 Project also contributed significantly to the development of methodologies for this new kind of archaeology, particularly in the recognition of features and artefacts not normally encountered in Flemish archaeology's more usual kinds of work. While the VIOE's archaeologists were used to excavating prehistoric and medieval sites, with distinctive and well-documented pottery, burials and structures, they were now confronted with largely unfamiliar Great War landscapes and material culture. Artillery-shell craters, evolving trench systems and gun emplacements were now archaeological features, and bombs, bullets, grenades, rifles and uniforms were archaeological finds. And interspersed with all these were the remains of men appearing like images from a horror movie – skeletons wearing steel helmets and boots, or pieces of the body blown apart by high explosive. All human remains had to be carefully and sensitively treated, but what, for example, constituted a 'body'? Did a leg bone represent a body? An arm? A head? And what happened if no identity tag was found?

It was clear that creating innovative methodologies for Great War archaeology required philosophical and theoretical issues to be raised, as well as new practical techniques developed, and knowledge gained. For example, archaeologists need to consider that in their initial archaeological reconnaissance their finds would vary, not least because after 1918 the Ypres Salient had seen unequal levels of battlefield clearance. The reasons for this remain unclear, although they could be linked to individual landowners' decisions about such activity. So the density of remains today will not necessarily reflect the battlefields during the war, the battles fought on them, or even the situation in 1919. As with all archaeological investigations, post-depositional factors have been at work.

There is also the issue of that most basic kind of archaeological prospection – fieldwalking. Is fieldwalking and tracing concentrations of mostly metal scrap the best way of locating sites for excavation, especially in landscapes that have been officially cleared of battlefield debris during the interwar years? And, in uncleared or partially cleared areas, what should be the role of metal detecting in an archaeological landscape defined by its metallic nature? What, in such conditions, are the possibilities for geophysical research? How can we recognise and best excavate bomb craters, and can we identify telltale signs indicating the presence of human remains among the debris of industrialised war?

Although these are difficult methodological issues, the discovery of human remains is not a new phenomenon. Ever since refugees had returned to the battlefields of the Ypres Salient in 1919, soldiers' remains had been found on a yearly basis (although they were not investigated by archaeologists). While the VIOE's archaeologists have professional issues to consider, the treatment of human remains follows a well-established practice. The bodies are recorded in the normal way – by drawing, photography and initial on-site examination by physical/forensic anthropologists. The local police then take possession of the

Reburial of nine unidentified French soldiers from Boezinge, at the war cemetery of St Charles de Potyze, Ypres. *(Courtesy and © Aurel Sercu)*

bones and the items associated with them, such as buttons, badges, miscellaneous military equipment and personal belongings. Where time permits, a more detailed forensic examination may be made. The remains are then given to the war graves authorities of the appropriate country, each of which follows its own procedures that culminate in the formal reburial of the remains.

The identification (where possible) and reburial process is another distinguishing feature of Great War archaeology, where human remains are placed back in the ground, rather than shelved in storage boxes in a university or museum. In this way, Great War archaeology shares a moral as well as a methodological set of concerns with those kinds of archaeology that deal with indigenous peoples across the world, and who themselves seek to identify, repatriate and rebury their dead (see Hubert 1989; Zimmerman 1989). Learning to 'read' and interpret this new kind of archaeological evidence remains a challenge for all who specialise in the archaeology of war.

Modern archaeology is not only concerned with the theoretical and practical investigations at ground level, but has over the past two decades increasingly taken advantage of new technological developments – some of which can be traced back to the First World War. One of these developments became an integral part of the A19 Project, and has since broadened its remit to include the interpretation of aerial photographs, and analysis and manipulation of these images using powerful computer imaging software. While the potential of aerial photography in archaeological investigations is well established, in Great War archaeology it can be combined with different kinds of information, such as that offered by trench maps and detailed documentary records. The photographs themselves belong to different eras – wartime, the interwar period and today. It is only recently that this wealth of aerial images has been modified and interpreted by integrating them with Geographical Information System (GIS) computer programs.

Recent work by Birger Stichelbaut included digitising over a thousand aerial photographs from the First World War in Belgian Flanders, and entering them into a GIS program at the University of Ghent (Stichelbaut 2006). The exact locations of 1,039 out of a total of 1,128 images were identified, overcoming, for the main part, such problems as correlating the wartime names of landscape features with modern ones, and the expansion of some villages since 1918. As wartime aerial photography became more sophisticated, armies on both sides learned to camouflage the telltale appearance of their bunkers and artillery emplacements, although stereoscopic pictures often overcame these efforts. Digital stereoscopic images called anaglyphs have proved equally successful at revealing such hidden features some ninety years later. The identified sites were then inventoried, with information concerning size, coordinates, nationality and date.

While this project was developed for studying the First World War, its results also proved useful for more traditional kinds of archaeology. The information yielded not only revealed information on Great War sites, but also on environmental features and the presence of prehistoric and medieval sites, some of which were destroyed during the course of the war and were hitherto unknown. The majority of features did, however, belong to the war, and, despite local differences in geology and topography, it was possible to distinguish between gun emplacements, infantry locations and a variety of structures behind the front line, as well as to discern otherwise invisible features such as deep dugouts and mines.

So sensitive was this computer-aided technique that it was also possible to identify dummy trenches (originally dug to mislead aerial photographers during

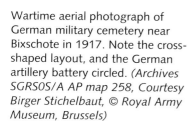

Wartime aerial photograph of German military cemetery near Bixschote in 1917. Note the cross-shaped layout, and the German artillery battery circled. *(Archives SGRSOS/A AP map 258, Courtesy Birger Stichelbaut, © Royal Army Museum, Brussels)*

the war) by observing the absence of shadows due to their shallow construction. Barbed wire could also be identified because of the geometrical arrangement of the wooden stakes that held it in place, bunkers housing German *Minenwerfer* (trench mortars) revealed themselves by a rectangular roof opening, narrow-gauge Decauville railways could be seen because of their curving lines, and even listening posts showed up as small round spots on the landscape. Artillery emplacements were often set in horseshoe-shaped embankments, easily seen from above, and ammunition dumps have paths leading to them. One of the most spectacular images is of German war cemeteries near to the front-line trenches and contemporary with the war. These were often laid out as huge decorative figures in the landscape, such as the cross-shaped one nearby Bixschote north of Ypres (which also has an identifiable German artillery battery adjacent to it).

The remarkable detail revealed in these digitised images, their accompanying information, and the ability of computerised cartography to produce time-sensitive layers that can be removed or added at will to show the changing nature of the front line, represents a significant advance for Great War archaeology. Equally important in this respect was the work of Mathieu de Meyer, who made an inventory of First World War features in the Ypres Salient using aerial photographs on behalf of the VIOE and the In Flanders Fields Museum.

This research was directly tied to public education and to changing public perceptions of the war, when it was used by the In Flanders Fields Museum in the ambitious exhibition on war landscapes, The Last Witness, in 2006. This research into the potential of aerial photography in Great War archaeology (and beyond) by a new generation of scholars means that today we have the potential for a far greater appreciation of the war than was available during the conflict itself (de Meyer 2005; Stichelbaut 2005, 2006, 2009, Stichelbaut *et al.* 2009) – a fact reflected in a groundbreaking, international conference on this topic held in Ypres in October 2006 (and sponsored jointly by the European Union, Ghent University and the In Flanders Fields Museum).

Another aspect of the unique nature of Great War archaeology also became apparent during the VIOE's A19 Project. It was clear that in order to document and interpret the vast quantities of largely unfamiliar Great War materials, the VIOE required the cooperation of many different kinds of specialist, amateur and professional, in Belgium and internationally. Fortunately, the First World War has inspired many such individuals, who focus almost entirely on one or two specific kinds of feature, whether military maps, regimental badges, firearms, artillery shells, uniforms, memorabilia, or the various techniques of trench construction (e.g. Chasseaud 1999; Williamson 2003). As Marc Dewilde, the VIOE's chief archaeologist, observed, 'a unique feature of the First World War is that, in addition to military historians, it attracts a large and wide-ranging number of specialist groups. Together, they form a rich repository of specialised knowledge . . .' (Dewilde *et al.* 2004).

This knowledge was necessary if Great War archaeologists were going to be able to identify British, Belgian French, and German bullets, to discern the difference between shrapnel and gas artillery shells, to identify a German bunker, to distinguish between a French and British trench, or identify the fragmentary remains of a rifle or mortar. Not only could the VIOE call on this wealth of outside expertise in its analysis of excavated materials, but, at the same time, it became a legal and professional focus for the networks of dedicated experts across the world.

A further challenge to the A19 excavators, and an issue that has (and will continue to have) a profound impact on the ways in which future generations will view Great War archaeology, was the amount of media attention the project received, and the effect of this on the public. Newspapers from the United Kingdom, Canada, Australia, the United States and even Japan regarded this new kind of archaeology as newsworthy. This, in turn, and together with word of mouth, stimulated the interest of considerable numbers of the public, many of whom visited the excavations – far more than would come to see the excavation of a Bronze Age burial or a Roman fort.

Schoolchildren (from Belgium, France and the United Kingdom), visitors on a battlefield package tour, knowledgeable Great War enthusiasts, and the simply curious all turned up on site, visiting the place where, some may have believed, a relative could have fought or died. Such were the numbers of visitors

Excavation becomes
commemoration.
Poppies placed where
human remains were
found during the
excavation at the
Cross Roads site, near
Wieltje, in the Ypres
Salient. *(Courtesy
and © VIOE)*

that on occasion the VIOE's excavation team was overwhelmed. Faxes, e-mails
and letters expressing appreciation, giving information and offering help flowed
into the offices of the VIOE and to the team on site.

The presence of many different kinds of visitors emphasises the
anthropological dimension of Great War archaeology, and highlights
the problems and potential of excavating such recent and sensitive layers of
history. More than just an archaeological dig, the A19 Project (and similar
excavations on the Somme) connected to the cultural memory of the war, and
was underlined by the emotional resonances that link generations by tying
people to places, either by historical fact or imagined associations. At one
point during the excavations at Cross Roads, the remains of a Northumberland
Fusilier soldier were found, and visitors covered the ground with poppies and

remembrance crosses, objects more usually associated with larger-scale and meticulously orchestrated 11 November Armistice commemorations.

The investigations at the Cross Roads site were designed to test the potential of archaeology to identify and document the area's Great War heritage, but had another, equally significant, result. Archaeological activity was seen to be visibly extending the landscapes of remembrance, and connecting the public with wider notions of commemoration that hitherto had been focused almost solely on official war grave cemeteries and monuments to the missing, such as the Menin Gate and Tyne Cot cemetery. In other words, archaeology was actively contributing to a more nuanced and personal understanding of the First World War by temporarily creating places (the archaeological excavation itself) where the public could stand on a battlefield and observe the retrieval of a long-dead soldier. Arguably more than any other kind of archaeology, the excavation of Great War sites was producing an intimate relationship with the general public.

A more problematic development, as we have already seen, was the advent of a television archaeology of the war. As with excavations in France, 2003 and 2004 saw Canadian television companies actively financing a series of programmes according to a commercial rather than a strictly academic research agenda, albeit with the involvement of professional archaeologists. The series of programmes that were produced ranged over Great War sites in France and Belgium, providing opportunities to investigate hitherto untouched battlefield locations, and making significant discoveries.

Most recently, in the Ypres region, television excavations have taken place at Bixschote, and at the Great War locations known as 'Forward Cottage' and 'Caesar's Nose'. Here, as in France, the results of these excavations have not yet been published at the time of writing, and those who were involved cannot yet comment on them. The issue of publication is, of course, something which future television archaeology – with its central role of promoting and financing, rather than just recording other people's investigations – will have to address. This is particularly the case in Belgium, where there is currently no equivalent to the popular publications that the French regional archaeological services (DRAC) publish concerning their investigations. This fact also accounts for the comparative lack of detailed archaeological information available concerning Great War excavations as compared to the situation in France.

While television archaeology of the kind described here has many advantages for professional archaeologists investigating the First World War, its influence on such a new kind of archaeology, which is still formulating its own methodologies, is a double-edged sword.

Television crew filming excavations in the Ypres Salient in 2005. *(Courtesy and © Birger Stichelbaut)*

Recent advances in the recognition and practice of a modern scientific archaeology of the First World War in Belgian Flanders have been rapid and dramatic, although this new discipline is still in its infancy. Most importantly, there has been a sea change in attitudes. There is now no doubt that professional investigation of the material culture of the First World War is a scientifically and culturally worthwhile endeavour. Indeed, Great War archaeology is a prime example of what has recently been called 'the archaeologies of the contemporary past' (Buchli and Lucas 2001), and is therefore firmly situated in the vanguard of new kinds of archaeological investigations.

Equally important is the fact that the change in professional attitudes towards Great War archaeology has been accompanied by official recognition that the physical traces of the conflict must be fully integrated into Flanders' overall archaeological heritage. In other words, the Flemish government's 1993 decree that dealt with the management, research and protection of the region's

Excavation of the British line known as Ealing Trench at Caesar's Nose in the Ypres Salient. Note the inverted A-frame that supports the duckboards and allows water to drain away beneath. *(Courtesy and © VIOE)*

The postwar marker stone at Caesar's Nose in the Ypres Salient, marking the maximum advance of German soldiers. *(© Author's collection)*

archaeological heritage is now extended to the First World War, and can be legally enforced. Great War sites and finds now have to be reported to the authorities, and the granting of excavation permits and use of metal detectors are strictly controlled, just as they would be with prehistoric and medieval remains. The application of the act to First World War remains thus regulates and minimises damage to sites by construction activities, and by those who engage in illicit digging. As everywhere else around the world, however, the existence of legislation is one matter; having the time and financial resources available to enforce it is quite another.

One consequence of this new professional approach has been efforts to identify and define areas that require legal recognition as heritage locations. In 2004, in the framework of the Central Archaeological Inventory, a new project began with the aim of documenting all Great War archaeological sites in Western Flanders. Once completed, this inventory allows for sites to be evaluated and for some to be listed for protection as designated war landscapes, and perhaps, eventually, to be investigated. By registering and classifying war-related sites, the public are also drawn in by a heightened awareness of the heritage value of these locations, and can sometimes be organised in support for their protection. A sympathetic local population can be crucial to monitoring the sites, and when considered altogether, these developments should make illicit digs far more difficult.

Apart from these official developments, the professional excavations along the old Ypres Salient have highlighted the true value of a modern archaeology of the war. They have shown that information retrieved by professional archaeologists is more accurate, detailed and nuanced than that which can be gained only by looking at trench maps and aerial photographs in a more traditional military history approach. Archaeological fieldwork can identify sudden changes in the conditions of war, such as trench repairs made after heavy shelling, and the presence of soldiers in a particular spot for a short period. Excavation can reveal unexpected structures, such as the entrance to a deep dugout or an ammunition depot, and the extent to which it may have changed hands between Allied and German forces. A more detailed understanding of the evolution of trench construction can also be gained, where, for example, the dimension of duckboards may indicate a date for their construction and for the trench within which they are found. Excavation also uncovers the terrible effects of industrialised war on the human bodies, and the emotive artefacts belonging to or made by individuals.

Such fine-grained details, uncovered by archaeologists, and interpreted with the help of the many specialists referred to above, can add new insights into the conduct and human cost of particular battles at specific locations, and clarify ambiguities that are beyond the abilities of other kinds of investigation to resolve. Archaeology can test the assumptions and interpretations of military history, offer a soldier's-eye view of a skirmish or battle, and bring an intimacy to the experiences of soldiers through the objects they left behind.

As in France, arguably the most significant and sensitive contributions of Belgium's new approach to the war's archaeology is in the locating, documenting and recovering of the dead. Archaeologists always take painstaking care when uncovering human remains, but in the archaeology of the First World War there is a unique and overriding imperative at work. These are not Bronze Age warriors, Roman legionaries or medieval peasants, forever divorced in time and space from the archaeologists who excavate them and from those who come to visit. The soldiers of the Great War are, essentially, our own and very recent ancestors, to whom we still feel intimately connected.

As many soldiers who fought in the battles around Ypres have no known grave, not even the smallest fragment of battlefield evidence can be neglected because it may contribute to the identification of an individual. In other words, archaeology can bring back those who are lost to us, either by complete identification or partially, as was the case with Private George Herbert Parker from Barnsley in Yorkshire, who had served with the 5th Battalion, York and Lancaster Regiment, and was killed in action aged 23 on Sunday 11 July 1915 at Boezinge. Along with those of thirty other men from his battalion who died in No Man's Land during the attack, Parker's remains have never been identified, and his name is engraved on panel 55 at the Menin Gate memorial to the missing at Ypres.

Parker's case, like that of the German soldiers Jakob Hönes and Albert Thielicke at Serre, in France, shows the power and poignancy of Great War objects in a heart-rending way. In August 2000, during excavations by The Diggers at Boezinge, an old-fashioned 'cut-throat' razor was found with Parker's service number, 716, scratched onto it. When Aurel Sercu, one of the team members at the time, published an article in the *Barnsley Chronicle*, hoping to find relatives, he was contacted by Mr John Hutchinson, the widower of George Parker's granddaughter – and unsuspectingly opened a Pandora's box of tangled emotions and memories.

Instead of asking for the razor to be sent back to England, Hutchinson sent Sercu a package that contained a photograph of the young soldier George Parker and his war service medal. George Parker's widow Beatrice had kept these two items from her tragically short first marriage, and they had been retained by the family. It was explained to Sercu that the photograph and medal of George Parker

The 'cut-throat' razor inscribed '716' found by The Diggers at Boezinge near Ypres. *(Courtesy and © Aurel Sercu)*

The 'memory card' of Private George Herbert Parker, with Parker's inscribed razor, war medal and details of his military service, death and commemoration. *(Courtesy and © Aurel Sercu)*

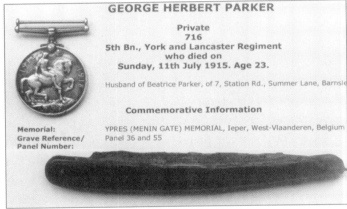

GEORGE HERBERT PARKER

Private
716
5th Bn., York and Lancaster Regiment
who died on
Sunday, 11th July 1915. Age 23.

Husband of Beatrice Parker, of 7, Station Rd., Summer Lane, Barnsle

Commemorative Information

Memorial: YPRES (MENIN GATE) MEMORIAL, Ieper, West-Vlaanderen, Belgium
Grave Reference/   Panel 36 and 55
Panel Number:

Photograph of Private George Herbert Parker, sent to Aurel Sercu by John Hutchinson, the widower of George Parker's granddaughter. *(Courtesy and © Aurel Sercu)*

should not only be reunited with the razor, but that all three objects belonged more to those who had found a trace of him on an almost forgotten Flanders battlefield than to himself. Perhaps it was felt that sending the two items to Belgium would have been Beatrice's last wish (Aurel Sercu, pers. comm.).

Here was a transference of what might be called an 'orphan memory', a way of making sure that a young soldier of the First World War was never forgotten despite the circumstances of his death. Ironically, The Diggers, and perhaps Aurel Sercu most of all, despite being total strangers to George and Beatrice Parker, had become almost a substitute family, the sole inheritors and keepers of a young man's life. The medal, photograph and razor were donated by Sercu and The Diggers to the In Flanders Fields Museum in Ypres, where they rest alongside so many other items returned to the museum by the descendants of Great War soldiers (Dendooven 2007). After almost ninety years, a single object – the inscribed razor – had reclaimed the identity, appearance and memory of a missing soldier.

Great War archaeology, as this example shows, has the potential to reclaim some of 'the missing', to identify, perhaps name individuals, on occasion permitting a formal reburial in a war cemetery, and bringing closure to the descendants, whether Allied or German, after almost a century. In this sense, Great War archaeology (in Belgium, France, Italy, Greece and beyond) connects the past directly to the present, and in the most emotive and personal way.

One of the most important advantages of excavating Great War sites is that it changes our perspective by redirecting attention away from the grand strategies of military history towards the everyday realities and experiences of the ordinary soldier. Furthermore, it has the power to associate particular events with a specific topography, linking the physical experience of landscape – a sense of changing heights and the textures and smells of different terrains – to details of a battle or skirmish known hitherto only from documentary evidence.

As Great War archaeology begins to mature in Belgian Flanders, excavations such as the A19 Project play a crucial role in shaping a highly focused methodology for this new kind of archaeological investigation, where landscapes themselves are seen as artefacts that not only preserve the past, but also define and redefine people through time. Beyond the theoretical considerations and technical developments, the existence and practice of a professional archaeology of the war also attracts a wider particpation in, and a deeper understanding of, the complex relationships between excavation, commemoration, heritage and tourism. As in France, Great War archaeology in Belgium must become a truly interdisciplinary endeavour, calling on all kinds of expertise if it is to fulfil its ethical as well as its scientific and historical responsibilities and potential.

CHAPTER 6

Legacies and Visions of War

Bullets or battlefields, the artefacts of the First World War are part of the twentieth century's cultural heritage, a universal legacy of conflict for Europe and the wider world. The ways in which this heritage is treated and understood depends in large part on how it is investigated and presented, in archaeologicial excavations, museum exhibitions, private collections, school visits, and, increasingly, on television and the Internet. Great War archaeology itself is only one aspect of this broader understanding of the war and its aftermath. It is linked, inevitably, to the wider archaeology of twentieth-century conflict, but also embraces such important issues as identity, nationality, memory, tourism and the nature of material culture.

The objects of the First World War have a curious and unique character. Not only are they mud-covered artefacts excavated from the earth, but also cherished mementoes in people's homes, captioned exhibits in museum displays, exquisitely polished objects in private collections, and commercially valued items for sale in militaria fairs and in cyberspace. Any effort to investigate the material culture of the First World War is, by definition, a social archaeology of the conflict that cuts across many sections of society, each with its own interests, motives, prejudices and knowledge. As we have seen throughout this book, it also involves many kinds of specialists, each of whom brings invaluable experience and insight to the interpretation of the physical remains of the war.

Great War objects, like all items of material culture, possess their own 'social lives' in a world now distanced by almost a century from the conflict that gave them birth. Excavating war objects, interpreting them, exhibiting them, collecting them or selling them, are all different but inextricably linked aspects of how the war is seen and understood today. The First World War does not stand alone as a single indisputable legacy that we are only now discovering; it is a heritage that we are all creating and shaping as we come into contact with new and different understandings and presentations of its physical remains, and of the personal experiences embodied in them.

MUSEUMS AND REPRESENTATION

Archaeology meets the public through the displays of its found objects in museums more often than on ephemeral excavations. Yet, unlike the artefacts from more traditional kinds of archaeology, artefacts excavated from Great War sites are not valued and appreciated for their age, their rarity, their technical virtuosity, their beauty or their serendipitous survival. Most Great War objects have no such intrinsic worth; their significance comes from their associations, not only with other archaeological finds, but also with memories, imagination and a wealth of historical documentation.

A bullet carved into a crucifix after being dug out of a wound, a metal matchbox cover, an identity tag, a woollen blanket, an army boot, a corroded roll of barbed wire, a fragment of carved wood or chalk, or a hundred other everyday objects from a soldier's life in (and out of) the trenches connect directly to people's lives in ways that Neolithic flints, Roman amphorae and medieval sculptures cannot.

The very ordinariness of these often mass-produced objects is matched only by their unusual (sometimes extraordinary) qualities. Superficially, of course, they are the same as hundreds of thousands of other items that are already in museums and in people's homes across the world – the latter usually in better condition than those that have been recently dug up. What makes the excavated items significant is not their rarity or wondrous craftsmanship, but the fact that they were found on the battlefield, and sometimes in association with human remains. Location provides context, and context bestows historical importance and (sometimes) commercial value to everyday items from 1914–18. The unusual qualities of Great War objects offer many challenges to museum curators and others in terms of how they should be displayed, and shown to new generations of visitors.

Only in recent years have some war museums along the old Western Front become interested in showing this archaeological and anthropological face of war – a willingness stimulated in part by the enthusiastic (and sometimes contentious) public reaction to archaeological excavations in Great War landscapes. Hitherto (and sometimes still today), museum curators were motivated solely by acquiring Great War objects through a network of connections in the professional worlds of militaria dealers and collectors, sometimes the art world, and also, in some cases, donations and private sales. By and large, the items acquired reflected the wider collecting world's interest in objects in perfect condition – i.e. an item obviously associated with the war, but preferably not damaged by the war.

This way of representing the war to the public led to exhibitions in the major war museums (though not always the smaller ones) of often stunning, visually attractive (if sometimes troubling) displays of bright, highly polished bullets, artillery shells, trench-art items, miscellaneous souvenirs and beautifully preserved (and often conserved) uniforms, weapons and helmets (particularly the distinctively spiked German *Pickelhaube*), laid out with almost military precision. The idea of exhibiting war-damaged objects, incomplete or abandoned items – with mud and rust incrustations – was not thought appropriate. It was almost as if the war had to be sanitised through the display of clean and undamaged items.

As Great War archaeology gathered momentum, first through amateur digs, and more recently through modern scientific excavations, attitudes began to change. Some museums seized the moment, and mounted exhibitions that not only displayed war-shattered and uncleaned objects, but also trench sections and dugouts reconstructed from the original materials retrieved during the archaeological excavation, or accurately modelled on original forms but with modern materials. This was a fundamental shift of emphasis, driven equally by archaeology, anthropology, and new ideas and thinking in the museum world. It acknowledged the changing role of museums in catering for and perpetuating the public's developing relationship with the war, and particularly the education of new generations of schoolchildren who were visiting Great War battlefields in ever-greater numbers.

There are, as we saw briefly in Chapter 2, several different kinds of Western Front museums that exhibit the material culture of the Great War. The two main museums are the Historial de la Grande Guerre, at Péronne, on the Somme, and the In Flanders Fields Museum at Ypres. Somewhat smaller are the Somme 1916 Trench Museum at Albert on the Somme, and the Memorial Museum Passchendaele 1917 at Zonnebeke near Ypres. Smaller still are a number of privately owned café-museums, such as the Tommy Café on the Somme, and the Hooge Crater and Sanctuary Wood museums just outside Ypres. There are also a host of other small private museums (sometimes with no café) scattered along the Western Front, such as those at La Targette, and Notre Dame de Lorette, both near to Vimy Ridge, and until recently at Hill 60 near Ypres. Each museum projects a different view of the war, from the intimately personal to the impressively large, and each has a place in representing the First World War.

The Historial de la Grande Guerre (Péronne)

Behind the imposing façade of the medieval castle at Péronne lies the modern building which houses the most important Great War museum on the Somme. The Historial de la Grande Guerre was conceived during the mid-1980s, and was funded by the Conseil général de la Somme. The founding impulse was that

The imposing façade of the medieval castle at Péronne, which houses L'Historial de la Grande Guerre. (© Author's collection)

it should be a museum for all nationalities, and concerned with the war in its entirety, and not just with the 1916 Battle of the Somme.

It opened in August 1992, with an innovative display of soldiers' uniforms (Allied and German) and equipment, laid out in depressions in the floor, symbolically recalling and commemorating the dead. Alongside are extraordinarily well-preserved rifles, machine guns and mortars, as well as a poignant display of medical equipment and artificial limbs. In the more traditional display cases are exhibited stunning arrays of Great War artefacts – from clocks made of shell cases and bullets to wartime posters, commemorative sculptures and delicate fans painted with war scenes. Small audio-visual units constantly play contemporary film, and the masterful drawings of the German artist Otto Dix add a nightmarish vision of the war he observed.

Apart from its eye-catching design, what makes the Historial significant is that it has its own research centre that promotes and supports academic research into various aspects of the First World War, and into the museum's own extensive collections. Since its inception, this function of the Historial has been guided by several prominent cultural historians of the war: Annette Becker, Jay Winter,

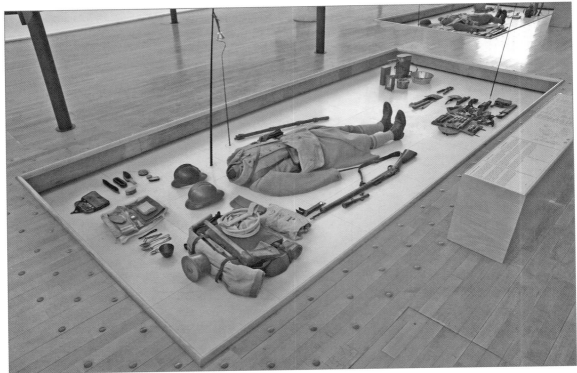

The distinctive sunken-floor display of soldiers' uniforms and kit in L'Historial de la Grande Guerre at Péronne. (© *Author's collection*)

Stéphane Audoin-Rouzeau and Gerd Krumeich. In addition to the research centre, the Historial also supports a documentation centre and an education service.

Since its foundation, the Historial has organised numerous conferences, and mounted many themed exhibitions of Great War material culture and events. It has also supported a programme of lavish publications of both its conferences and its exhibitions that are indicative of its wider interests in global conflict. The most notable of these have been Mémoires d'Outre-mer (Overseas Memories) in 1996, Camouflages in 1997, Histoires de familles – Cartes postales et culture de Guerre (Family Histories – Postcards and Culture of War) and De la transformation des tapis afghans (Transformations of Afghan Carpets), both in 2000, and the innovative Petites histoires de la Grande Guerre – Les Objets insolites de l'Historial (Little Stories of the Great War – Unusual Objects from the Historial) in 2001, which saw a potent combination of cultural history, anthropology and museology that explored the museum's wealth of small-scale three-dimensional material culture (Thierry 2001).

Apart from the Historial's exhibitions and publications, it also has an important relationship with the battlefield landscape of the surrounding Somme area through its development of a *circuit de souvenir* – a self-guided itinerary around the region's Great War battlefield sites, monuments and war cemeteries, which are flagged, en route, by emblematic poppy signs (Compère-Morel 2000). This route takes visitors to, among other places, the town of Albert, the cemeteries at Rancourt, the monument to the missing at Thiepval, the Australian memorial at Villers Bretonneux, and the memorial to the South Africans at Delville Wood, at Longueval. These sites, and others, represent the international aspect of the Allied armies, linking the Somme landscape with the exhibits and films on display at the Historial.

A more visceral connection, where archaeological objects from excavations on the Somme are exhibited, conserved or studied at the Historial has not developed, perhaps because, and as we have seen, the importance of Great War archaeology was not evident in 1992, and maybe also because this was beyond the historical remit of the original planners. Yet it is interesting to consider whether archaeology would be left out of the planning if the Historial were being built today.

Despite the Historial's absence of any overt archaeological dimension, its research centre played an important role in highlighting the urgent need for a truly interdisciplinary archaeology of the Great War. As we saw in Chapter 1, the Historial's own journal – *14/18: Aujourd'hui. Today. Heute* – dedicated its second issue to the archaeology of the war despite the fact that the directors and staff of its research centre were cultural historians and museum professionals, not archaeologists. This snapshot of archaeological research as of 1999 remains a key source for Great War archaeology in France almost a decade after it was published.

Although the Historial's collections are mainly 'high-end' items – unusual, rare, top quality, complete and mainly in perfect condition, its research centre has shown what can be done in terms of high-quality interdisciplinary investigations into Great War material culture. While no true exibition of Great War archaeology has yet been organised, the Historial has recently arranged a temporary display of objects found on the battlefields – a mass of damaged, incomplete, and dirt-encrusted items that give a sense of archaeological finds, and contrast dramatically with the otherwise pristine exhibits on display.

The Somme 1914–1918 Trench Museum (Albert)

Altogether smaller than the Historial is the The Somme 1914–1918 Trench Museum at Albert, west of Péronne, in the centre of the old Somme battlefield.

The museum, called until recently the Musée des Abris (Museum of the Shelters), was opened by the town's municipal authorities in 1992, and by 2003 was attracting 37,000 visitors annually, some 60 per cent of whom were British. Built in a series of underground tunnels, it has a mix of traditional and more modern displays, including glass cases of trench art and associated souvenirs, and, more strikingly, a series of dioramas showing dugout life on the Somme for British, French and German soldiers. Apart from the occasionally quizzical look on the faces of the mannequins, the uniforms, weapons and associated Great War memorabilia – together with the dank surroundings – give an unusual and sometimes chilly insight into the subterranean lives of Great War soldiers and civilians.

Along with the change in the museum's name, other recent developments include – interestingly for the shape of future battlefield tourism – a new website to which a German version has been added to the original English and French ones. Also, while ten years ago there were but a few (and mainly original) Great War souvenirs for sale in the café area, today there is an extensive shop selling commercially made commemorative items (glasses, cups, plates, etc.), books and genuine battlefield debris. The museum seems to have recognised (and capitalised on) a change in tourist behaviour. Previously, visitors liked to buy 'nice', clean and complete souvenirs, but increasingly it seems that authenticity (or the appearance of it) might be becoming more popular. As the museum's

The Somme 1914–1918 Trench Museum at Albert on the Somme, France. (© *Author's collection*)

Diorama of a dugout with French and Indian soldier mannequins in the tunnels of the Somme 1914–1918 Trench Museum at Albert on the Somme, France. (© *Author's collection*)

publicity says, 'We have noted with admiration how passionate our British visitors are about the (often rusty) WW1 items we sell.' Perhaps, as Great War archaeology and its mud-covered artefacts become better known and more valued, aesthetic attitudes are becoming modified by other, more poignant, kinds of meanings.

In Flanders Fields Museum (Ypres)

The Ypres Salient Museum had been the main Great War museum in Belgian Flanders for decades. Despite being located in the post-1918 reconstruction of the medieval cloth hall in the city's main square, its organisation was simply a straightforward affair that focused on objects and their captions, in the same way as smaller private museums and café-museums in the surrounding area, albeit on a larger scale. The museum had no funding, and no professional or scientific staff, and was operated solely on the efforts of volunteers.

By the mid-1990s, with Ypres becoming the centre of a boom in battlefield tourism, with changing attitudes towards museum exhibitions, and with the museum itself failing to attract the new (and often younger) wave of visitors, the town council decided on a dramatic change of direction. Whereas the Ypres Salient Museum was a traditional (some would say old-fashioned) war museum, a new museum was envisioned to reflect the status of Ypres as a 'town of peace', not conflict. While this was (and remains) a contentious idea for some, it was decided that the new museum, christened 'In Flanders Fields' after the famous 1915 poem by John McCrae, should be set up and operated by a professional staff of historians and museum specialists. The impressive collection of objects from the old museum was recycled and presented in a completely different way (Madoc & IFFM 1998).

While the expertise of the volunteers was employed in checking the detail and accuracy of everything to do with the objects, the concept of the new museum lay with Piet Chielens, who had undertaken years of Great War research in the museum's documentation centre, and proposed many new ideas as to how the redesigned museum should work.

In keeping with museum developments elsewhere, the In Flanders Fields Museum was built on the idea of 'history from below', telling the stories of ordinary soldiers and civilians on all sides, rather than the grand strategies of generals and politicians (almost always from the Allied side). War poetry, the experiences of refugees and events such as the Christmas truces gave a common touch and a universal appeal to the new museum. Museum artefacts and displays illustrated this 'everyman' view of the war, and were designed to tell the stories of people, rather than being an interesting but essentially miscellaneous collection of military objects that were the remainders of war.

This new concept saw the objects of war in much the same way as a new generation of archaeologists and anthropologists were seeing and investigating material culture – exploring the 'life stories' of objects as they passed through the hands of people whose lives they intersected (Baert *et al.* 1999). Equally new were displays that appealed to all the senses (not only sight), and included the sounds and smells of a deafening artillery barrage, smoke, and the taped words and cries of the soldiers (as interpreted by actors) involved in the 1917 Third Battle of Ypres (Passchendaele). In an adjacent room was a reconstructed casualty clearing station, where the figures and equipment were brought to life by the spoken contemporary words of doctors and nurses. And throughout the new exhibition hall were multilingual interactive panels where visitors could feel their way in English, French, German and Dutch to different aspects of the war. The new In Flanders Fields Museum was opened in 1997, and gave

The reconstructed 'medieval' cloth hall at Ypres, which houses the In Flanders Fields Museum. (© *Author's collection*)

its visitors juxtaposed and contextualised experiences and images of the First World War in a way that the old Salient Museum could never have done.

Together with these new ideas, the staff of the museum developed an innovative programme of smaller, temporary exhibitions, conferences and associated events, in a similar way to the Historial in France. In 1999, the museum initiated a series of annual artists in residence, whose role was to create an artwork of some aspect of war. In 2003, the museum invited the British artist Mark Anstee to become artist in residence, and he created a picture composed of thousands of identical small pen-drawn soldiers in full view of the public, which was then destroyed so as to become, in the artist's words, 'a memory not an artefact'.

International conferences explored many issues, such as the executions of Great War soldiers, the use of gas in warfare, refugees, the role of battlefield landscapes as witnesses to war, and, most recently, military aerial photography and archaeology. The 2006 landscape exhibition, together with its publication – both called *The Last Witness* – not only explored the war landscapes of Belgian Flanders, but also assessed the underlying relationship between museums, archaeology, anthropology and military history. Such ambitious events have been supplemented by smaller exhibitions, including one that displays archaeological material from The Diggers' excavations at Yorkshire Trench at Boezinge, and includes a diorama of the trench and dugout system, another that documents the Australian presence in the Ypres Salient, and, beginning in 2004, a five-year rotating exhibition on different themes in trench art.

The new museum and its multidisciplinary approaches, exhibitions, conferences and associated publications has been extraordinarily successful. Nevertheless, by 2005 annual visitor numbers had exceeded its capacity, and visitors' interests were also outrunning the original 1997 concept. Museum design and technology had moved on, as had knowledge about the First World War and the visitors' expectations. Anthropological ideas about the material culture of conflict, and especially the progress of Great War archaeology, have reinforced and widened the possibilities of what the museum could be in the minds of its staff and visitors.

Not only have archaeological discoveries opened up a whole new world of objects, large and small, that give different insights into the war, but increasingly anthropology has also influenced the museum's activities. The multicultural dimension of the Allied armies has been acknowledged especially in relation to the presence of Chinese labourers in the Ypres area, and, equally significant and insightful, Native Americans from Canada conducted a 'Homecoming Ceremony' in October 2005 at the Menin Gate for the spirits of their comrades who fell while serving in the Canadian army during the war.

As the material culture and memories of the war in Belgium have been reassessed and represented from an increasingly international perspective, so it became clear to many that the museum's relationship with its surrounding landscape needed to be reconfigured to include the whole of Belgian Flanders, and not only the old Ypres Salient. The single most powerful idea is a new concept that creatively redesigns the museum in accordance with landscape – and that plans to be finished and open its doors in 2012. This very anthropological notion builds on the recent landscape conference and exhibition, and regards landscape as the most authentic (and soon to be the only surviving) witness to the war – an idea not obvious (and to an extent also not true) in 1997, when so many Great War veterans were still alive.

Memorial Museum Passchendaele 1917 (Zonnebeke)

The other major, civic-funded museum in the immediate Ypres Salient region was until recently the Streekmuseum at Zonnebeke. It was housed in the old Zonnebeke Château that had been built on the devastated battlefield in 1924,

A unique sight. Representatives of Native American peoples in full regalia honouring their ancestors during the Last Post ceremony at the Menin Gate, Ypres, on 1 November 2005. *(Courtesy and © www.greatwar.be)*

and had traditional displays of Great War material culture, photographs and dioramas, and included a rare trench-art toolkit that had belonged to two local trench-art makers from nearby Passchendaele.

In 2003, Franky Bostyn of ABAF was appointed curator, and the Streekmuseum underwent a complete redesign of its structure, displays and ethos, emerging in April 2004 as the Memorial Museum Passchendaele 1917. Perhaps more than any other museum in Belgian Flanders, this new museum reflects the influence of archaeological discoveries by virtue of Bostyn's participation in ABAF's excavations of the dugout at Beecham Farm, Bayernwald and elsewhere (described in Chapter 5). This influence is seen most dramatically in the 'Dugout Experience', a permanent display that impressively and accurately reproduces a British underground dugout system, with a dressing station, headquarters, work area and dormitories, and which, from the smell of the wood to the dark and cramped conditions, captures a very sensual aspect of war life under ground.

A reconstructed dugout, part of an impressive display of the underground war at the Memorial Museum Passchendaele 1917 at Zonnebeke near Ypres. (© *Author's collection*)

One important reason for the founding of the new Memorial Museum Passchendaele 1917 was to prepare for the 90th commemoration of the Battle of Third Ypres (Passchendaele) in 2007. This involved an extensive programme of conferences, exhibitions, public talks, educational activities, themed walks, living-history events and the opening of the newly built visitor centre at Tyne Cot cemetery. An innovative development was to establish 'The Passchendaele Archives', which seeks to find photographic evidence for each of the names carved onto headstones and memorials to the missing involved in the 1917 battle. The aim is to produce a database of all the casualties, to include identifying photographs and personal information that, where possible, includes details from the soldiers' families.

In addition, as already briefly mentioned, 2 kilometres of the old Ypres–Roulers railway were cleared, excavated and converted into a foot and cycle path, allowing visitors to walk and cycle between Zonnebeke and Tyne Cot – a clear example of what has been called public archaeology. This archaeological dimension, made possible by the museum's close ties to ABAF, is also evident at Bayernwald and the Letteberg – sites that are linked to Passchendaele because the fighting at the former was a precursor to the bitter struggle at the latter, and was carried on by the same Allied troops (British, Irish and ANZACs). In other words, the concept of the new Passchendaele museum is not just a building and its exhibits, but embraces the linked landscapes of war, involves archaeology as well as traditional museum research, and seeks to engage with an international audience.

Ijzer Tower (Diksmuide)

One last major museum in Belgian Flanders must be mentioned; this is the Ijzer Tower at Diksmuide, north of Ypres. It was at Diksmuide, by the banks of the River Ijzer, that the Belgian army experienced constant bombardment, sniping and underground tunnelling attacks by the Germans on the other side of the river from 1914 to 1918. Virtually all the Belgian army units passed through the front-line trenches, reconstructed today with concrete sandbags as the 'Trenches of Death'.

A few hundred yards away stands the Ijzer Tower, some 85 metres tall, and bearing the sign 'No More War' in the four languages of the conflict – Dutch, English, German and French. The tower is not a museum in the traditional sense, as its origins were as a monument to Flemish nationalism, which came to the fore during the Great War and developed considerably afterwards. This political dimension is clear from the giant letters on the nearby monumental cross – 'AW–WK' – which stands for *'Alles voor Vlanderen, Vlanderen voor Kristus'* ('All for Flanders, Flanders for Christ').

The tower itself is divided into themed floors, with exhibition space for the First World War, the peace that followed, the Flemish people today, and the panorama hall at its summit that gives magnificent views of the Ijzer battlefield landscape. As Flemish nationalism and Great War tourism have developed, so the Ijzer Tower has been home to a number of rotating exhibitions about the conflict, including a temporary display on trench art, and a recent semi-permanent installation of underground dugouts excavated from the Ypres Salient by ABAF, and reconstructed in the tower by Johan Vandewalle, one of the excavators.

Private museums and café-museums

During the interwar years of 1919–39, the Somme and Belgian Flanders especially became a focus of national and international battlefield tourism. The visitors were often bereaved wives, mothers and sisters who wished to visit the places where their loved ones had served and died. An informal economy (often run by returning refugees) developed to cater for them, offering accommodation, food and drink, and an inexhaustible supply of war souvenirs made from recycled battlefield debris.

The itineraries of these tours included (and in turn stimulated the establishment of more) café-museums that offered rest and recuperation, the opportunity to meet other bereaved individuals, as well as being favourite places to view and buy items from the surrounding battlefields. The private museums, café-museums and more temporary souvenir stalls presented Great War material culture to the civilian war generation in a very specific way. The women tourists desired to make a connection with their husbands, sweethearts, fathers and brothers who had not returned from the war, and did so by purchasing items that they believed came straight from the landscapes that contained the remains of the missing. The men who visited were either the older generation also in search of the places where younger family members had died, or veterans of the war who returned to see the places where they had fought, been wounded and perhaps lost their comrades. Interwar battlefield pilgrims and tourists helped rebuild the war-torn economies of France and Belgium, and the various kinds of small-scale museums played an important role in this.

Many of these museums, so reliant on the tourist trade, disappeared after 1939 when a new war loomed. Although some private war museums survived into the 1950s (and occasionally longer), it was the resurgence of battlefield tourism during the 1960s, and especially the 1980s and 1990s, that led to the establishment of new and revamped café-museums, such as that belonging to André Becquart at Bayernwald near Ypres. Today there is a constantly changing tourist landscape of such places, blending almost imperceptibly with an ever-increasing number of war-themed pubs, restaurants and hotels.

Of the surviving or redesigned café-museums, the most popular – and thus the most influential in shaping visitors' understandings of the war – are the Tommy Café at Pozières on the Somme, and Hooge Crater and Sanctuary Wood just outside Ypres. Many others have long since disappeared, their collections of military memorabilia sold and dispersed, and their role in interwar tourism all but forgotten.

The Tommy Café is located on the infamous Bapaume Road at Pozières, an area that saw fierce fighting and terrible losses during the Battle of the Somme in 1916. In the mid-1990s, it was bought by Dominique Zanardi, a Great War enthusiast, and converted into a café-museum, its entrance guarded by two uniformed mannequins, a display of trench-art shell vases on its windowsill, and a garden transformed into a pair of opposed front-line trenches, one British, the other German. This was an artifical landscape created for tourists, not a reworking of original trenches. Nevertheless the dugouts, duckboards, machine

An Allied trench scene created in the garden of the Tommy café-museum at Pozières in the middle of the Somme battlefield. (© *Author's collection*)

guns, artillery shells and rolls of barbed wire give a flavour of the real thing, albeit with a twist of the surreal.

The café-museum was redesigned in 2005, with a new entrance and an extension to the café area in advance of the 90th anniversary of the 1 July Battle of the Somme, which brought thousands of extra visitors to the area. Coach tours feature so large in the business that they have a special section on Zanardi's website, and it is clear that the café rather than the museum aspect is currently more visible, as indicated by the removal of the original trench-art display. It is an interesting fact — and indicative of the diversity of battlefield tourism — that the Tommy Café's commercial success has been based partly on the triumph of its make-believe trenches over its authentic memorabilia.

Opposite the Hooge Crater CWGC cemetery on the Menin Road, outside Ypres, is a memorial chapel to the fallen. In 1994, the building was bought by Roger de Smul, and transformed into the centrepiece of the Hooge Crater café-museum. The museum contains uniforms, weapons, ammunition, souvenirs,

The patio at the Tommy café-museum at Pozières, showing a characteristic mix of war objects and tourist facilities. (© *Author's collection*)

and one of the best collections of trench-art artillery-shell-case vases on public display. It also houses a special exhibition of objects dug up by The Diggers at Boezinge. Hooge Crater museum is a frequent stop on battlefield tour itineraries, providing thousands of adults and schoolchildren with a well-organised first-hand experience of the material culture of the First World War.

Nearby, Sanctuary Wood café-museum offers a different experience to many of the same visitors who stop at Hooge Crater museum. Unlike the latter, Sanctuary Wood museum has a longer pedigree, as it was begun in 1923 by the Schier family, who owned the wood, and who capitalised on the burgeoning numbers of battlefield tourists in the postwar years. It is much less organised than Hooge Crater, with a haphazard arrangement of trench art (including two large trench-art clocks), a dusty but magnificent collection of helmets, original 1920s slide-viewers (and rare contemporary slides), and a section of trenches that the current owner, Jacques Schier, says is original, albeit regularly tidied and protected.

Although the café-museum has changed its shape and form since 1923 – particularly as it was rebuilt and revamped in 1947 and again in 1980 – it has

The café-museum at Hooge Crater on the Menin Road outside Ypres. It houses an impressive display of Great War armaments, memorabilia and trench art. *(© Author's collection)*

the atmosphere of an original interwar museum. Eighty per cent of its visitors are schoolchildren, who are particularly attracted by the trenches and slide-viewers, and so it plays an important if uninvestigated role in shaping ideas of the First World War in impressionable minds.

What is evident from the variety of French and Belgian museums that display Great War objects is the sometimes explicit, sometimes unspoken (and almost stealth-like), influence of Great War archaeology and anthropological studies of material culture. These linked disciplines have led museum curators to re-evaluate their collections, building on the wealth of historical sources, local knowledge, international expertise, and on advances in military history, cultural history, museum studies and audio-visual technologies, and capitalising on the financial revenues of an expanding battlefield tourism industry.

As the First World War slips deeper into memory, and the last soldiers pass away, archaeology and anthropology almost inevitably join military history in a sometimes formal, sometimes informal, cooperation to understand and show the public different views of the war. Hand in hand with these developments

Visitor looks at rare pictures of the First World War through original 1920s viewer at the café-museum at Sanctuary Wood near Ypres. *(© Author's collection)*

The trenches at the Sanctuary Wood café-museum are one of its main attractions. *(© Author's collection)*

are other changes in the ways that Great War material culture is viewed, valued, packaged and displayed to the world.

THE COMMERCE OF WAR

Large, well-funded and professionally organised museums, together with their smaller, privately run counterparts, offer different views and understandings of the First World War. Both, of course, are made possible (albeit in different ways) by revenues produced by battlefield tourism (see Crouch and Lübbren 2002, and Diller and Scofidio 1994 for recent examples). Commerce and the entrepreneurial spirit is not a new combination for the First World War – it was present during the war itself in catering to soldiers' needs and desires, and after the war, when individuals and businesses offered different services to bereaved battlefield pilgrims and visitors. Nevertheless, the commercial incentive in presenting the war to the public is probably more widespread and nuanced today than at any time since the 1920s and 1930s.

Not only is it possible to experience the war through a multitude of general and tailored battlefield tours, but, thanks to the Internet, individuals can now take virtual tours around the Western Front (and beyond), purchase original Great War memorabilia from the comfort of their own homes, and make their views and understanding of the war, as well as their tour experiences, available to a global community in Great War chat rooms.

Every year, hundreds of thousands of visitors tramp the trenches of the Somme, shed a tear at the Last Post at the Menin Gate in Ypres (Dendooven 2001: 113–52), stand in awe at the Thiepval monument on the Somme, visit Great War museums, and walk around countless war cemeteries and associated sites. The collective total for the Western Front is probably more than a million individual visits, though no single place experiences (or would be able to accommodate) such numbers. Many of these are schoolchildren gaining a formative experience of the war, and who sometimes run unaware across the old killing fields that still conceal the remains of the dead.

The café-museums and private museums of the Somme and Belgian Flanders are stopping points on such battlefield tours, and carry on a tradition that began in the 1920s, albeit modified to suit modern tastes, and coach, train and ferry timetables. Emerging out of this tradition is yet another way of presenting the war to the touring public that takes the form of a more general commercialisation of war heritage in the towns at the centre of tourist itineraries.

Elaborate trench-art clock bought on the Internet in 2005. Note the British, Australian, Scottish and Indian soldiers, and the biplanes, Zeppelin airship, battleships and cavalry. *(Courtesy and © David Cohen Fine Arts)*

Great War heritage has seeped almost imperceptibly into the fabric of places such as Ypres, where a baker's shop may display a few trench-art shell cases, a café where 'Tommy cakes' are served, a pub where 'Remembrance beers' are brewed, and shops where 'Great War mints' and chocolates in the shape of a Tommy's helmet can be bought, and where the poppy motif is a uniquitous marketing device. Bed and breakfast establishments offer a shelf of Great War books for sale or consultation, perhaps a piece of modern trench art for sale, and sometimes also a video or DVD of a First World War programme. Great War bookshops, too, have artillery shell cases, bullets and miscellaneous souvenirs for sale alongside the serried ranks of military history books.

Schoolchildren study the headstones at Tyne Cot cemetery, near Passchendaele. (© *Author's collection*)

Ypres, in particular, is not only a post-1918 replica of its medieval self, and thus a strange commemorative monument to the Great War dead, but is also a living example of how ideas of the war are constantly being reshaped and renewed by commercial interests. Whatever individuals think about such commercialisation of the war, it is inescapably as much a part of Great War heritage as objects in museums, war cemeteries and battlefield landscapes. Today, as during the 1920s, the First World War is for sale at Ypres (and elsewhere), though there are none of the children selling war souvenirs that so upset and angered some of the visiting pilgrims during the interwar years.

Memorabilia

Archaeology's focus on the contextual relationships between landscape and material culture is lost when artefacts are taken from the earth with no (or scant) record being kept of exactly where they were found. Nevertheless, as we have seen many times with Great War objects, similar items survive in museums, private collections, and as family heirlooms, and in usually far better condition than

A Remembrance Week display in a chocolate shop in Ypres. Each November, trench-art shell cases, a British soldier's uniform, chocolates in the shape of a British Tommy's helmet, and wooden crosses and poppies are placed in the window along with John McCrae's poem 'In Flanders Fields'. (© *Author's collection*)

those buried in the ground. Most of these objects, whether weapons, uniforms or miscellaneous souvenirs, have been the objects of desire at the heart of a long-established international trade in military memorabilia, where their condition and commercial value have usually outweighed any deeper anthropological significance.

Investigating such objects is a kind of social archaeology, where artefacts are retrieved not from the ground, but from car-boot sales, militaria fairs and salerooms, flea markets, museum storerooms, and people's garages and attics (and sometimes living rooms). The stories these objects can tell are of a different kind than those of similar items excavated by Great War archaeologists, although they all resonate with experiences and memories of the conflict.

Unlike ancient antiquities traded on the international art market, Great War artefacts from non-archaeological sources have a uniquely anthropological value becase of the life stories, photographs and associated memories that sometimes accompany them. By contrast, many of the antiquities in the world's museums came from the earth over the past several hundred years, were then sold on, and

The 'Shell Hole Bookshop' in Ypres, whose window display includes Great War souvenirs and a highly polished trench-art artillery-shell flower vase. (© *Author's collection*)

thus have no stories attached to their original makers or owners (except where they have a written inscription). Great War items may have been in the same family for ninety years – perhaps made, bought or acquired during the war itself, and treasured by a family ever since. Collectors and museums also often have value-adding information about the objects they own. So, while Great War artefacts do not possess the intrinsic value of antiquities, they can be embedded in an information-rich (and sometimes emotional) context.

This single fact establishes the importance and research potential of objects widely referred to simply as militaria or military memorabilia, and would seem to contradict the idea that by virtue of being bought and sold in militaria fairs and on the Internet, they are anonymous and meaningless objects.

The best-known example of how such items can be studied and analysed to reveal a rich and different view of the First World War and its legacy is that of trench art (see Chapter 2). Quite apart from the study of an inherently interesting and hitherto uninvestigated kind of material culture, the analysis of these objects

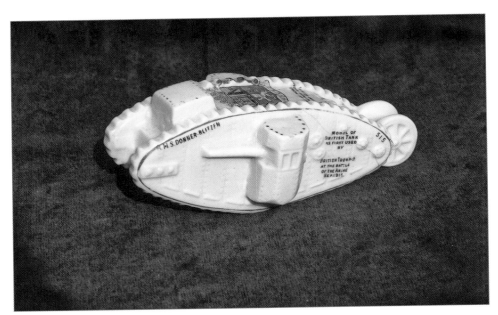

Heraldic china miniature British tank. (© *Author's collection*)

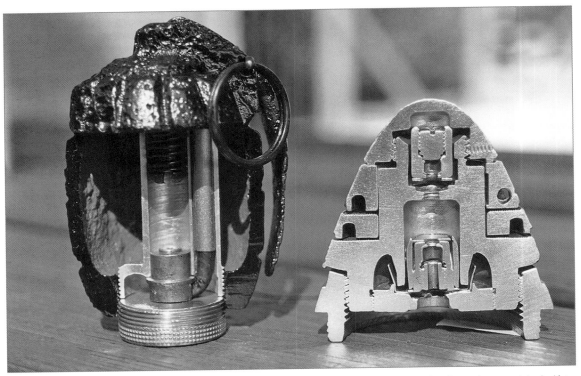

Battlefield souvenirs for sale on the Somme. The grenade (left) and fuse-cap (right) have been cut in half to reveal their internal structure. (© *Author's collection*)

revealed how they connected in unexpected ways to many other issues of the war. Trench-art objects could embody, represent or be otherwise associated with such varied issues as religious faith, ethnicity, wounding and recuperation, the locating of experiences in particular battlefield locations, creating identity and affinity, influencing art and artists, affecting tourism and commercialisation, bringing together anthropological and archaeological research, and influencing the design of museum exhibitions, to mention only the most obvious.

The power of trench art – which is, after all, only one kind of memorabilia – to overlap with, and cast an interpretative net over, so many different issues is an indication of the future potential of the many other kinds of memorabilia. Uniforms, helmets, weapons, writing materials, smoking equipment, identity tags, munitions, heraldic china and other commercially made souvenirs, postcards, ornamental textiles, soldiers' personal effects, clothing and footwear are just a few of the many kinds of artefacts whose study could yield new insights into what, in effect, is a social archaeology of the First World War.

The potential of these items to educate (particularly schoolchildren) is equally significant, as many objects were made, owned and used by young soldiers hardly older than today's school-trip visitors. The ability to handle, touch and smell these artefacts, to understand how and why they were made (and sometimes by whom) – as well as perhaps buying an example – adds a new dimension of experience that physically connects today's visitors to the soldiers of the First World War. This experience may then be given depth and breadth by the details of military history, whether an account of a particular battle, or an old soldier's personal reminiscences. The power of memorabilia to sensitise, educate and ultimately connect today's generations with those of the war is as significant as it is currently unrealised.

Archaeology and anthropology overlap in creative ways in museum exhibitions and the commercialisation of the war. In this overlap, professional and financial incentives create new commemorations of the First World War, some of which would be familiar to interwar battlefield pilgrims and visitors, while others would be undreamt of. One consequence of these new developments is that today's generations are, in a sense, remaking the war in the present, rather than merely recalling it from the past, and there is little sign that this process will cease in the foreseeable future.

A further consequence highlights the issue of exactly what is Great War heritage. To what extent are new tourist destinations authentic landscapes, and can heritage itself go some way towards healing individual pain and loss, and create a new understanding of the war? The answers to these questions lie in the future.

CHAPTER 7

Beyond the Western Front

The archaeology of the First World War has, until recently, focused almost exclusively on the Western Front, with only limited investigations elsewhere, such as in Britain, northern Italy, and to a lesser extent at Gallipoli in Turkey. Vast areas of the old Eastern Front (and especially the Balkan region) have so far remained virtually untouched. What reveals the anthropological nature of Great War archaeology, and the more inclusive nature of modern archaeology itself, is the realisation that war affects different areas in different ways, and can leave a variety of distinctive physical traces. Each of these has its own significance, and each can contribute a piece to the jigsaw of how the war was experienced and remembered by ordinary soldiers and civilians during the war and afterwards.

Investigating the First World War beyond the Western Front is at an even earlier stage of development than the admittedly still young archaeology of the battlefields. It depends to a great extent on political and cultural attitudes to the war as heritage, and on attitudes to the war held by the professional archaeological community in each of the affected countries. Added to this is the problem that many of the First World War's constructions were ephemeral – wooden buildings to house transient populations – which after the war were dismantled, pillaged and reused. In Britain, where more than one million acres were used for military purposes during the war, a number of individual projects, and English Heritage's 'Monuments Protection Programme' (MPP), have compiled a record of Great War activities and remains (English Heritage 2000), but across Europe at least, this is the exception rather than the rule.

HOMELAND ARCHAEOLOGY: THE FIRST WORLD WAR IN BRITAIN

One of the most important and innovative kinds of Great War archaeology beyond the Western Front is that which investigates facsimile battlezones – the training areas where soldiers were prepared for, or at least partially familiarised with, the conditions that would confront them on the real battlefields. These practice trench systems are today often only visible from old aerial photographs. Many have become silted up, or were deliberately filled in after 1918. While some are small, and were obviously dug on an ad hoc basis, others are large and impressive systems stretching across the countryside.

In England and Wales, training trenches are found from Penally in Pembrokeshire to Cannock Chase in Staffordshire, Salisbury Plain in Wiltshire, and Dartmoor in Devon. In 2006, preliminary investigations were carried out at Cannock Chase by No Man's Land to assess its archaeological potential (Martin Brown, pers. comm.). Two training camps, Brocton and Penkridge, were established at Cannock Chase at the outbreak of war, and more than 40,000 soldiers stationed there. A hospital, power station, and the infrastructure of roads and a railway were included, and the camps opened in the spring of 1915, with special areas for practice trench digging and bombing ranges.

No Man's Land investigations included excavating sections across a practice trench, a rubbish dump (midden), the base of a wartime hut, the survey of a previously unmapped area of the Chase, and initial recording of various structural remains. The practice trench revealed part of its architecture, and also evidence of original barbed-wire entanglements. The midden yielded a wealth of material culture, including ceramic and glass items, some of which were probably bought by the soldiers themselves. The pottery, most of which was locally made at the Stoke-on-Trent kilns, was mainly tableware, and many items had the 'crow's foot' stamp indicating that they were official army purchases. Glass items included various bottles, used for medicine, sauce, beer and lemonade. Martin Brown and Jon Price, who led the investigation, also noticed layers of ash, which may have come from a nearby forge belonging to the Royal Horse Artillery. The remains of brick, concrete and salt-glazed pipes revealed the site of a toilet block. While this was only an initial investigation of a huge site, it became clear that Cannock Chase has great potential for future work.

The most complete, extensive and best-documented examples of army training landscapes, however, lie on Salisbury Plain in southern England. The area was bought by the British War Office in 1897, and practice trenches have been dug since at least 1902, when the army constructed and evaluated S-shaped trenches that had been used by the Boers against the British in South Africa (Brown and Field 2009).

The Salisbury Plain trenches accurately replicated those on the Western Front in many respects. They had a front line, and support and reserve trenches, all of which were connected by a series of communication trenches that featured shelters for command posts and first aid stations. At Perham Down, no less than three separate trench systems cover an area of more than 100 hectares, and show how successive crenellated firing lines were dug as the 'battle' moved on (McOrmish *et al.*, in press, quoted in Schofield 2004). Indicating the relationship between Great War and traditional archaeology, the Perham Down trenches (now only visible in aerial photographs) are superimposed over a large area of prehistoric 'Celtic fields' that have in turn influenced the layout of the practice trenches (*ibid.*). Indeed, the existence and extent of some of training trenches were first realised during archaeological assessments of these areas.

Different kinds of trenches survive to varying degrees at various locations. Some can be seen as earthworks at ground level, while others are only visible from the air as crop marks. Some are small, about 0.25 hectare, while others can sprawl across the landscape for 26 hectares. On Orcheston Down there is a trench system composed of three lines of trenches – a front line, a support trench and a reserve line. The system is about 1 kilometre in length, and has no less than twenty-five communication trenches connecting the front and rear lines. The existence of another trench, and eight smaller ones leading to it some 120 metres beyond the original front line, may indicate a practice 'advance' from the original position.

One of the most extensive and best-preserved trench systems to have been investigated archaeologically in this area is at Beacon Hill, which was probably one of the main training areas for the troops living near the army towns of Bulford and Tidworth. Two lines of trenches, covering around 7 hectares, were cut on Beacon Hill's south slope, and still today have a depth of around 1.5 metres.

Some parts of the trenches are very well preserved, and the positions of a possible machine-gun bay and several saps (small trenches leading out into No Man's Land) are still visible. At its eastern edge, the front-line trench appears unfinished, and behind it the support trench preserves its original zigzag shape. No less than eleven communication trenches connect the front-line and support-line trenches, along each of which are situated T-shaped bays, possibly used as command or first aid posts. Interestingly, three communication trenches stretch back from the support line to a 1-metre-deep Bronze Age ditch which leads to the lowland valley floor – an example of how Great War trenches incorporated prehistoric landscape features into modern (albeit facsimile) battlezones.

Archaeological work was also carried out on a second trench system inside the nearby Bulford Rifle Range, which is itself part of a larger unexplored system. The excavations revealed that Great War practice trenches had been cut into two prehistoric Bronze Age landscapes, one dating to around 1500 BC, and the other around 1000 BC. The typically crenellated front-line trenches had six identifiable firing bays, and there were also two communication trenches associated with these. As if to illustrate the constant reuse of this landscape, the army's present-day firing range overlies both of these earlier landscapes.

It was not only the British army that trained on Salisbury Plain. The Great War was a world war, and men from all over the British Empire came to practise here before being sent to the real war in France and Belgium. Another example of the homeland practice of archaeology of the Great War took place when the Australian War Memorial in Canberra requested help from the British Ministry of Defence (MOD) to investigate the activities of the Australian 3rd Division. In particular, it was decided to excavate part of the training trenches known as 'Bustard trenches', where the Australians had practised, in order to see how realistic they were, and how they had survived (Osgood *et al.* 2006).

While little trace of these trenches survived above ground, a 1916 trench map and a 1920s aerial photograph enabled archaeologists to identify the Bustard trench system and excavate two test pits – one in a communication trench, the other in the front line. The trenches were found to be too shallow to afford adequate protection had they been in the battlezone. Although they must have been cleaned then reused to train other soldiers (and probably cleaned again after the war), the trenches yielded several 1917 fired .303 bullets, as well as a pair of scissors and part of a shrapnel shell. Bovril jars and bottles originally filled with Anzora hair cream were found in nearby craters.

After training, which, as a contemporary Battalion history revealed, had been extremely realistic, the Australian 3rd Division moved to Ploegstreet Wood on the Western Front in Belgium. They were soon part of the Allied attack that followed the explosion of the huge British mines at Messines in June 1917.

The Anzora hair-cream bottle found during excavations near the Bustard Trenches on Salisbury Plain. *(Courtesy and © Richard Osgood)*

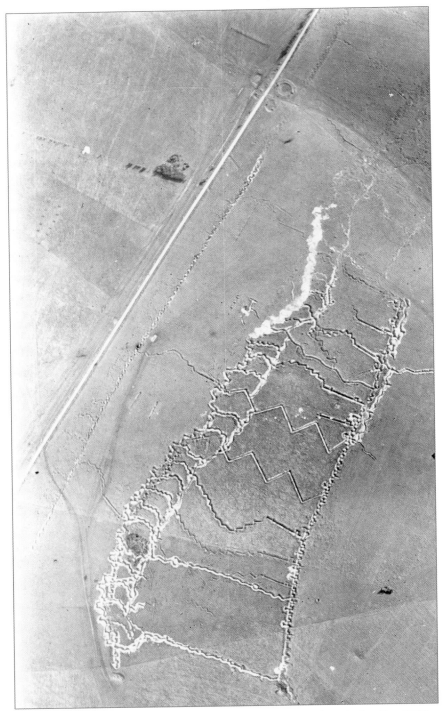

Aerial photograph of the Bustard Trenches on Salisbury Plain during the 1920s.
(Courtesy and © English Heritage, NMR SUO847/5)

In an innovative example of Great War experimental archaeology, the MOD archaeologists intend to excavate a section of the Ploegstreet trenches, in order to see how reality compared to prior training on Salisbury Plain.

Salisbury Plain and other facsimile battlezones also contain other material traces of the war, some predictable, others quite unexpected. At various places, bomb or mine craters can still be seen, indicating training with explosives. At Chapperton Down the practice trenches are peppered with shell holes, though it is not known if both features are contemporary. New technologies have also left an archaeological signature, as at the trench system near the Iron Age hillfort at Yarnbury, where innumerable small craters are the result of the Royal Flying Corps (RFC) aircrew practising dropping their primitive hand-held bombs from aircraft (O.G.S. Crawford 1924: 34, quoted in Brown and Field 2009).

Even newer than aircraft, the world's first tanks have also left their mark on the Salisbury Plain landscape. At Shrewton Folly a 65-hectare anti-tank range was built in 1916, and included a firing line for artillery, and a tank-shaped canvas screen that was mounted on a trolley pulled along a railway track (Brown and Field 2009).

Great War archaeology has an intimate relationship with the anthropology of landscape and material culture, as we have seen with the study of trench art, where personal, social and cultural features can overlap in artistic imagery. This is as true for training areas in wartime Britain as it is for the Western Front battlefields of France and Belgium. As at certain locations on the chalky battlefields of the Somme, and in the underground limestone caverns at Confrécourt, so too on the chalk downlands of southern England, where giant images were carved into the turf.

Around the Wiltshire villages of Fovant, Compton Chamberlayne and Sutton Mandeville, Allied soldiers undergoing training on Salisbury Plain, and those waiting to be transported to France, left their mark on the landscape. These took the form of large regimental badges and insignia cut into the ground on the slopes below the prehistoric hillfort of Chiselbury. The tradition began during the First World War, but was carried on after the Second World War, during which time, ironically, they had been turfed over so as not to offer any navigational aid to Hitler's Luftwaffe bombers. In 1961, the Fovant Badges Society was formed to protect the images, and in 2001 they were further protected by being officially designated as a site of cultural heritage. Today, nine of the original nineteen images are still visible (through recutting and preservation), although currently several others, including a map of Australia, have not been restored (Holyoak 2001a).

The earliest badge appears to have been made by the 5th Battalion of the London Rifle Brigade in 1916, and a year later they had moved on and were

The 'Rising Sun' – a giant landscape image of the General Service badge of the Australian Commonwealth Military Forces at Fovant, Wiltshire. *(Courtesy and © Richard Osgood)*

replaced by the Australian Imperial Force. The Australians created the famous 'Rising Sun' landscape image, a monumental 51 × 32 metre version of the General Service badge adopted by the Australian Commonwealth Military Forces in 1911 (Brown and Field 2009). Other insignia belong to the Post Office Rifles, the Wiltshire Regiment and the Devonshire Regiment. All are monumental traces of men's lives in wartime, and part of the poignant archaeological and anthropological heritage of the First World War.

Training landscapes are not the only remains of the First World War in Britain to have left archaeological traces. Defence against invasion and attack, prisoner-of-war and internee camps, and the production of war munitions on a vast and hitherto unseen scale all led to tailormade constructions, many of which have left a distinctive footprint on the land.

To defend against a German invasion by sea, and then overland, so-called 'stop lines' of blocking fieldworks, entrenchments and pillboxes were constructed to slow down the enemy advance. These features were built at various strategic locations – north and east of London, between Maidstone and the River Swale in Kent, and along the east coast in Suffolk and Norfolk – and were already manned by 300,000 soldiers by the end of 1914 (Andrew Saunders

1989: 213, quoted in Schofield 2004). At Farningham in Kent, and North Weald in Essex, the buildings of Great War mobilisation centres have been preserved, and English Heritage's 'Defence of Britain Project' has identified fifty surviving examples of anti-invasion structures dating from 1914–18.

Although Britain was reasonably well protected by its coastal defences in 1914, the onshore artillery batteries were only ever used on one occasion. On 16 December of that year, there was a German naval bombardment against the town of Hartlepool that caused four military and 112 civilian deaths. The connection between this event, the archaeological traces of the coastal battery and the anthropological dimension of material culture is revealed by the cottage industry that arose after the attack of making trench-art souvenirs (jewellery, ashtrays and flowerpots) from the shrapnel fragments of the German shells fired at the town (Saunders 2003b: 141).

Apart from seaborne attack, the First World War also saw extensive construction of anti-aircraft (including Zeppelin airship) gun and searchlight positions. Research into these locations revealed how most of these sites were purpose-built, with fixed guns established at permanent sites (Dobinson 1996: 11–47; Anderton and Schofield 1999). Around 376 of these stations were built, though few are thought to have survived. Similarly associated with air defence were primitive 'sound mirrors', concrete acoustic dishes built around the south and east of England, designed to pick up aircraft engine noise at a distance of between 13 and 24 kilometres. While their reliability was questionable, and they were soon overtaken by radar, several of the east coast examples have survived (Dobinson 1999: 8–12).

While defence against German air attack has left one kind of material trace of war, Britain's own aerial forces have left another, with home defence stations and training aerodromes for the Royal Flying Corps (RFC) being established in eastern England from 1916, with even more being built as reserve stations for training pilots for the Western Front in 1917. The design of these early aerodromes was distinctive, as they comprised four groups of buildings: the officers' mess and quarters, regimental buildings, technical structures (including hangars), and the women's hostel (Francis 1996: 12, quoted in Schofield 2004).

Today, few traces of these buldings survive: 271 out of a total of 301 such sites have disappeared (dismantled or decayed), and only eight sites still have their Great War hangars, including Old Sarum in Wiltshire, and Calshot in Hamphire (Holyoak 2001b: 256–7; Lake 2000). Perhaps the largest surviving structures are two vast hangars at Cardington in Bedfordshire (one of which was built between 1916 and 1917) in which airships were constructed.

The First World War was, above all, a war of industrialised production. Mass-produced weapons of hitherto unimaginable power were made in their millions in factories built on land acquired by the government under the initial Defence of the Realm Act (DORA) of 8 August 1914. Many of these war-related industrial constructions (and sometimes their associated civilian structures) have survived, and, in one sense, belong as much to Britain's industrial archaeological heritage as they do its Great War archaeological patrimony (Stratton and Trinder 2000).

Three kinds of structures were built, and survive to various degrees today. The first was concerned with manufacturing propellants, of which the best preserved is at the old Royal Naval Cordite Factory at Holton Heath in Dorset. Here are the remains of a purpose-built plant where maize was fermented to produce acetone (necessary for cordite production), a process devised by Chaim Weizmann, an industrial chemist who later became President of Israel. Several structures survive, of which the most impressive are six of the original eight reinforced concrete fermentation vessels that later served as air raid shelters during the Second World War (Stratton and Trinder 2000: 97).

The second kind of construction was concerned with the manufacture of high explosives, especially TNT (trinitrotoluene), which was put into the millions of artillery shells made by women factory workers – the munitionettes – in the filling factories (see below, and Woollacott 1994). Again, purpose-built plants were constructed at such places as Oldbury in the West Midlands, and were supplemented by older factories that had been converted to TNT production, such as at Hackney Wick and Silvertown in east London. The third kind of specialist construction was that which housed the national filling factories, such as those at the Royal Arsenal at Woolwich in London, Lemington Point and Derwenthaugh near Newcastle, and Banbury in Northamptonshire, where today earthworks and concrete floor slabs still survive (Cocroft 2000: 170–1).

The overlap between the home-front aspect of Great War archaeology and industrial archaeology in Britain is made more complex (and fascinating) by what might be called a social archaeology (or perhaps an anthropology) of domestic architecture created for the munitions workers – most of whom were women.

The largest of the wartime explosives factories was at Gretna (and its surrounding area) on the Scottish borders, and employed over 20,000 workers at its height. Although the industrial buildings have long since been dismantled, many of their physical traces remain scattered across the countryside. Most intriguing, however, are the intact and still-occupied wartime dwellings – most of which have been converted to other uses, but at least one of which at nearby Eastriggs appears hardly different to when it was built (Cocroft 2000: 192). No fewer than eight Great War hostels were later converted into permanent houses, and it is possible that some of the original wooden huts also survive beneath later decorative cladding (Stratton and Trinder 2000: 98–9). Gretna's layout and the life histories of some of its public and private buildings are extraordinary archaeological legacies of the Great War, although have not been explicitly investigated.

Another material legacy of the war in Britain is the large number of prisoner-of-war and internee camps that were constructed (and which sometimes seem almost indistinguishable from each other). Prisoner-of-war camps such as Stobs near Hawick in Scotland, Brocton Camp on Cannock Chase, and internee camps like those at Handforth near Manchester, at Newbury and Lancaster, have each left behind their own material traces, of which it is sometimes the small handicraft objects made by the inmates that are best known.

Some sites, such as Stobs and those at Cannock Chase, would be challenging places to excavate, as they were evidently multi-purpose establishments. Stobs served as a training camp for Kitchener's Army, an internee camp, and a prisoner-of-war camp – whose 6,000 German inmates erected and maintained a memorial to the German general Hindenburg. Two hundred wooden huts were built to house the prisoners, and nearby are practice trenches, graffiti, concrete foundations and roads – all of which could be surveyed, photographed and selectively excavated. The same is true for the many similar sites that have left physical traces.

Perhaps the best-documented body of material culture to have survived from any of these camps comes from Knockaloe internment camp on the Isle of Man, where internees of German and Turkish origin (many of whom had lived in Britain for decades, and only spoke English) made a variety of objects. As already mentioned, these included painted and inlaid wooden boxes, fretwork, picture frames, model boats, ubiquitous flower vases carved from the shin bones of cattle devoured by the inmates, and even flat-packed furniture (Cresswell 1994). These items sometimes poignantly embodied prisoners' own feelings of alienation and longing to be free, and in this respect are similar to items made by prisoners of war. At various locations in both kinds of camps, the excavation of rubbish dumps would yield an insightful array of half-finished, broken and practice pieces – a truly social archaeology of everyday life between 1914 and 1919. The material culture of Great War imprisonment is an integral part of Great War archaeology, although there has been little investigation of this to date.

There are, of course, a large number of other Great War-related monuments, buildings and landscapes that could be studied from archaeological and anthropological perspectives – some of which have been well documented from the points of view of military or cultural history. Almost all of these are postwar commemorations of the war dead, such as the already intensively studied war memorials, and memorial hospitals and libraries that were erected between the wars (Borg 1991; Boorman 1988; Richardson 1998: 98–100).

Equally intriguing are the scattered and sometimes anonymous traces of the war, such as a bas-relief of a biplane flying over a warship, at Tregantle Fort, Cornwall, and a rare pencil sketch of 'Kaiser Bill' at Wigmore Abbey, Herefordshire. Other places have preserved the names of those involved, such as at the coast watcher's post at Garn Fawr, Fishguard, Wales, where an inscription tells us that 'J.J.W. Calderon. Commander. R.N. [and] D.J.W. Edwardes Deputy. C.W. R.N. 1914–15' looked out from this remote and windswept spot during the early years of the war (Cocroft *et al.* 2006: 36–7).

GREAT WAR ARCHAEOLOGY: AN INTERNATIONAL PERSPECTIVE

Great War archaeology has only recently begun along the Western Front, and is hardly even an idea in other countries that participated in or were affected by the conflict. In Finland, the Baltic States, Germany, Austria and Eastern European countries, the First World War is still mostly the domain of military history. The idea of an archaeology or a material culture anthropology of the 1914–18 conflict remains firmly outside the interests of both academic archaeology and anthropology, and museum exhibitions on the First World War follow a traditional military history approach where the focus is on uniforms and weaponry.

The only exceptions to this have been exhibitions on trench art held at the University of Tübingen, Germany, in 2002 (PTA 2002) and at the Museum of War History in Budapest in 2006 – perhaps an indication of the ability of these objects to cross the boundaries between traditional and new approaches to the material culture of war. Perhaps understandably in these countries, more attention is often given to the Second World War and the cold war, and their various political legacies, although even here there are but a handful of investigations that could be termed archaeological or anthropological.

In other areas, such as the different nations of the Balkans, East Africa, Iraq (formerly Mesopotamia), Israel (formerly Palestine) and Egypt, the intensity of different kinds of later conflicts – from the Second World War, independence struggles, ethnic conflicts, and the First and Second Gulf Wars – have seemingly left the First World War in limbo. So many momentous events have occurred since 1918 that the idea of spending time and money on the archaeology of the

First World War (rather than on each area's own unique prehistoric and medieval heritage) is perhaps an idea whose time has not yet come.

Nevertheless, there are notable exceptions to this state of affairs, primarily in Italy, and to a lesser extent in Turkey (Gallipoli) and Jordan. Doubtless, more will follow as the relevance of Great War archaeology to history, nationality, heritage and tourism becomes more obvious and (perhaps) commercially insistent.

Great War archaeology in Italy

The most impressive archaeological research beyond the Western Front is that currently under way in Italy. Although not at present well known in the English- and French-speaking worlds that dominate Great War archaeology, Italian investigators have made significant advances in recent years, especially in the north and north-east of the country, where, during the First World War, Italian forces confronted the Austro-Hungarian army.

The terrain of Italy's Great War battlefields was unlike any other, and consequently its archaeology is also distinctive. The Italian Front was high-altitude mountain country, which included snowfields and glaciers, and this has led to examples of astonishing preservation, as well as to unusual features of the battlezone landscape (Balbi 2009). The front line between Italy and Austria traversed some of the highest mountain ranges of the Alps, with altitudes approaching 4,000 metres in some places. In these hostile environments, the main enemy was not human, but rather the unforgiving environment and severe weather conditions. Never before had so many people been forced to live (and fight) at such high altitudes for such lengthy periods.

On the Italian Front, the commanders of the Italian and Austro-Hungarian armies had to contend with this harsh environment as a matter of priority, as more (perhaps two-thirds of) men lost their lives to cold, frostbite, illness and avalanches than to enemy action (Von Lichem 1995, 1: 65–6). Unlike today's mountain climbers, Italian and Austrian soldiers in the First World War did not have modern technologies; they used hemp ropes that stiffened in the cold, wore woollen sweaters that absorbed water, and used heavy iron crampons. While early twentieth-century technologies for destroying human life had become increasingly sophisticated, those for saving it were literally and figuratively still in the Iron Age.

Nevertheless, both armies innovated and adapted to the conditions, and the Italian alpine troops (*Alpini*) were matched by their Austrian

A replica wooden hut typical of those used by Italian soldiers at high altitudes. (© *Author's collection*)

equivalent, the *Kaiserschützen*. The Austrians in particular created specialised divisions composed exclusively of soldiers with expertise in mountaineering – the Hochgebirgskompagnien (high-altitude companies) and the Bergführerkompagnien (companies of alpine guides). Ironically, fighting this high-altitude war contributed significantly to development in the technologies of skiing and cable cars that greatly benefited postwar alpine leisure activities (Balbi 2009). In other words, the distinctive nature of the war in this region led to an equally distinctive relationship between conflict and tourism, quite different from that which developed along the old Western Front.

Environment and climate had a profound effect on the relationships between soldiers and the material culture of war. White camouflage suits were worn over the uniform, and soldiers' accessories and materiel – from helmets to cartridge boxes – were painted white, as were skis and artillery. In this way, men, equipment and weapons blended with the snowfields and glaciers, making all an integral part of the landscape, both above and below the icy surface. This relationship took a startling and unusual turn on the glaciers, where huts were built inside crevasses, and offered protection against enemy fire as well as extreme weather.

One advantageous peculiarity of such places was that a glacier's internal temperature was constant – a unique microclimate that enabled the Austrians to construct the so-called 'City of Ice' within the Marmolada Glacier (Bartoli and Fornaro 1993; Andreoletti and Viazzi 1977: 157–62, quoted in Balbi 2009). In the spring of 1917, Austrian soldiers began carving out caverns within the glacier, connecting them together, and linking the system to natural crevasses. They dug manually, and used pneumatic drills and explosives to create a huge and safe storage and living area, composed of dormitories, canteens and storerooms, as well as 12 kilometres of tunnels that led from rear areas to the front lines. In such a surreal environment, they also cared for their spiritual needs by excavating a cave where mass was celebrated. As with the tunnels and caves beneath Arras in France, electric lighting was installed, and the subterranean landscape signposted with names given to its various caverns and tunnels. For their part, the Italians created a similarly impressive tunnel beneath the Adamello Glacier that was 5,200 metres long and also electrically lit (Viazzi 1981: 249–50, quoted in Balbi 2009).

The harsh environmental conditions that made fighting the war so difficult have benefited archaeology, as preservation of material culture (especially of wood, leather and fabric) is excellent. Snowfall covered the battlefields, and eventually turned into ice, entombing human bodies, guns, bullets, helmets and uniforms, as well as newspapers, books, letters and even entire huts.

The downhill movement of glaciers, combined with the rising summer temperatures, has meant that in recent years live munitions and miscellaneous Great War objects have begun appearing at the melting mouth of the glaciers, neccesitating annual clear-up operations by the local authorities.

The distinctive environmental conditions of this part of the Italian Front have direct consequences for the material culture of the Great War, adding remarkable preservation to the already volatile mix of archaeology, anthropology, souvenir collecting, tourism and cultural heritage. Preservation affects large and small items in similar ways, and highlights the potential of modern archaeology to illuminate details both unexpected and intensely personal. In 2003, for example, a complete Austrian Skoda howitzer emerged from the ice of the Presanella Glacier, complete with its camouflage cover, ammunition and the sledge that had originally transported it.

This dramatic event was paralleled at the other end of the scale by finding of the *Kaiserschütze* kepi (hat) found on the Presena Glacier, perfectly intact with its feather and metal badges. One of the badges was a hand-made section of thin corrugated iron and a bullet, bearing the engraved name 'Presena' (Offelli 2001: 166). This artefact brings together a range of important features, including military identification, a recycled trench-art badge, the association of an individual with a named place in the battlefield landscape, and the unique preservation of a high-altitude landscape.

These well-preserved items are not the only material remains of the war. As along the Western Front during the interwar years, so along the old Isonzo Front after 1918. Returning refugees and ex-soldiers scoured the battlefields by day for the debris of war, and turned it into useful items and trench-art souvenirs by night. Iron, copper, lead, aluminium and brass were all collected and transformed. Helmets became braziers, bayonets refashioned as sickles, artillery-shell cases hammered into lamps and vases, and miscellaneous scrap became paperweights, bracelets and rings. In a curious turn of events, trench-art items were given as prizes in skiing competitions – a sport whose popularity (and technological innovations) was greatly enhanced by the war itself (Hellmann 2007).

The annual harvest of Great War objects eroding out of glaciers, together with the trade and collection of trench art, has led to discussions about how to treat these items of cultural heritage. For example, should the gifts of the glaciers be left in situ, where climate and collectors will wreak their own havoc, or be placed in museums? As elsewhere, part of the problem has been the status of Great War archaeology itself. The feeling that Great War heritage in Italy is inferior to the country's prehistoric, Roman and medieval remains is strong.

Austrian Skoda howitzer that emerged from the ice of the Presanella Glacier in 2003. *(Courtesy and © Marco Balbi)*

This attitude has also afflicted the Trentino region further west, in the foothills of the Dolomites – an area that saw fierce fighting during the conflict, and that is extraordinarily rich in physical traces of the war.

In the Trentino, nevertheless, there is a sophisticated appreciation of how the First World War should be treated as a cultural resource, as part of the region's unique archaeological heritage, and as a commercially viable strategic repositioning of its tourist industry. What is particularly significant about an integrated plan for the region supported by the local archaeological, heritage and tourist authorities, as well as Padua University, is its emphasis on exploring the social and cultural aspects of the war rather than retelling the political and military history. Grandfathers fighting on opposite sides during the war, the role of women carrying supplies to the front lines, feelings of belonging in such a distinctive and isolated area – all are seen as fostering an interest in the local communities with the First World War and its legacies.

The high-altitude war of the Trentino has left a distinctive signature on the landscape, not least in the great forts built to repel and defend against the enemy. The potential of battlefield tourism, or, perhaps more accurately for the Trentino, a battlefield element in tourist itineraries, is shown by the fact that one year after the huge and dramatically sited Fort Belvedere was restored and opened to the public, it attracted 40,000 visitors, and a smaller fort nearby had 5,000.

Modern trench-art Christ at Luserna, Italy. Made from Great War artillery shells by Max Nicolussi Castellan, 2001. *(© Author's collection)*

Fort Belevedere is now a Great War museum, with exhibitions of trench art, uniforms, photographs and weaponry, interspersed with original features such as the wartime morgue and operating rooms, and postwar memorials. In 1999, the local community of Lavarone (where Fort Belvedere is located) and the Austrian *Tiroler Kaiserjäger-Bund* in Innsbruck formed the 'Belvedere–Gschwent Foundation' – a symbolically international body to oversee and administer the fort, emphasise the cultural rather than the military memories of the area, and to promote peace rather than war (Prezzi and Pace 2004: 15).

In the surrounding and adjacent areas, archaeological excavation of Great War sites has been limited, although there is increasing awareness of the value of the war's objects, monuments and landscapes as heritage, and the need for these to be treated systematically, and integrated into regional cultural and educational initiatives. In 2006, an international conference was held in Luserna, near Trento, to discuss the future of Great War archaeology (and its associated approaches) for the region – one result of which was the 'Luserna Agreement', where delegates from many of the European nations that had been involved in the First World War undertook to cooperate in the archaeological investigation of Great War sites and material culture.

It was Austro-Hungarian troops that the Italian army confronted in the Trentino and further east, on the Isonzo Front. Today, Italy's old battlefront has political boundaries with two twentieth-century nations – Austria to the north, and Slovenia to the east. Both of these countries have significant Great War remains in need of archaeological investigation and protection. In Austria, there is little support for the First World War (or indeed the Second World War) from the Austrian archaeological community, and no protection of sites belonging to either conflict. Nevertheless, several investigators from Innsbruck University are conducting Great War research, most notably into the material culture of personal belongings of Austrian soldiers in the Tyrol during the conflict (Brandauer 2006). This work offers a soldier's-eye view of the war through objects rather than the traditional military history approach that has focused on official documents and the actions of famous generals and politicians.

Much of the area fought over between Italy and Austria between 1915 and 1918 now lies just inside the border of the new nation of Slovenia. As a bitterly contested battlefield landscape, the Isonzo region has a rich archaeological heritage of the war, and one that of course belongs to both countries. Great War archaeology on the Italian–Slovenian border region has had its own problems, not least during the post-Second World War period, when the

Memorial to Italian soldiers at Fort Belvedere near Trento, northern Italy. (© *Author's collection*)

Yugoslavian authorities repressed the memory and knowledge of the First World War. The Isonzo Front became a synonym for a forgotten past – another indication of the wider anthropological dimension of Great War landscapes and their physical traces.

Yet interest in, and knowledge of, the First World War did not fade among those who lived on the Yugoslavian – now Slovenian – side of the border. Perhaps inevitably, attitudes changed, and in 1990, a Great War museum was established at Caporetto. It acted as a catalyst for rejuvenating public interest in, and family memories concerning, the events of 1915–18 in this area. The museum has been memorably described as the first opportunity for Slovenians to think about their grandfathers. Today, the museum's collections and multi-media exhibitions are in eight languages, and attract around 86,000 visitors every year, most of whom are Slovenians, and the balance being Italians.

In Slovenia, as elsewhere, there is no special legislation for Great War archaeology, and rescue excavations treat First World War remains – such as an Austrian war cemetery at Gorizia encountered while constructing a new motorway roundabout – in the same way as those from traditional sites. Yet Great War archaeological heritage is different, and illegal excavations and a dynamic trade in Great War souvenirs (and the formation of many private collections) threaten battlefield landscapes in ways that are not found on prehistoric, Roman or medieval sites. Nevertheless, Slovenia's resources are such that in the absence of a proactive, well-funded research and conservation strategy, a halfway house has been proposed as part of the country's first heritage protection bill (currently before parliament). It recommends that collectors of Great War objects can justify their various activities if they open private museums (often in high-altitude, open-air locations) to the public – in other words 'professionalise' (and legalise) the amateurs who at least give some protection to their objects (Željko Cimpric, pers. comm.).

Great War archaeology in Italy, Austria and Slovenia has left a heritage shared by three countries, each with distinct attitudes towards its investigation, preservation, and incorporation into the wider field of cultural heritage and tourism. Italy has a strategy for developing this heritage in a multidimensional way, whereas in Austria and Slovenia positive developments have so far been fewer, although there are signs of change. As along the Western Front, the potential of the war's material culture to throw new light on the individual's experience of conflict is becoming evident, and there is increasing professional and public interest in developing archaeological and anthropological approaches to a conflict hitherto known mainly in terms of military history.

The battlefield at Gallipoli (Turkey)

In Turkey, a nation that owes its origins to the First World War, when it emerged from the collapse of the defeated Ottoman Empire, the tragedy of the Gallipoli campaign in 1915 has ensured its importance to the Turkish people, and also to the British, Australians, New Zealanders and French, whose soldiers suffered and died there. The heritage aspect of Gallipoli for all these nations, especially Australia, is where Great War archaeology has its first foothold, not only on the battlefields of the Gallipoli peninsula itself, but also in the waters surrounding it. In 1998, the wreck of the Australian submarine *AE2*, which had sunk in the Dardenelles on 30 April 1915, was discovered – with its conning tower, through which the crew had made their escape, still open.

The first archaeological record of wartime Gallipoli appeared as part of a 1990s assessment of the 'Gallipoli Peninsula Peace Park' – an area of over 33,000 hectares that was established in 1996, and was an expansion of the 1973 'Gallipoli Peninsula National Historic Park', that itself had emerged from the original 'ANZAC Area' established in the 1923 Treaty of Lausanne. The assessment, entitled *Gallipoli Peninsula Peace Park International Ideas & Competition* (Bademli 1997), recorded the history, archaeology, fauna and flora, and human settlement, and assessed likely developments in the area, but did not include small-scale archaeological features and items, such as Great War trenches and tunnels, personal and military equipment, and bullets. Consequently, by 2003, while some geological assessment had been made of the battleground (Chasseaud and Doyle 2005), there was no comprehensive archaeological survey of First World War sites and features, and Gallipoli's Great War heritage remained largely unknown.

In 2003, a team led by Australian archaeologist David Cameron made a preliminary archaeological survey of the ANZAC Gallipoli battlefields of 1915 (Cameron and Donlon 2005). The survey was restricted to the ANZAC battlefields, known as 'Focus Area II', which had been damaged by fire in 1994, and was receiving over 15,000 visitors in 2002 for the annual commemoration of ANZAC day that took place on 25 April. Within this area, four locations were examined (but not excavated) – 'Russell's Top', 'Turkish Quinn's', 'German Officers' Trench' and 'Lone Pine'.

At Russell's Top, trench systems were clearly visible, but, apart from pieces of barbed wire, broken pottery and rusty food containers, very little material culture was evident. This may be due to the fact that unofficial walking paths across the area had appeared – informal tracks taken by visitors to a nearby war cemetery.

Preserved ANZAC trenches at Gallipoli. *(Courtesy and © David Cameron)*

The site of Turkish Quinn's was held by Turkish troops and never gained by the Australians, despite a distance of only 5 metres between the opposing trenches at some points. The outlines of the Turkish trenches were clearly visible, and all seem to have been deliberately filled in. This may be explained by the fact that after the Allies evacuated the area, the Turkish army collected the bodies of their own troops (and possibly some ANZACs) and buried them in the trenches. In other words, this site is probably an impromptu battlefield cemetery, as well as a partially fossilised system of battlefield trenches. Almost nothing was found at the site, a situation again probably best explained by streams of visitors picking the area clean of its easily pocketable items.

Only 150 metres away, German Officers' Trench appeared similar to Turkish Quinn's, with intentionally filled-in trenches (maybe concealing bodies), and no artefacts remaining on the surface. At Lone Pine, some of the Turkish trenches have been backfilled, while others are still open and suffering erosion.

The artefacts that were discovered included (probably) human bone, ceramic fragments and metal cans. In addition, a human femur was found lying by the roadside at ANZAC Cove, near to where thousands of visitors alight from their tour buses.

Archaeology, heritage, battlefield tourism and not a little politics came together at the spot where the femur was found, for it was here that in 2005 bulldozers began clearing the area to improve road access to the site, and thereby destroyed the spiritual and commemorative, as well as the archaeological, integrity of what was, at least in part, an impromptu battlefield cemetery of the missing. Aspects of battlefield topography that had survived intact from 1915 to 2004 were destroyed, and many locations that had seen notable actions by Australian troops – that themselves had added significantly to the origins of modern Australian nationhood – were obliterated (Cameron and Donlon 2005: 136). This was particularly ironic (as well as tragic) inasmuch as these improvements seem to have been inspired by the desire of the Office of Australian War Graves to improve access and amenities for the 20,000 visitors (mainly Australians) who would attend the 90th ANZAC Day anniversary ceremonies held here in 2005.

The developments at Gallipoli set conservation against tourism. The archaeology of historically documented sites on the area known as Second Ridge was damaged, not only by road construction but also (and over decades) by endless streams of souvenir-collecting tourists. The 2003 archaeological assessment highlighted the problems and pressures on this area, but also considered that other, less accessible and less visited areas probably had a rich and perhaps mainly untouched archaeological record, below ground and above, and that this should be the focus of professional heritage management initiatives in the future (Cameron and Donlon 2005: 137).

It was perhaps partly in response to these developments that in September 2006 it was announced that Australia, Turkey and New Zealand would conduct a three-nation archaeological survey of the Gallipoli's Great War battlefields (Skatssoon 2006). The aim is not to excavate, but rather to map subsurface features with remote-sensing equipment, plot surface artefacts and identify trench lines, command posts and key battle areas. As Australian soldiers in 1915 wrote in their diaries that they encountered prehistoric artefacts while digging trenches, it is possible that this survey will also contribute to traditional archaeology as well as that of the First World War.

The archaeology of Lawrence of Arabia (Jordan)

During the First World War, the Ottoman Empire stretched south from Gallipoli to include what is today Syria, Lebanon, Iraq, Israel, Jordan and parts of Saudi Arabia. If a modern scientific archaeology of the First World War is only just beginning in Gallipoli, it is non-existent in all of these countries, with the sole exception of the southern part of what is today the Royal Hashemite Kingdom of Jordan.

North of the Red Sea holiday resort of Aqaba lie the desert battlefields where the British and their Arab allies – led by Colonel T.E. Lawrence (Lawrence of Arabia) – harassed, fought and defeated the imperial Ottoman

Aerial photograph of the trenches at Ma'an, southern Jordan. *(Courtesy of R. Bewley and © Aerial Archaeology in Jordan Project)*

army in what is called the Great Arab Revolt (1916–18). The political legacy of the war was the establishment of the British Mandate of Palestine that included an area east of the Jordan River called Trans-Jordan, the effective control of which the British gave to the Hashemite family. In 1946, when the mandate was revoked, Trans-Jordan became the independent Hashemite Kingdom of Jordan, and King Abdullah its first ruler. Despite these close connections between the First World War, the Great Arab Revolt, their collective aftermath and the founding of Jordan, almost no attention has been given to the archaeological heritage of these events. Until recently, Western interest in the Great Arab Revolt had focused on the charismatic figure of Lawrence, whose legendary exploits were burnished by Peter O'Toole in David Lean's 1962 epic, *Lawrence of Arabia*.

In 2005, a long-term investigation known as the 'Great Arab Revolt Project' (GARP) began by initiating a brief survey of part of the battlefields north of Aqaba (GARP 2006). This was a first step designed to show the archaeological and heritage potential of Great War sites in southern Jordan. The initial results were encouraging, and, beginning in 2006, a fully-fledged archaeological team has conducted an annual survey and excavation of sites along the route of the Ottoman Hejaz railway between Ma'an and the Saudi Arabian border.

GARP's research has revealed the potential of Great War archaeology in the area between Ma'an and Aqaba, the latter being a major Turkish–Ottoman port during the war. Near the village of Abu Al-Lissan, for example, two major battles were fought on 30 June and 2 July 1917, the latter being the decisive engagement of what is known as the Aqaba Campaign. Despite this, knowledge of the battle relies mainly on Lawrence's account in his *Seven Pillars of Wisdom*, published in 1927, and so archaeological reconnaissance is needed to identify and date battlescape features and debris. In addition, an anthropological investigation was felt necessary in order to collect and assess surviving village memories of the event, in much the same way as the battlefield ethnography conducted by the VIOE in Belgian Flanders.

The project began in earnest by investigating the extensive and well-preserved system of Turkish–Ottoman trenches that were cut along the ridges surrounding the Hejaz railway station at Ma'an – an ancient oasis and caravan stop on the pilgrimage route to Mecca, and a major centre for the Turkish–Ottoman army during the First World War. These trenches are known from recent aerial photographs, and ground-level investigation has shown that substantial earthworks still survive, including front-line firing trenches,

Turkish trenches at Ma'an, southern Jordan at ground level. Trench system on right, artillery positions on left, and redoubt in foreground. (© *Author's collection*)

Conflict archaeology and public archaeology at Ma'an, southern Jordan, November 2006. The excavation of a Turkish artillery position is explained to local schoolchildren. (© *Author's collection*)

communication trenches, dugouts and artillery bays, as well as bomb craters. Metal detecting and excavation revealed a distinctive array of incoming .303 bullets (from the Arabs and British) and empty Mauser cartridges from outgoing Turkish rifle fire, as well as shrapnel evidence of British artillery bombardment of the Turkish positions.

As with similar places on the Western Front, the trench landscape at Ma'an is under threat from modern quarrying, natural erosion, the presence nearby of industrial development and, ironically, a modern Jordanian army training area. Nevertheless, the Ma'an trenches represent one of the largest and best preserved of all First World War conflict landscapes. This fact, combined with Ma'an's status as a major railway station, and its location on the main highway between Petra and Wadi Rum (both important modern tourist destinations), offers a unique opportunity for Great War archaeologists to investigate not only the site's physical remains, but also to establish a community-based heritage resource of exceptional educational and economic potential. Considerable effort has been made to embed the Ma'an investigations in the community by involving politicians, the Aqaba Railway Corporation and local schools in what is a pioneering exercise in public archaeology as well as conflict archaeology.

The second focus of GARP's investigations is the abandoned Hejaz railway station at Wadi Retm, where three Ottoman-period buildings were fortified during the First World War (and possibly also during the later Hejazi War of 1924–5), with a blockhouse, improvised loopholes and a possible rooftop parapet. In addition to an assessment of these surviving standing buildings, the project discovered several new sites clearly associated with the period 1916–18, which illustrated the distinctive and dramatic ways in which the ancient cultural landscape (of Bedouin encampments, a medieval caravan route, and even a *c.* 200 BC Nabatean site) had been reconfigured into a twentieth-century conflict landscape. The excavation of a small Turkish army tented camp nearby revealed aspects of daily life for these isolated troops, but no evidence of fighting – a discovery that highlights the inappropriateness of the term 'battlefield archaeology' and emphasises the value of the more inclusive term 'conflict archaeology'.

The GARP investigations incorporated geophysical and surface survey, professional metal-detector sweeps, landscape assessment and targeted excavation, and is developing these approaches within a wider multidisciplinary project in cooperation with local archaeologists and Jordan's Department of Antiquities.

Conflict archaeology in contested landscapes. Armoured Humvee of the Jordanian army parked on the edge of the First World War Turkish trenches at Ma'an, southern Jordan, in November 2006. (© *Author's collection*)

Excavation of a Turkish tent circle near the Hejaz railway station site of Wadi Retm, southern Jordan, in November 2006. (© *Author's collection*)

CONCLUDING COMMENTS: FUTURE HERITAGE

Unlike most kinds of archaeology, the excavation of Great War sites is a memory-making activity. Along the old Western Front in particular, it sees excavators, landowners and innumerable tourists struggling to imagine today's verdant woods and fields as monochrome images of Hell, just as returning refugees in 1919 struggled to see devastated landscapes as fertile pastures and farms. The tension between the scientific objectivity of modern archaeology, the intensity of emotions that investigations can produce, and the almost inevitable momentum towards commemoration at such locations, reveals Great War archaeology as a uniquely interdisciplinary endeavour.

As we have seen throughout this book, it is impossible completely to disentangle all the individual threads of this spider's web, although a rigorous scientific approach to excavation and post-excavation analysis remains a priority. It is perhaps inevitable that at this early stage of its development, Great War archaeology remains a largely untheorised kind of investigation, although its connections with industrial archaeology, historical archaeology, cultural history and anthropology offer rich sources of theoretical understanding. Ultimately, however, the archaeology of the First World War is about industrialised conflict and its aftermath during the twentieth century, and so needs to develop its own distinctive methodologies.

Archaeology is now established as one of the many different futures for our understanding of the First World War. As excavation joins history to interpret the evidence, our views of the Great War, its legacies and its meanings, will be transformed. The challenges facing Great War archaeology are considerable, for they mix and juxtapose materiality with spirituality, experience with memory, and science with emotion. In the archaeology of the First World War, imagination is everywhere, and so, ironically, are 'the missing'.

CHAPTER 8

Recent Developments

As the 2014 centenary of the First World War approaches, there is little doubt that the archaeology of the Great War has established itself firmly in the public mind, in the world of professional archaeology and in the academic world of universities in the United Kingdom and beyond. The last few years have seen many new books appear, each adding to our store of knowledge and understanding, and offering different perspectives on how archaeology can make sense of the recent past in time of war. Yet, the idea behind *Killing Time* remains distinctive. It was always to present an overview, to explore how modern archaeology of the First World War must heed its responsibilities and embrace its multidisciplinary potential, helping new generations to understand the legacies of war and its heritage – for themselves and for others.

Since the first edition was published in the spring of 2007, advances in First World War archaeology have been so rapid that a paperback version of the book required a substantial update. The opportunity has been taken to make minor adjustments throughout the book and update the bibliography, but mainly to offer an overview of recent developments in this new chapter.

* * * * *

Anthropology, which has shaped much of First World War archaeology, has continued to exert a profound influence, though few of those involved would call themselves anthropologists. Studies of the material culture of the Great War, from trench art souvenirs to whole conflict landscapes, have informed new exhibitions, conferences (and associated publications), particularly at the In Flanders Fields Museum in Ypres and the Historial de la Grande Guerre at Péronne. The explosion of new publications, in French and Flemish as well as English, attest to a new kind of scholarship, avowedly archaeological, but drawing variously on cultural history, military history, art history and the work of heritage professionals.

The men and women who were involved in, or who were affected by the war, have now closed the door on our world. Henry Allingham and Harry Patch, First World War British veterans, both died in 2009 cutting the links between the living and the dead. All three veterans in the photograph at the beginning of this book are now gone, and the image itself has taken on a new resonance. We are now truly in the world of archaeology, where our understanding of the past can no longer be refined or corrected by talking to those who took part. Their voices are silent, but their message lives on.

In conflict landscapes, museums and private collections, objects are consequently of increasing importance to our understanding of the war. Interpretation is not only enriched by the countless diaries and official papers of military and cultural history, but also by the insights gained by archaeologists who crouch in excavated trenches first dug and last occupied by the men whose lives and experiences they seek to comprehend. The breadth of new investigations is impressive. While archaeologists find a pipe, a tobacco box, or a lighter made of bullet cartridges, others, such as Patrice Warin – the doyen of French trench art collectors – publish books that provide astonishing images and details of the social and material worlds of tobacco smoking during the war (Warin 2009).

Television has continued to fund new Great War excavations, though for some this remains controversial. Of the many programmes that have been produced in the last three years, perhaps the most emotionally resonant has been the YAP Films documentary called *Vimy Underground*, first broadcast in 2007. It focused on Maison Blanche, an underground cave near Vimy Ridge, which gave shelter to Canadian and British soldiers during the war, was visited during the inter-war years, and also provided refuge during the Second World War.

What makes this subterranean bolt-hole so fascinating is that it has preserved a gallery of images, names, and insignia carved and scrawled on the limestone walls. YAP Films' researcher Judy Ruzylo tracked down Aleck Ambler in Saskatchewan, Canada, whose stonemason father, Private A.J. Ambler, carved some of the regimental images with a professional flourish. Aleck was flown to northern France and filmed as he encountered with eye and finger-tips the work of his long-dead parent. The following year, Aleck's wish that his father's work be repatriated was fulfilled when plaster casts of the originals arrived in Canada – Aleck passed away just a few days later.

Graffiti naming Canadian soldiers underground at Maison Blanche, Vimy, and dated 16 March 1917. (© Author's collection)

Museums have also taken a lead, organising exhibitions and conferences that have pushed forward the boundaries in our understanding of the cultural experiences of the war and its aftermath. Epitomising this approach is the research of Dominiek Dendooven at In Flanders Fields Museum in Ypres, which focuses on the multicultural contribution to the First World War in Belgian Flanders, presented to the public in the extraordinary exhibition *Man – Culture – War* in 2008 (Dendooven and Chielens 2008; Anon. 2010). Equally significant, though in a more technical sense, was the publication of *Images of Conflict: Military Aerial Photography & Archaeology* (Stichelbaut *et al.* 2009), based on an earlier conference also organised by the In Flanders Fields Museum. For the first time, the diversity of military aerial images from the first fifty years of the twentieth century was set in a broad context, where empirical knowledge and theoretical analysis appeared side by side.

The aspiration expressed in the first edition of *Killing Time* has been realised through the influence of First World War archaeology in extending its interdisciplinary approach to all conflicts of the twentieth and twenty-first centuries, whether these are traditional wars between nation states – such as the Second World War and the Vietnam War, or civil conflicts, such as the Bosnian War of 1992–5. Embracing this wider notion, First World War archaeology has been in the vanguard of the emerging discipline of 'Modern Conflict Archaeology', and is no longer trapped inside the straitjacket of traditional 'Battlefield Archaeology', where so many opportunities for investigation are ignored due to the absence of a formal battlefield.

Particularly important has been a growing interest in the archaeology of the Second World War, where the influence of anthropology has marked the most innovative of studies to appear so far. The work of Gabriel Moshenska has begun laying the foundations of a sophisticated and multidisciplinary approach to this second global conflict (2009), for example in a study of the shrapnel collecting habits of children between 1939 and 1945 (2008). Equally distinctive has been the path followed by Gilly Carr, whose work on the material culture of occupation on the Channel Islands is opening up a new field of research (2009).

This broadening of horizons has resonated with younger generations, and not only the schoolchildren who visit the battlefields on organised tours. At universities, too, the archaeology of modern conflict is finding a home, attracting an increasing number of students interested in an archaeological approach to the First World War and other recent conflicts. The current research of postgraduate students at Bristol University, for example, promises to significantly extend the breadth of modern conflict archaeology on an international scale.

Commemoration, too, forges new links between the First World War, its archaeology, and more recent conflicts. The Remembrance Day ceremonies of 11 November show how visceral and emotive such connections can be. The Remembrance Poppy, with its origins in the Great War, is surely one of the most powerful (and ironically, fragile) artefacts created during the twentieth century. It has renewed its pull on the collective souls of Britain and Canada especially, through the seemingly constant flow of the dead and maimed repatriated from conflicts first in Iraq and now Afghanistan.

By far the most obvious development over the past few years, however, has been the increase in the number of archaeological excavation projects, large and small, that have begun, or gathered pace, in France, Belgium, the United Kingdom, and beyond. The following is an overview of these new endeavours.

ARCHAEOLOGY ON THE HOME FRONT

First World War archaeology, as we have seen, is not only tied to investigating places where battle has raged. Nowhere is this better seen than in projects that have recently begun in the United Kingdom, and that investigate conflict landscapes that owe their existence to the war, but never saw actual fighting.

Investigations into First World War training grounds began before 2006 and have continued apace over the past few years, accelerated by the work of Martin Brown and Richard Osgood of the Defence Estates (Ministry of Defence) on Salisbury Plain. Brown, especially, is concerned with a much wider appreciation of training trenches in the United Kingdom, particularly at Cannock Chase, the Silloans trenches on the Otterburn Traning Area, and at RAF Halton. Building on their previous investigations, Brown and Osgood have supervised a team from Bristol University in excavating the Bustard training trenches and surrounding area since 2008. The results so far support the view that these trenches were cleaned up before being backfilled after the war, as one prehistoric flint, but

Section of an excavated training trench at the Bustard trenches on Salisbury Plain in 2008. The duckboard stain can just be made out running along the trench floor. (© Author's collection)

Arborglyph at Half Moon Copse, Salisbury Plain, identified for Corporal Alexander Todd of the Anzac 3rd Division, who died of wounds in France in October 1918. (© Author's collection)

no cartridges or military debris have been found. One trench floor did however preserve the dark staining of a wooden duckboard.

Hardly a stone's throw from these trenches is Half Moon Copse, and an extraordinary living memorial to men who have passed through the area from the First World War to the present day. Carved into the bark of beech trees are the names and insignia (arborglyphs) of the soldiers who trained here during the Great War, such as the Australian Lance Sergeant Clyde Henry Walker, who won the Military Medal for bravery under fire in France in 1917. A year later he returned to England for training on Salisbury Plain where he carved his name with a penknife or bayonet on a beech tree at Half Moon Copse (Summerfield n.d.:51,54–55). Lance Corporal Alexander Todd of the Anzac 3rd Division was another soldier traced from his arboreal graffiti (Brown and Osgood 2009: 45–46). He died of wounds in France in October 1918, but left his evocative mark on Salisbury Plain. Other names and images appear on beech trees in nearby Polo Wood. Both areas have been the subject of an innovative study over several years by Chantel Summerfield (2009), creatively combining painstaking recording and archival searches of names, and subtly blending ideas of landscape, identity, and commemoration.

Proof of the vibrancy and diversity of this new kind of archaeology is the addition of a recent conflict dimension to a well-established public archaeology project in Norfolk. The 'Sedgeford Historical and Archaeological Research Project' began in 1996 and continues today. While mainly concerned with the excavation of an Anglo-Saxon village and cemetery of *c.*AD 750–950, project archaeologists began to investigate Sedgeford Aerodrome in 2009, which was home to a Royal Flying Corps (RFC) training airfield during the First World War.

Aerial photographs and archaeological remains indicate that by 1918 the aerodrome was virtually a small town, with hangars, workshops, barracks, tents, and its own railway. Hundreds of people lived and worked here, transforming the everyday life of the surrounding area. Fortunately, since 1919, the aerodrome has been used mainly for farming, and during the Second World War it was only a decoy airfield. Consequently, the remains of this First World War aerodrome are exceptionally well-preserved and even include several intact buildings.

Sedgeford Aerodrome is an unusual time capsule, an important site for conflict archaeology, though not for battlefield archaeology as no fighting occurred there. Its remains are being explored with a combination of desktop research, GPS survey, standing-building recording, sample excavation, and analysis of the rich finds that have been recovered. The aim is to reconstruct the society of the airfield and assess its economic, social, and cultural impact on a relatively remote rural community during the First World War, and to a lesser extent, the Second World War – a key element of conflict archaeology's anthropological approach.

The first investigations in the summer of 2009 focused on a mortuary, an air-raid shelter, the site of former barrack-blocks, and a rubbish dump which spanned both the First and Second World Wars, and included a large number of bottles. Every archaeological site has at least one feature which seems to define its uniqueness in often strange and unfamiliar ways. At Sedgeford Aerodrome, this is the mortuary – a grim reminder of a well-known historical fact that more First World War airmen died in training and air accidents than in combat. Sedgeford Aerodrome, while not a battlefield, was nevertheless a place of death. The casualties here were no less victims of the Great War than the infantry mown down by machine-guns on the Somme in 1916 or at Passchendaele a year later.

The mortuary was a building whose decorative architectural flourishes were appropriate to housing the honoured war dead, but which was also concealed

The mortuary at Sedgeford Aerodrome. (© Keith Robinson for Sedgeford Historical and Archaeological Research Project)

from general view. It lies hidden in a wood at the centre of the airfield, in a liminal part of the landscape, where ambiguity reigns. Some of the young men whose bodies passed through its portals were buried in local cemeteries, while others, it must be assumed, went home.

The new investigations at Sedgeford Aerodrome show how modern conflict archaeology is associated with traditional archaeology, how it differs utterly from battlefield archaeology, and how it can ask, and hopefully sometimes answer, hitherto unspoken questions about the experiences of those whose lives were changed forever by occupying a conflict landscape which was hundreds of miles away from the battle-zones of France and Belgium. The work at Sedgeford Aerodrome demonstrates how modern industrialised war blurs the distinction between front line and Home Front, and how archaeology can yield insights into a Home-Front phenomenon known previously only from historical sources.

The archaeology of First World War aerodromes is a new endeavour and as yet hardly begun. It also extends into a wider analysis of the relationship between landscape and airscape, not least concerning the Zeppelin raids on Britain from 1915 to 1918. Wartime damage inflicted by Zeppelin bombs has been called 'The First Blitz' and Zeppelin crash sites have already been investigated (Faulkner and Durrani 2008). None of these are battlefields, but all are conflict zones where buildings were destroyed and people (mainly civilians) were killed and injured. The afterlife of crashed Zeppelin aluminium airframes, which saw the metal scavenged by the curious as mementos, or reworked as souvenir trench-art pins and badges, is a virtually untouched topic for the anthropological side of modern conflict archaeology (Saunders 2003: 93, 96, 139–141).

Sedgeford Aerodrome typifies these multidimensional issues because *L70*, the last Zeppelin to raid Britain, was shot down in August 1918 just off the Norfolk coast with the loss of all its crew. The victorious British biplane lost its way coming home, but saw the night-lights at Sedgeford Aerodrome, which did secondary service as a reserve landing-strip for Britain's First World War air-defence. Sedgeford, and other similar aerodromes, were not simply airfields, but rather part of a complex new weapons system, geared to war in the third dimension. Once again, we see that the First World War's industrialised nature of mass production and cutting-edge war technology played havoc with traditional ideas of dangerous battlefields and safe homes.

On a grander scale, but evoking similar ideas and a multidisciplinary approach, is 'Digging Dad's Army' (DDA), an ambitious long-term project based at Bristol University, but focused on exploring the archaeological and anthropological traces of the First and Second World Wars and the Cold War in London. The project's wider interests, and its orientation, are clear in its subtitle – 'The East and South-East London People's War Project'.

The DDA's investigations began in 2009, seeking to add an archaeological dimension to the term 'People's War', a phrase commonly used in historical sources, but hardly ever defined. Its key aim is to explore archaeologically and anthropologically all aspects of twentieth-century conflict in a densely populated urban landscape, and to record popular experiences of modern conflict between 1914 and 1952. To achieve this, investigations include research into official and community archives and oral history, as well as archaeological reconnaissance, survey, and excavation.

Archaeologists have initially focused on an area which extends from Eltham and Shooters Hill in southeast London, through the Woolwich

Arsenal/Creekmouth area, to Wanstead Flats in northeast London, which housed anti-aircraft sites, a POW Camp, and an Army Transit Camp for the 1944 D-Day invasion force. This geographical study area has extraordinary potential, not least of which is the size and importance of the Woolwich Arsenal, whose arms research, production, and distribution complex operated during the entire first half of the twentieth century. The research area also corresponds to a First World War air-defence line (with two known balloon-aprons, one at Creekmouth, one at Wanstead Flats), and AAA positions at Woolwich Garrison, Shooters Hill, and One Tree Hill, and incorporates also the Second World War anti-invasion 'Stop Line B'.

There is an already-established project in the Shooters Hill area of Woolwich which contains a wealth of known military and civilian sites, including anti-aircraft defences, military defences, and Civil Defence buildings. This investigation was filmed for a *Time Team* television episode called *Blitzkrieg*, broadcast in 2008 (Brockman 2009; Brockman and Barton 2009).

DDA brings together a diversity of approaches to studying a range of issues under the umbrella of modern conflict archaeology. These include the development of British air-defence systems from 1915 to 1945, and the refinement of 'stop-line' anti-invasion defences in London's heavily urbanised landscape between 1939 and 1945. Equally important, is the intention to chart the popular experience of the militarization of East London during the Second World War, particularly in relation to working-class politics and institutions such as the Home Guard. Post-war realities too will be investigated, not least the culture of commemoration as displayed in war memorials, personal items, and the listing and preservation of wartime buildings.

A crucial element of the DDA investigations is that they are seen not only as an example of modern conflict archaeology, but also by their very nature are responding to an urbanised People's War with a People's Archaeology. In other words, DDA projects are an exercise in what has come to be called Public Archaeology – where the local community is fully involved in research and in the dissemination of knowledge. Local newspapers, radio and television coverage attract local views and memories of past events and places, and schoolchildren are invited to excavate archaeological trenches.

At Eaglesfield Park, Shooters Hill, DDA archaeologists have forged a relationship with several local schools, and when excavations are undertaken pupils can gain hands-on experience of surveying and digging the heritage of their own community. They are also invited to examine the same maps and

DDA Open Day at Eaglesfield Park, Shooters Hill, London, in June 2009 (© Andy Brockman and DDA)

aerial photographs that the archaeologists use to guide their research, and then walk the landscape with a team member and point out the features on the ground that they have seen in the documents. In an instant, archaeology casts off its remote and academic nature, and becomes an integral part of understanding a landscape – of stories of parents and grandparents, and of how the local community came to be what it is today.

By the end of 2009, important advances included an exploration of the Creekmouth area where debris from crashed Zeppelins was stored during the First World War; the excavation of a Second World War zig-zag trench; the investigation of features associated with London Barrage Balloon sites, and a number of field schools held to train volunteers in the various skills of modern archaeology. Most exciting of all, was the discovery, investigation, and temporary public display of a First World War AAA gun site at Eaglesfield Park. Local interviews combined with documentary sources and geophysical survey identified the location, which soon became the first of its kind to be excavated.

DIGGING UP PLUGSTREET (BELGIUM)

The Western Front remains not only a symbolic landscape for our time, but also the centre of attention for much First World War archaeological investigation. In the last few years, several new projects have added significantly to our understanding of the war itself, and also of its often tangled and contentious legacies.

Although the Ypres Salient in Belgium and the Somme in France have dominated our understanding of First World War conflict landscapes, many other sites of epic struggle exist. One of these lies in western Belgium, in an area known as Ploegsteert-St Yvon (called 'Plugstreet' by the English-speaking soldiers of 1914–18). It was the scene of bitter fighting in 1917, and memorably saw the detonation of nineteen Allied mines beneath German front-lines on the morning of 7 June of that year at the opening of the Battle of Messines.

In August 2007, a team of archaeologists led by Martin Brown and Richard Osgood began excavating at Plugstreet, across an area which included the Allied front line (held by the Australian 3rd Infantry Division), the opposing German trenches, and the No Man's Land in-between (Brown and Osgood 2009). The project was ambitious, international, and interdisciplinary from the start, and sought to extend an understanding of the Australian experience of war which had begun in the Salisbury Plain trenches where the Australians had trained. The Plugstreet team included professional archaeologists and anthropologists, but also a host of technical experts, such as conservation specialist Rob Janaway from Bradford University, aerial photograph expert Birger Stichelbaut from Ghent University, geophysics professional Peter Masters from Cranford University, and Peter Chasseaud, who combines his flair as a landscape artist with being the authority on Great War trench maps.

Ploegsteert-St Yvon, like all First World War battle-zones, is simultaneously an agricultural landscape, an industrialised slaughter house, a tomb for 'the missing', a place for returning refugees, a tourist destination, a location of memorials and pilgrimage, a site for archaeological research, cultural heritage development, and, of course, a still deadly location of unexploded shells and bombs. The Plugstreet Project aimed to 'unpack' each of these landscapes, in order to understand them as ways in which different people engage with the area, and thereby to acknowledge, interpret, and preserve the various juxtaposed histories of the region.

The events of 1917 destroyed a largely medieval landscape, finely balanced between architectural splendour, and such rural features as the sophisticated medieval drainage systems, field boundaries, coppices, and moated-farms. This landscape became a factory of industrialised death – 'drenched with hot metal', cut by trenches, undercut by mining tunnels, swathed in barbed wire, poisoned with gas, soaked with human blood, and disfigured by blasted trees and shell craters. At the Factory Farm site, an upturned German bunker now sits just below the water level of the flooded mine crater blown on 7 June. The crater is fringed by willows, and nearby, the modern fields are defined by post-1918 boundary ditches that in fact are a testament to a re-emergent medieval landscape.

The area had been explored by local investigators before the Plugstreet Project began. In 2003–4, the remains of two German soldiers had been found in the debris thrown up by the mine explosion which destroyed the Factory Farm bunker. Amongst the artefacts was a fragmentary identity disc which allowed one of the bodies to be identified as Julius Wilhelm Brugger of the 2nd Company of the 5th Bavarian Regiment, killed when the mine detonated (Brown and Osgood 2009: 135). This discovery indicated that, while the Plugstreet Project was a multidisciplinary investigation of a battle-zone landscape, and not a 'bone hunt', it was not impossible that its archaeologists might encounter human remains.

Plugstreet Project archaeologists at the Factory Farm site at Ploegsteert-St Yvon in August 2007. The water-filled crater of the mine blown on 7 June 1917 is in the background. (© Author's collection)

During excavations near to Ultimo Crater – in an adjacent part of the investigation area – the remains of an anonymous Australian soldier of 33rd Btn, 3rd Australian Division, were discovered on 5 August 2008. He was one of the missing soldiers recorded on the Menin Gate at nearby Ypres. The skeleton was damaged, but mostly complete, and there were no signs that he had been buried by his comrades or the Germans, or that any of his possessions had been removed. In other words, he was found as he fell. In addition to barbed wire, shrapnel balls, fired German Mauser cartridges, and a small box respirator, the archaeologists noticed that his left hand still clasped the stock of his Lee Enfield rifle.

Although his nationality was established by the presence of collar badges and a shoulder title with the Australian 'Rising Sun' design, there was nothing which identified him by name. Later investigation revealed that thirty-eight men went missing in this area at this time, but that twenty-four were recorded as being buried in temporary graves. Of the remaining fourteen, isotope analysis at the University of Leuven further narrowed the possibilities down to five individuals. One of these men is the anonymous Australian.

Several items opened the door to this dead soldier's social world from 1917. Amongst his possessions was found a spiked German *pickelhaube* helmet, probably from a Hessian regiment and belonging to an NCO. These were popular souvenirs amongst Allied soldiers. It is possible that the anonymous Australian picked it up in the German front-line trench as he passed through, though more likely he acquired it as a war souvenir en route to the front and kept it with him to avoid the danger of it being pilfered. A small altered copper bullet casing was also found, and this may have served as an amuletic charm. Both items humanised the skeletal remains, and connected him to the world of souvenir collecting during the war, and to the battlefield superstitions that attached themselves to men about to face death.

Project archaeologists and specialists have ranged over the Ploegsteert-St Yvon area for three years, surveying and excavating Great War trenches, a Lewis machine gun position, the remains of a concrete blockhouse, and miscellaneous features. Bullet cartridges, barbed wire, shrapnel balls, shell fragments, and unexploded artillery shells – the normal debris of war – have all been found, but so have fragments of rum jars, HP sauce bottles, and a variety of surprisingly intact glass bottles once containing medicines. More personal was a beautifully preserved pocket knife, and more surreal, the contorted remains of pre-war crockery and glass fused into strange shapes by the heat of the exploding mines.

Excavation of the remains of a concrete blockhouse near Ultimo Crater at Ploegsteert-St Yvon in August 2007. (© Author's collection)

Between 2007 and 2008, sixteen hectares of the investigation area were surveyed using a gradiometer, and revealed a scene invisible to the naked eye today – a lunar landscape of trenches, craters, and metal fragments lying just beneath the modern surface. Aerial photographs taken during the war often show clearer detail, but while camouflage tactics might fool the camera, they are exposed by modern geophysical prospection. The use of such techniques, when combined with trench maps and a GIS inventory of aerial photographs, gives an unprecedented view of the palimpsest of Plugstreet's battle-zone landscapes (Masters and Stichelbaut 2009).

CONTESTED BODIES OF FROMELLES (FRANCE)

More contentious than the investigations at Ploegsteert-St Yvon has been the excavation of Australian and British soldiers' bodies from a mass grave at Fromelles over the border in France. This investigation epitomises some of the fundamental issues concerning First World War archaeology, and indeed, the excavation of many conflict landscapes of the twentieth and twenty-first centuries. For these landscapes are a complex layering of human actions, experiences, emotions, and memories that have mingled with the physical remains of war for almost a century.

The Battle of Fromelles took place between 19–20 July 1916, and was intended partly as a diversion from the Battle of the Somme further south. Australian and British soldiers joined forces to take a German position nearby the village of Fromelles, some 16km from Lille. The attack was a disaster, no ground was won, and the allies suffered terrible casualties – some 5,533 Australians and 1,500 British soldiers killed, wounded, or taken prisoner. Jimmy Downing, a survivor, recalled how 'The air was thick with bullets, swishing in a flat, criss-crossed lattice of death. Hundreds were mown down in the flicker of an eyelid.' (Murray 2010).

The victorious Germans buried the allied dead in mass graves, and most of the bodies were relocated and reburied by the Imperial War Graves Commission during the 1920s. Rumours persisted that another mass grave lay undiscovered nearby. In 2007, Tony Pollard and archaeologists from Glasgow University followed up a lead given by Lambis Englezos, an amateur Australian historian, whose research identified a field near Bois Faisan ('Pheasant Wood'), just outside Fromelles. Commissioned by the Australian government, the Glasgow team conducted geophysical and metal detector surveys that indicated the presence of mass burials, and in addition discovered Australian Army artefacts. In May 2008, an exploratory excavation uncovered human remains, as well as badges and buttons that confirmed the identity of the bodies as Australian and British. The magnitude of the discovery was unique in First World War archaeology, and a few months later it was announced that all the bodies would be exhumed and reburied with full military honours by the Commonwealth War Graves Commission in a new war cemetery to be built nearby.

Retrieving the dead of the Great War is never straightforward. While the initial investigations had been carried out by Glasgow University, the responsibility for full-scale excavation and exhumation was put out to tender, and eventually the project was awarded to 'Oxford Archaeology', a well-respected commercial archaeological practice which quoted significantly less than rival university-based bids. The Oxford Archaeology team included not only archaeologists, but also forensic anthropologists, a pathologist, and an anatomical mortuary technologist, as well as bone specialists, surveyors, and finds experts (Loe 2009). Part of the strategy was to take DNA samples in the hope of identifying as many individuals as possible. The excavation of the remains lasted from May to September 2009, and in total some 250 bodies were recovered.

The bodies of the dead at Fromelles soon found themselves in the eye of a gathering storm. Accusations were made against the Oxford Archaeology team concerning their procedures, the secrecy of the operation, and a timescale for retrieval considered too short by some for DNA analysis. In Australia especially, descendants of soldiers lost at Fromelles voiced their frustration. Tim Whitford, whose great uncle, Private Henry Victor Willis, is among the dead, was angry that the identification process was reportedly being hurried. 'What's the rush? They've waited 93 years', he said (Dayton 2009).

To calm these feelings, and restore confidence in the exhumation process, senior figures from the world of archaeology, and British and Australian government officials, visited the excavation to see for themselves. Shortly afterwards, official statements were issued that all were fully satisfied with the professionalism of the Oxford team and the results of the work.

The remains of the soldiers recovered from Pheasant Wood will be reburied over a period of months in 2010, in the first new CWGC cemetery to be built in fifty years. There are currently no headstones, as the hope is that ongoing analysis of the DNA and other artefacts may provide definitive identifications. A commission of specialists will deliberate each case, and for those whose names have been agreed, permanent headstones will begin appearing in April. The first interment of a single unnamed soldier took place under a blanket of snow on 30 January. As flags were lowered, the Last Post sounded, and a volley of three shots pierced the air.

THE ARCHAEOLOGY OF LAWRENCE OF ARABIA REVISITED (JORDAN)

Since 2006, the Great Arab Revolt project (GARP) has continued to explore and investigate the archaeological traces of Lawrence of Arabia's war in southern Jordan. It has made dramatic progress in understanding how the Arab-British desert insurgency succeeded in containing and ultimately defeating the Ottoman forces in this region – insights aided by the cooperation of Jordanian archaeologists from the al-Hussein bin Talal University at Ma'an and Wadi Mousa. It has also generated much official interest from the Jordanian government concerning the potential for heritage tourism and a broader understanding amongst Jordanians of the course and consequences of the Arab Revolt. In many respects, these investigations have focused attention on the potential of the distinctive interdisciplinary approach of modern conflict archaeology.

As GARP investigations continued after 2006, it became increasingly clear, in those areas associated with the defence of the Hejaz Railway, that there existed many archaeological traces of a hitherto unknown Ottoman militarization of the landscape. These defences were a response to the widespread low-level guerrilla activity that occurred in the area after the Arab-British capture of the Red Sea port of Aqaba in July 1917. Camel-borne Bedouin, Arab regular troops, and British and French specialist units combined their forces to attack the fixed positions of the Ottoman army, advised and trained by Germany. These tactics put into practice the ideas of guerrilla warfare which T.E. Lawrence was beginning to advocate: operating in small local groups, avoiding set-piece battles, making war on *matériel* not men, and being an omnipresent, but almost always invisible threat. It was identifying the archaeological imprint of this 'war of detachment' which became a central feature of GARP's work from 2007 onwards.

Survey and excavation at the major Hejaz railway station of Ma'an continued in 2007, mainly along the nearby ridge known as the 'Hill of the Birds', which has preserved almost intact a wartime Ottoman trench system. Today, there is still a well-defined crenellated firing trench which stretches 725m along the ridge, with a second trench extending for 500m along the south-west approaches. Communication trenches criss-cross the area, three redoubts anchor the system, and four artillery emplacements were located near to the best-preserved of these strong-points – the so-called Northern Redoubt.

The analysis of the previous year's metal detecting survey, and the results of 2007's excavations, suggest that many of the artefacts recovered probably represent archaeological traces of the First Battle of Ma'an in April 1918, during which Arab forces briefly occupied part of Ma'an station before being thrown back by Ottoman counter-attacks. The careful investigation of the site's horizontal stratigraphy indicated two periods of development, with earlier shallow linear trenches later reinforced or replaced by deeper ring-trench redoubts. The reasons for this are unclear, though it is possible that they were a response to advice from the visiting German general Erich von Falkenhayn, whose new ideas of defending landscape abandoned linear defences (as used in the 1916 Battle of the Somme) and replaced them with interrelated strong-points (as deployed in the 1917 Battle of Passchendaele).

Excavation and survey also continued during 2007 at the small Hejaz railway station of Wadi Retm, some 60km south of Ma'an. The previous year's recording of the ruinous station buildings was completed, as was the

Ruined Ottoman Hejaz Railway station building at Wadi Retm. It shows impromptu loopholes and Arabic graffiti. A building from the 1960s refurbishment of the station is visible through the doorway. (© Author's collection)

excavation of the nearby Ottoman tented camp. This campsite sits on a hill which commands views of the nearby railway to the north-east, and the traditional route through the wadi to the south-west. The site has firing dugouts with stone parapets, some twenty stone-lined tent-rings, an oven, and a latrine. The tent rings were similar to those made by the Bedouin, but revealed their military origins by being laid out with linear regularity, and yielding tent pegs, pieces of tent canvas, sand bags, and many Ottoman army uniform buttons.

Landscape walking in the Wadi Retm area added a new dimension to understanding these desert surroundings. It soon became clear that the isolated railway station sat within an extensively militarized landscape, which had not been recognised or mentioned by Lawrence, or other historians. Only the Bedouin, it seems, had known of these military features, and they had told few outsiders.

As one field reconnaissance expedition followed another, a pattern began to emerge. It seems that to control the Wadi Retm area, the Ottomans depended on the inter-visibility of isolated military sites in a landscape whose tortuous geography conspired to block direct lines of sight between the railway station and outlying strong-points. They overcame these obstacles by building strong-points at critical locations, such as a defended observation point/machine-gun position on a small hill lying 200m north-west of the station. Similarly well-sited was a large rectangular fortified position perched atop a 1,130m-high sandstone ridge, and overlooking the station from the north-east. German Mauser cartridges, Ottoman army buttons, and artillery shell fragments were found at this well-defended location. From both these points of inter-visibility, flag semaphore or heliograph could have conveyed messages to the railway station.

A new discovery at the end of 2007 shaped the following year's investigations. At the northernmost part of the wadi, a large cliff-top fort was discovered. Never mentioned in the military histories of the Great Arab Revolt, this impressive structure overlooks a strategic bend in the Hejaz Railway as it descends from the stony desert plateau to the sandy wadi floor. In 2008, investigations at the site, called 'Fassu'ah Ridge', revealed fortified gun-points, administrative buildings, and internal trench systems.

Inside view of the Ottoman administrative command centre at Fassu'ah Ridge, showing the remains of paths belonging to a small 'parade ground'. (© Author's collection)

Scattered along the ridge itself were the remains of other tented encampments, gun positions, observation points, and a mule-tethering site. The Fassu'ah Ridge site itself has the remains of a military road leading down to a presumed halt on the railway, possibly for Ottoman officers to ascend to what probably was the local command-and-control centre.

While these investigations were underway, another team of archaeologists were excavating the remains of a large tented camp at the site of another (and now disappeared) Hejaz Railway station known as Batn Al-Ghoul, lower down the slope from Fassu'ah Ridge. Metal detecting and excavation uncovered many more Ottoman Army buttons, fragments of an Ottoman uniform and a miscellany of pre-war items indicating that long before the Hejaz Railway was built, this place was a stopping point for camel caravans descending into the wadi, en route south to Medina and Mecca. There was no doubt that the archaeology of the Great Arab Revolt of 1916–18 was embedded in a landscape which, while it appeared as a desert wilderness, had been used for hundreds, perhaps thousands of years by people moving north and south for trade and pilgrimage.

GARP's latest research took place in 2009, and completed the excavations at Batn Al-Ghoul. At the same time, a 50km walking survey of the Hejaz Railway from Ma'an to Batn Al-Ghoul was also completed, mapping every location associated with the Arab Revolt. Exploration, survey, and excavation then moved north-west to the area around the town of Wuheida, in whose nearby wadi the Arab tribes gathered together with their British and French allies between 1917 and 1918.

This large wadi is, on one side, dominated by Ottoman bunkers and trenches, whose excavated remains indicate that the area was fought over by the Turks and the Arabs (and their allies). The Ottoman Turks abandoned their positions which were then occupied by the victors. Across the wadi are the archaeological traces of the Arab encampment – whose tents and connecting pathways are still outlined by stones, and whose investigation yielded a rich and varied array of artefacts. Future work will investigate further at Wuheida, and the surrounding area, as well as survey a recently located Ottoman burial ground further south, on the outskirts of Ma'an.

References

This bibliography has several purposes. First, it includes the references that appear throughout the book. Second, it offers many additional references that are not directly cited in the text. The reason for this is that Great War archaeology is a new and quite different kind of archaeology, which incorporates many varied types of research that are not archaeological in the traditional sense. Investigations from anthropology, military history, cultural history, geography, geology, art history, tourism and heritage studies all contribute to the archaeology of the First World War. Many important books and articles from these various disciplines are often unfamiliar to the student and general reader primarily interested in archaeology, and a cross-section of these is included here. It is hoped that bringing together in one place a representative selection of important references will allow all who are fascinated by, and wish to read more about, this newest kind of archaeology, to find the multidisciplinary path both stimulating and just a little easier to follow.

As some readers might wish to participate in, or at least learn more about, the various projects described in this book, I include here a brief list of the appropriate websites.

The Great Arab Revolt Project (Jordan) is at: www.jordan1914-18archaeology.org
The Plugstreet Project is at: http://plugstreet.blogspot.com
The Sedgefield Aerodrome Project is at: http://ccgi.sedgeford.plus.com/blog
The Great War Archaeology Group is at: www.gwag.org
Digging Dad's Army (DDA) is at: www.diggingdadsarmy.org.uk
The Durand Group is at: www.durandgroup.org.uk
My own website is under construction at: www.conflictarchaeology.com
The University of Bristol new MA in '20th Century Conflict Archaeology' can be accessed at: www.bris.ac.uk/archanth/postgrad/conflict

Adam, Frédéric (1991). *La Sépulture collective de Saint-Rémy-la-Calonne, Quart-en-Réserve (Meuse)*. DRAC Lorraine: Service regional de l'Archéologie

Adam, Frédéric (1999). 'L'Archéologie et la Grande Guerre', *'L'Archéologie et la Grande Guerre Aujourd'hui'*. *Noêsis: Revue Annuelle d'Histoire*, 2: 29–35

Adam, Frédéric (2006). 'Alain-Fournier et ses compagnons d'arme. Metz: Editions Serpenoise

AIPS (1996). Association pour l'Inventaire et la Préservation des sites, *Les Carrières de Confrécourt: Soissonais 14–18*. Vic-sur-Aisne: Imprimerie Lepigeon

Allison, Penelope M. (1999). 'Introduction', in Penelope M. Allison (ed.), *The Archaeology of Household Activities*. London: Routledge, pp. 1–18

Anderton, M. and Schofield, J. (1999). 'Anti-Aircraft Gunsites – then and now', *Conservation Bulletin*, 36: 11–13

Andreotti, A. and Viazzi, L. (1977). *Con gli alpini sulla Marmolada 1915–1917*. Milan: Mursia

Anon. (1999). 'Sikhs in the Salient', *Flanders Fields Magazine*, 1/1: 16

Anon. (2010). Toiling for War: Chinese workers in World War One. *In Flanders Fields Magazine* 12 (1): 1–4.

Appleyard, B. (1929). *Burgate Memorial Shrine*. Eye: Comer and Phillips, privately published

Audoin-Rouzeau, Stéphane (1992). *Men at War 1914–1918: National Sentiment and Trench Journalism in France during the First World War*. Oxford: Berg

Audoin-Rouzeau, Stéphane (1995). *Combattre*. Péronne: Historial de la Grande Guerre

Audoin-Rouzeau, Stéphane and Becker, Annette (2002). *1914–1918: Understanding the Great War*. London: Profile

AWM. *Australian War Memorial Military Heraldry Catalogue Worksheets/Accession Numbers*. Canberra: Australian War Memorial

Baccarne, R. and Steen, J. (1975). *Boezinge na 1914–1918*. Wervik: privately published

Bademli, R. (1997). *Gallipoli Peninsula Peace Park International Ideas & Competition: The Book and The Catalogue (II)*. Ankara: Middle East Technical University

Baert, Koen, Boone, Jean-Pierre, Chielens, Piet, Debruyne, Tony, Dendooven, Dominiek, Dewilde, Jan, Fierens, Edward, Steen, Jan and Verbeke, Roger (1999). *In Flanders Fields Museum: Catalogue of the Objects*. Ieper: In Flanders Fields Museum

Bailey, Paul (2000). 'From Shandong to the Somme: Chinese Indentured Labour in France during World War I', in Anne J. Kashen (ed.), *Language, Labour and Migration*, Aldershot: Ashgate, pp. 179–96

Balbi, Marco (2009). 'Great War Archaeology on the Glaciers of the Alps', in Nicholas J. Saunders and Paul Cornish (eds), *Contested Objects: Material Memories of the Great War*, pp. 280–290 Abingdon: Routledge

Barbusse, Henri (1988). *Under Fire*. London: Dent

Barbusse, Henri (2003). *Under Fire*. London: Penguin

Bartoli, M. and Fornaro, M. (1993). *La città di gliaccio. Guida agli itinerary e al museo della Guerra 1915–1918 in Marmolada*. Trento: Publilux

Barton, Peter (2005). *The Battlefields of the First World War: From the First Battle of Ypres to Passchendaele*. London: Constable and Robinson

Barton, Peter, Doyle, Peter and Vandewalle, Johan (2004). *Beneath Flanders Fields: The Tunnellers War 1914–1918*. Staplehurst: Spellmount

Barton, Thomas A. (1997). *American Indians in World War I: At Home and at War*. Albuquerque: University of New Mexico Press

Becker, Annette (1996). *Croire*. Péronne: Historial de la Grande Guerre

Becker, Annette (1998). *War and Faith: Religious Imagination in France, 1914–30*. Oxford: Berg

Becker, Annette (1999). 'Graffiti et Sculptures de Soldats', 'L'Archéologie et la Grande Guerre Aujourd'hui'. *Noêsis: Revue Annuelle d'Histoire*, 2: 117–27

Belk, R. (2001). *Collecting in a Consumer Society*. London: Routledge

Bender, Barbara (1993). 'Stonehenge: Contested Landscapes (Medieval to Present-Day)', in Barbara Bender (ed.), *Landscape: Politics and Perspectives*. Oxford: Berg, pp. 245–79

Bender, Barbara and Winer, M. (eds), *Contested Landscapes: Movement, Exile and Place*. Oxford: Berg

Berliner Illustrirte Zeitung (1917). 'Three Advertisements for Decorative War-Rings (Finger Rings) and Armbands', *Berliner Illustrirte Zeitung*, 46: 599–60

Beurier, Jöelle (2004). 'Death and Material Culture: The Case of Pictures during the First World War', in Nicholas J. Saunders (ed.), *Matters of Conflict: Material Culture, Memory and the First World War*. Abingdon: Routledge, pp. 109–22

Black, Jonathan (2004). '"Thanks for the Memory": War Memorials, Spectatorship and the Trajectories of Commemoration 1919–2001', in Nicholas J. Saunders (ed.), *Matters of Conflict: Material Culture, Memory and the First World War*. Abingdon: Routledge, pp. 134–48

Blunden, Edmund ([1928] 1982). *Undertones of War*. Harmondsworth: Penguin

Bonnard, Jean-Yves and Guénoff, Didier (1999). *D'Attiche aux Cinq Piliers: Les Souterrains de la Grande Guerre*. Saint Quentin: L'Aisne Nouvelle

Boorman, D. (1988). *At the Going Down of the Sun: British First World War Memorials*. York: Sessions

Booth, A. (1996). *Postcards from the Trenches: Negotiating the Space between Modernism and the First World War*. Oxford: Oxford University Press

Borg, A. (1991). *War Memorials*. London: Leo Cooper

Bostyn, Franky (1999). *Beecham Dugout, Passchendaele 1914–1918*. Zonnebeke: Association for Battlefield Archaeology in Flanders, Studies 1

Bostyn, Franky and Vancoillie, Jan (2000). *Bayernwald: Het Croonaertbos in de Eerste Wereldoorlog*. Zonnebeke: Association for Battlefield Archaeology in Flanders, Studies 2

Boura, Frédérique (1999). 'Une tombe des soldats à Saint-Remy-La-Calonne', 'L'Archéologie et la Grande Guerre Aujourd'hui'. *Noêsis: Revue Annuelle d'Histoire*, 2: 71–83

Bourke, Joanna (1996). *Dismembering the Male: Men's Bodies, Britain and the Great War*. London: Reaktion Books

Brandauer, Isabelle (2006). *Solldatenalltag in den Dolomiten im Ersten Weltkrieg, 1915–1917* (Soldiers' Daily Life in the Dolomites in the First World War, 1915–1917), Ph.D. thesis, University of Innsbruck

Brandauer, Isabelle (2007). *Menschenmaterial Soldat: Alltagsleben an der Dolomitenfront im Ersten Weltkrieg 1915–1917*. Innsbruck: Golf Verlag.

Brandt, S. (2004). The Historial de la Grande Guerre in Peronne, France: a museum at a former First World War battlefield. *Museum International* 56 (3): 46–52

Braybon, G. (1995). 'Women and the War', in S. Constantine, M.W. Kirby and M.B. Rose (eds), *The First World War in British History*, London: Edward Arnold, pp. 141–67

Brazier, J. (1998). 'Re-burial of 27 Soldiers from 13th Bn Royal Fusiliers at Monchy-le-Preux', *Western Front Association Bulletin*, 50: 39

Brittain, H.E. (1917). *To Verdun from the Somme: An Anglo-American Glimpse of the Great Advance*. London: Bodley Head

Brockman, Andy (2009). Shooters Hill – Digging Up Dad's Army. *Current Archaeology* 228 (XIX): 35–42.

Brockman, Andy, and Barton, Kevin (2009). 'Air Photographs, Military Archaeology and Human Memory: A Case Study from South East London'. In, Birger Stichelbaut, Jean Bourgeois, Nicholas J. Saunders and Piet Chielens (eds) *Images of Conflict: Military Aerial Photography and Archaeology*, pp. 221–240. Newcastle: Cambridge Scholars Press

Brown, Martin (2005). 'Journey back to Hell: Excavations at Serre on the Somme', *Current World Archaeology*, 10: 25–33

Brown, Martin (2009). '"Slowly our Ghosts Drag Home": Human Remains from the Heidenkopf, Serre, Somme', in Nicholas J. Saunders and Paul Cornish (eds), *Contested Objects: Material Memories of the Great War*, pp. 266–279. Abingdon: Routledge

Brown, Martin and Osgood, Richard (2009). *Digging up Plugstreet: The Western front unearthed*. Yeovil: Haynes Publishing

Brown, Graham and Field, David (2009). 'Training for Trench Warfare: The Archaeological Evidence from Salisbury Plain', in Nicholas J. Saunders and Paul Cornish (eds), *Contested Objects: Material Memories of the Great War*, pp. 291–300. Abingdon: Routledge

Buchli, V. (2002) (ed.). *The Material Culture Reader*. Oxford: Berg

Buchli, Victor and Lucas, Gavin (2001) (eds). *Archaeologies of the Contemporary Past*. London: Routledge

Buckley, Francis (1920–1). 'Finds of Flint Implements in the Red Line Trenches at Coigneux, 1918', *Proceedings of the Prehistoric Society of East Anglia for 1920–21*, 1–9

Buffetaut, Yves (1997). *The 1917 Spring Offensives: Arras, Vimy, Le Chemin des Dames*. Paris: Combined Books

Burl, Aubrey (1985). *Megalithic Brittany*. London: Thames and Hudson

Cameron, D. and Donlon, D. (2005). 'A Preliminary Archaeological Survey of the ANZAC Gallipoli Battlefields of 1915', *Australasian Historical Archaeology*, 23: 131–8

Carr, Gillian (2009). *Occupied Behind Barbed Wire*. Jersey: Jersey Heritage Trust

Carlin, J. (2003). 'Ordnance Collecting: Collecting German Large Calibre Ammunition of WW1 & WW2', *The Armourer*, 56 (March/April): 34–7

Carmichael, D.L., Hubert, J., Reeves, B. and Schanche, O. (1994) (eds). *Sacred Sites, Sacred Places*. London: Routledge

Caunt, Pamela M. (1994). *Military Sweethearts*. London: ARBRAS

Cecil, Hugh and Liddle, Peter (1996) (eds). *Facing Armageddon: The First World War Experienced*. London: Leo Cooper

Chasseaud, Peter (1999). *Artillery's Astrologers: A History of the Field Survey Companies*. Lewes: Mapbooks

Chasseaud, Peter (2002). 'British, French and German Mapping and Survey on the Western Front in the First World War', in Peter Doyle and Matthew R. Bennett (eds), *Fields of Battle: Terrain in Military History*. London: Kluwer, pp. 171–204

Chasseaud, Peter and Doyle, Peter (2005). *Grasping Gallipoli: Terrain, Maps and Failure at the Dardanelles, 1915*. Staplehurst: Spellmount

Chielens, Piet (2001). 'Diggers Dig for Remains of a War', *Flanders Fields Magazine*, 3/5: 13–15

Cieraard, I. (1999) (ed.). *At Home: An Anthropology of Domestic Space*. Syracuse, NY: Syracuse University Press

Clack, Timothy (2006). 'Living Archaeology: Conflict and Media', in John Schofield, Axel Klausmeier and Louise Purbrick (eds), *Re-Mapping the Field: New Approaches in Conflict Archaeology*. Berlin/Bonn: Westkreuz-Verlag GMBH, pp. 89–93

Classen, Constance (2005). *The Book of Touch*. Oxford: Berg

Clout, Hugh (1996). *After the Ruins: Restoring the Countryside of Northern France after the Great War*. Exeter: University of Exeter Press

Cocroft, Wayne D. (2000). *Dangerous Energy: The Archaeology of Gunpowder and Military Explosives Manufacture*. London: English Heritage

Cocroft, Wayne D., Devlin, Danielle, Schofield, John and Thomas, Roger J.C. (2006). *War Art: Murals and Graffiti – Military Life, Power and Subversion*. Bootham: The Council for British Archaeology

Compère-Morel, Thomas (2000). *L'Historial de la Grande Guerre et le Circuit du souvenir*. Tournai: La Renaissance du Livre

Connerton, Paul (1989). *How Societies Remember*. Cambridge: Cambridge University Press

Corbin, Alain (1999). *Village Bells: Sound and Meaning in the Nineteenth-Century French Countryside*. London: Papermac/Macmillan

Coombs, R.E.B. (1994). *Before Endeavours Fade* (7th edn). London: Battle of Britain Prints International Ltd

Cork, Richard (1994). *A Bitter Truth: Avant-Garde Art and the Great War*. New Haven: Yale University Press

Cornish, Paul (2004). '"Sacred Relics": Objects in the Imperial War Museum 1917–39', in Nicholas J. Saunders (ed.), *Matters of Conflict: Material Culture, Memory and the First World War*. Abingdon: Routledge, pp. 35–50

Cresswell, Yvonne M. (1994) (ed.). *Living with the Wire: Civilian Internment in the Isle of Man during the Two World Wars*. Douglas: Manx National Heritage, The Manx Museum & National Trust

Crouch, D. and Lübbren, N. (2002) (eds). *Visual Culture and Tourism*. Oxford: Berg

CWGC. (Commonwealth War Graves Commission). n.d. website: http://www.cwgc.org/fromelles. Accessed 27 January 2010

Davidson, A.H.G. (1990) (ed.). *The Somme and the Butte de Warlencourt*. Western Front Association

Das, Santanu (2005). *Touch and Intimacy in First World War Literature*. Cambridge: Cambridge University Press

Dayton, Leigh (2009). Fromelles DNA Fears. *The Australian*, 3 June.

Decock, Benoit (1996). 'L'Art rupestre des soldats de la Grande Guerre: La Carrière du "Premier Zouaves" de Confrécourt', *Guerres mondiales et conflits contemporains*, 46/183: 141–9

Decoodt, H. (2002). 'Forged Photographs during WWI', *In Flanders Fields Magazine*,4 (June): 12–14

Degaast, M.G. (1917). 'La Bijouterie des tranchées'. *Almanach illustré du petit Parisien*, 99–104

Dellouche, D. (1994). 'Cubisme et camouflage', in J.-J. Becker, J. Winter, G. Krumeich, A. Becker and S. Audoin-Rouzeau (eds), *Guerre et cultures, 1914–1918*. Paris: Armand Colin, pp. 239–50

de Meyer, M. (2005). 'Houthulst and the A19-Project: Inventory of World War I Heritage Based on Wartime Aerial Photography and Trench Maps', in J. Bourgeois and M. Meganck (eds), *Aerial Photography and Archaeology 2003: A Century of Information* (Archaeological Reports Ghent University, 4). Ghent: Academia Press, pp. 87–99

de Meyer, Mathieu and Pype, Pedro (2004). *The A19 Project: Archaeological Research at Cross Roads*. Zarren: Association for World War Archaeology (AWA) Publications

Dendooven, Dominiek (2001). *Ypres as Holy Ground: Menin Gate & Last Post*. Koksijde: De Klaproos

Dendooven, Dominiek (2009). 'The journey back: On the nature of donations to the "In Flanders Fields Museum"'. In, Nicholas J. Saunders and Paul Cornish (eds.), *Contested Objects: Material memories of the Great War*, pp. 60–72. Abingdon: Routledge

Dendooven, Dominiek and Dewilde, Jan (1999). *The Reconstruction of Ieper: A Walk through History*. Sint-Niklaas: Openbaar Kunstbezit in Vlaanderen/In Flanders Fields Museum

Dendooven, Dominiek and Chielens, Piet (eds) (2008). *World War One: Five Continents in Flanders*. Tielt: Lanoo

Dennis, Mark J.R. and Saunders, Nicholas J. (2003). *Craft and Conflict Masonic Trench Art and Military Memorabilia*. London: Savannah

Derez, Marc (1997). 'A Belgian Salient for Reconstruction: People and *Patrie*, Landscape and Memory', in P.H. Liddle (ed.), *Passchendaele in Perspective: The Third Battle of Ypres*. London: Leo Cooper, pp. 437–58

Desfossés, Yves (1999). 'Préserver Les Traces', *'L'Archéologie et la Grande Guerre Aujourd'hui'*. *Noêsis: Revue Annuelle d'Histoire*, 2: 37–51

Desfossés, Yves and Gorczynski, Philippe (2002). 'Un exceptionnel témoin de la bataille de Cambrai, le char de Flesquieres', *14–18 Aujourd'hui. Today. Heute. Revue Annuelle d'Histoire. Noêsis*, 5: 14–25

Desfossés, Yves and Jacques, Alain (2000). 'Vers une définition et une reconnaissance de l'archéologie de la Première Guerre mondiale'. *Actes des colloques 'La Bataille en Picardie, combattre de l'Antiquité au XXème siècle'*. Amiens, pp. 203–20

Desfossés, Yves, Jacques, Alain and Prilaux, Gilles (2002). 'Actiparc. Premier bilan de l'operation d'archéologie preventive', *Histoire et Archéologie du Pas-de-Calais*, 20: 3–26

Desfossés, Yves, Jacques, Alain and Prilaux, Gilles (2003). 'Arras "Actiparc", les oubliés du "Point du Jour"', *Sucellus*, 54: 84–100

Desfossés, Yves, Jacques, Alain and Prilaux, Gilles (2003). *Archéologie en Nord-Pas de Calais*. Arras: Zac Actiparc

Desfossés, Yves, Jacques, Alain and Prilaux, Gilles (2004). 'Archéologie de la Grande Guerre: Le Cas de la région d'Arras, Pas-de-Calais', in Jean-Paul Demoule, collectif, Ulysse Cabezuelo, Jean-Pierre Giraud and Laurence Bourgignon (eds), *La France archéologique: Vingt ans d'aménagements et de découvertes*. Vanves: Hazan, pp. 218–25

Desfossés, Yves, Jacques, Alain and Prilaux, Gilles (2005). *Archéologie en Nord-Pas de Calais: L'archéologie de la grande guerre*. DRAC Nord-Pas de Calais. Service régional de l'Archéologie. Villeneuve d'Ascq

Desfossés, Yves, Jacques, Alain and Prilaux, Gilles (2008). *L'archéologie de la Grande Guerre*. Rennes: Éditions OUEST-FRANCE

Dewilde, Marc (1991). 'Opgravingen in de Augustijnenabdij van Zonnebeke', *Biekorf*, 91: 375–80

Dewilde, Marc and Saunders, Nicholas J. (2009). 'Archaeology of the Great War: The Flemish Experience', in Nicholas J. Saunders and Paul Cornish (eds), *Contested Objects: Material Memories of the Great War*, pp. 251–265 Abingdon: Routledge

Dewilde, Marc, Pype, Pedro, de Meyer, Mathieu, Demeyere, Frederik, Lammens, Wouter, Degryse, Janiek, Wyffels, Franky and Saunders, Nicholas J. (2004). 'Belgium's New Department of First World War Archaeology', *Antiquity*, 78 /301, Project Gallery: http://antiquity.ac.uk/ProjGall/Saunders

Dicker, Kathy (2009). 'Family Trees'. *Estatement* (Summer) 67:19–20

Dieudonné, G. (1999). 'Experimental Archaeology and Education: Ancient Technology at the Service of Modern Education at SAMARA, France', in P.G. Stone and P.G. Planel (eds), *The Constructed Past: Experimental Archaeology, Education and the Public*. London: Routledge, pp. 206–16

The Diggers (2001). *Saved from Progress*. Boezinge–Ieper: privately printed

Diller, Elizabeth and Scofidio, Ricardo (1994) (eds). *Back to the Front: Tourisms of War*. New York: Princeton Architectural Press/ FRAC Basse-Normandie

Dobinson, C. (1996). 'Twentieth-Century Fortifications in England. Vol. 1. Anti-Aircraft Artillery 1914–46', unpublished report for English Heritage, London

Dobinson, C. (1999). 'Twentieth-Century Fortifications in England. Vol. 7. Acoustics and Radar: England's Early Warning Systems, 1914–45', unpublished report for English Heritage, London

Dolamore, M. (2000). *Ground Penetrating Radar and Digital Terrain Modelling Survey at the Canadian Memorial Parks at Vimy Ridge and Beaumont Hamel France*. Durand Group Report

Doyle, Peter (1998). *Geology of the Western Front, 1914–1918*. London: The Geologist's Association

Doyle, Peter (2008). *Tommy's War: British Miliary Memorabilia 1914-1918*. Marlborough: The Crowood Press.

Doyle, Peter and. Bennett, Matthew R. (eds) (2008). *Fields of Battle: Terrain in Military History*. London: Kluwer

Doyle, Peter, Barton, P. and Rosenbaum, M. (2001). 'Geohazards – Last Legacy of War?', *Geoscientist*, 11/1: 4–7

Doyle, Peter, Bostyn, Franky, Barton, Peter and Vandewalle, Johann (2001). 'The Underground War 1914–18: The Geology of the Beecham Dugout, Passchendaele, Belgium', *Proceedings of the Geologists' Association*, 112: 263–74

Dunn, J.C. ([1938] 1997). *The War the Infantry Knew 1914–1919: A Chronicle of Service in France and Belgium*. London: Abacus

Durand, Nicole (2006). *De l'Horreur à l'art : Dans les tranchées de la Première Guerre Mondiale* (Relié). Seuil.

Dyer, Geoff (1995). *The Missing of the Somme*. London: Penguin

Eksteins, Modris (1990). *The Rites of Spring: The Great War and the Birth of the Modern Age*. Boston: Houghton Mifflin

Eksteins, Modris (1994). 'Michelin, Pickfords et La Grande Guerre: Le Tourisme sur Le Front Occidental: 1919–1991', in J.-J. Becker, J. Winter, G. Krumeich, A. Becker and S. Audoin-Rouzeau (eds), *Guerre et cultures, 1914–1918*. Paris: Armand Colin,pp. 417–28

English Heritage (2000). *MPP 2000: A Review of the Monuments Protection Programme 1986–2000*. London: English Heritage

Fabi, Lucio (1998) (co-ord.). *1918, la Guerra Nella Testa: Arte popolare, esperienze, memoria nel primo conflitto mondiale* (catalogue for exhibition held at Musei

Provinciali di Gorizia, Gorizia and Museo della Grande Guerra, Borgo Castello, 4 November 1998–28 February 1999). Trieste: LINT Editoriale

Fabiansson, Nils (2000–2005). 'The Archaeology of the Western Front 1914–1918', unpublished paper, ex website

Fabiansson, Nils (2004). 'The Internet and the Great War: The Impact on the Making and Meaning of Great War History', in Nicholas J. Saunders (ed.), *Matters of Conflict: Material Culture, Memory and the First World War.* Abingdon: Routledge, pp. 72–89

Fair, C. (1998). 'The Lost Villages of the Camp de Suippes, Champagne: La Journée des Villages Détruits', *Western Front Association Bulletin*, 51: 32

Faulkner, N. and Durrani, N (2008). *In Search of the Zeppelin War: The Archaeology of the First Blitz.* Stroud: Tempus

Faulkner, N., and Saunders, Nicholas J. (2007). 'Archaeology, Lawrence, and Guerrilla Warfare'. *History Today* (August): 5–6

Faulkner, N., Saunders, Nicholas J., and Thorpe, David (2007). 'Trains, Trenches and Tents: The Archaeology of Lawrence of Arabia's War'. *Current World Archaeology* 23: 26–34

FBS (2002). Fovant Badges Society website www.fovantbadges.com

Ferguson, Niall (1998). *The Pity of War.* Harmondsworth: Penguin

Filippucci, Paola (2009). Postcards from the past: War, landscape and place in Argonne, France. In, Nicholas J. Saunders and Paul Cornish (eds.), *Contested Objects: Material Memories of the Great War*, pp. 220–236. Abingdon: Routledge

Finn, Christine (2005). 'Artefacts of Occupation: The Enduring Archaeology of Jersey, Channel Islands', in Bernard Finn and Barton C. Hacker (eds), *Materializing the Military.* London: Science Museum, pp. 121–39

Forty, A. and Kuchler, S. (2001) (eds). *The Art of Forgetting.* Oxford: Berg

Fraser, Alastair H. (2004). *The Identification of a German Soldier Found in the Heidenkopf at Serre.* Hellfire Corner website www.fylde.demon.co.uk/fraser.htm

Fraser, Alistair and Brown, Martin (2007). 'Mud, Blood and Missing Men: Excavations at Serre, Somme, France'. In, T. Pollard and I. Banks (eds.), *Scorched Earth: Studies in the Archaeology of Conflict*, pp 147–171. Brill: Leiden.

Fraser, Alistair, Robertshaw, Andy and Roberts, Steve (2009). *Ghosts on the Somme: Filming the Battle, June–July 1916.* Barnsley: Pen & Sword

Freeman, P.W.M. and Pollard, A. (2001) (eds). *Fields of Conflict: Progress and Prospect in Battlefield Archaeology* (British Archaeological Reports (BAR) International Series 958). Oxford: Archaeopress

Fussell, Paul (1977). *The Great War and Modern Memory.* New York: Oxford University Press

GARP (2006). Great Arab Revolt Archaeological Project (GARP). *Report on Preliminary Desktop Research and Field Reconnaissance, 20–27 February 2006*. GARP

Gilbert, Martin (1994). *First World War*. London: HarperCollins

Gilchrist, Roberta (2003). 'Introduction: Towards a Social Archaeology of Warfare', *World Archaeology*, 35 /1: 1–6

Girardet, Jean-Marie, Jacques, Alain and Letho Duclos, Jean-Luc (2003). *Somewhere on the Western Front, Arras 1914–1918*. Arras: Documents d'Archéologie et d'Histoire du XX Siècle, No. 8

GODA (2001). Website www.Greatwar.org/diaries/awirelessoperator

Goebel, Stefan. (2007). *The Great War and Medieval Memory*. Cambridge: Cambridge University Press.

Gough, Paul (1997). '"An Epic of Mud": Artistic Impressions of Third Ypres', in P.H. Liddle (ed.), *Passchendaele in Perspective: The Third Battle of Ypres*. London: Leo Cooper, pp. 409–21

Gough, Paul (1998). 'Memorial Gardens as Dramaturgical Space'. International Journal of Heritage Studies 3 (4): 199–214

Gough, Paul (2006). 'Beaumont-Hamel: The Recovery, Construction, and Reconstruction of a Site of National Memory', *Stand To!* 75: 13–19

Gough, Paul (2009). '"Calculating the future": Panoramic sketching, reconnaissance drawing and the material trace of war'. In, Nicholas J. Saunders and Paul Cornish (eds.), *Contested Objects: Material Memories of the Great War*, pp. 237–250. Abingdon: Routledge

Gregory, Adrian (1994). *The Silence of Memory: Armistice Day 1919–1946*. Oxford: Berg

Gwinell (1919). 'Souvenirs', in *The Golden Horseshoe: Men of the 37th Division B.E.F.* London: Cassell, pp. 46–7

Gygi, Fabio (2004). 'Shattered Experiences – Recycled Relics: Strategies of Representation and the Legacy of the Great War', in Nicholas J. Saunders (ed.), *Matters of Conflict: Material Culture, Memory and the First World War*. Abingdon: Routledge, pp. 72–89

Gygi, Fabio (2009). 'Shaping matter, memories and mentalities: The German steel helmet from artefact to afterlife'. In Nicholas J Saunders and Paul Cornish (eds.), *Contested Objects: Material Memories of the Great War*, pp 27–44. Abingdon: Routledge

Hanna, E. (2007). 'A small screen alternative to stone and bronze: The Great War series and British television'. *European Journal of Culture Studies* 10 (1): 89–111

Harvey, Oliver (2000a). 'Trading on Sick Black Market', *The Sun*, Saturday 11 November, p. 7

Harvey, Oliver (2000b). 'Ghouls Dig up Bodies of our Hero Tommies', *Sun*, Saturday 11 November, p. 6

Hawkes, Jacquetta (1939). *The Prehistory of the Channel Islands*. Vol. 2. *The Bailiwick of Jersey*. Jersey: Société Jersiaise

Higonnet, M.R. (2008). 'Souvenirs of Death'. *Journal of War and Culture Studies* 1 (1): 65–78

Hirsch, E. (1995). 'Introduction: Landscape: Between Place and Space', in E. Hirsch and M. O'Hanlon (eds), *The Anthropology of Landscape: Perspectives on Place and Space*. Oxford: Clarendon Press, pp. 1–20

Hohnnadel, Alain and Goby, Jean-Luis (1990). *La Mémoire des Forts: Peintures murales des soldats de la Ligne Maginot et des forts de Metz 1914–1940*. Metz: Éditions Serpenoise

Holmes, Richard (2004). *Tommy: The British Soldier on the Western Front 1914–1918*. London: HarperCollins

Holyoak, Vincent (2001a). 'Chalk Military Badges on Fovant Down', English Heritage schedule entry

Holyoak, Vincent (2001b). 'Airfields as Battlefields, Aircraft as an Archaeological Resource: British Military Aviation in the First Half of the C20th', in P.W.M. Freeman and A. Pollard (eds), *Fields of Conflict: Progress and Prospect in Battlefield Archaeology* (British Archaeological Reports (BAR) International Series 958). Oxford: Archaeopress, pp. 253–64

Horne, Alistair (1981). *The Price of Glory, Verdun 1916*. Harmondsworth: Penguin

Hoskins, J. (1998). *Biographical Objects: How Things Tell the Stories of People's Lives*. London: Routledge

Howe, Glenford Deroy (2002). *Race, War and Nationalism: A Social History of West Indians in the First World War*. Oxford: James Currey

Howes, David (1991). 'Introduction: To Summon All the Senses', in David Howes (ed.), *The Varieties of Sensory Experience*. Toronto: University of Toronto Press, pp. 3–21

Howes, David (2006). *Sensual Relations: Engaging the Senses in Culture & Social Theory*. Ann Arbor: The University of Michigan Press

Hubert, Jane (1989). 'A Proper Place for the Dead: A Critical Review of the "Reburial" Issue', in Robert Layton (ed.), *Conflict in the Archaeology of Living Traditions*. London: Unwin Hyman, pp. 131–66

Huss, Marie-Monique (2000). *Histoires de famille: Cartes postale et culture de guerre*. Paris: Éditions Noêsis

Hynes, Samuel (1990). *A War Imagined: The First World War and English Culture.* London: Bodley Head

Iles, J. (2008) 'Encounters in the Fields – Tourism to the Battlefields of the Western Front'. *Journal of Tourism and Cultural Change* 6 (2): 138–154

Isyanova, Gulya (2009). 'The Consumer Sphinx: From French Trench to Parisian Market', in Nicholas J. Saunders and Paul Cornish (eds), *Contested Objects: Material Memories of the Great War*, pp. 130–143. Abingdon: Routledge

Jockenhövel, A. and Smolla, G. (1975). Le Dépôt de Juvincourt-Damary (Aisne). *Gallia Préhistoire*, 18/1: 289–313

Jones, B. and Howells, B. (1972). *Popular Arts of the First World War*. London: Studio Vista

Jünger, Ernst (2003). *Storm of Steel*. London: Allen Lane

Kavanagh, Gail (1994). *Museums and the First World War: A Social History.* Leicester: Leicester University Press

Keegan, John (1991). *The Face of Battle: A Study of Agincourt, Waterloo and the Somme*. London: Pimlico

Keegan, John (1998). *The First World War*. London: Hutchinson

Kenyon, David (2005). *Thiepval Wood, France: Historical Analysis and Archaeological Assessment*. Belfast: Somme Association

Ketchum, J.D. (1965). *Ruhleben – A Prison Camp Society*. Toronto: University of Toronto Press

Kimball, J.A. (2004). *Trench Art: An Illustrated History*. Davis (CA): Silverpenny Press

King, Alex (1998). *Memorials of the Great War in Britain: The Symbolism and Politics of Remembrance*. Oxford: Berg

Krell, Alan (2002). *The Devil's Rope: A Cultural History of Barbed Wire*. London: Reaktion

Laffin, John (1987). *Battlefield Archaeology*. London: Ian Allan

Laffin, John (1993). *Digging Up the Diggers' War: Australian Battlefield Archaeology*. Kenthurst: Kangaroo Press

Lake, J. (2000). 'Survey of Military Aviation Sites and Structures: Summary Report', unpublished report of the Thematic Listing Programme, English Heritage, London

Leeds, Eric J. (1979). *No Man's Land: Combat and Identity in World War I.* Cambridge: Cambridge University Press

Linder, A.P. (1996). *Princes of the Trenches: Narrating the German Experience of the First World War*. London: Camden House

Liulevicius, V.G. (2000). *War Land on the Eastern Front: Culture, National Identity, and German Occupation in World War I*. Cambridge: Cambridge University Press

Lloyd, D.W. (1994). 'Tourism, Pilgrimage, and the Commemoration of the Great War in Great Britain, Australia and Canada, 1919–1939', Ph.D. thesis, Cambridge University

Lloyd, D.W. (1998). *Battlefield Tourism: Pilgrimage and the Commemoration of the Great War in Britain, Australia and Canada, 1919–1939.* Oxford: Berg

Loe, Louise (2009). 'Exploring Fromelles'. *In Touch: Oxford Archaeology Newsletter.* 10

Longworth, P. (1985). *The Unending Vigil: A History of the Commonwealth War Graves Commission 1917–1984.* London: Leo Cooper

Lunn, J. (1999). '"Les Races Guerrières": Racial Preconceptions in the French Military about West African Soldiers during the First World War'. *Journal of Contemprary History* 34 (4): 517–536

MacLeod, R. and Johnson, J.A. (2007). *Frontline and Factory: Comparative Persepctives on the Chemical Industry at War, 1914–1924.* Springer

Madoc & IFFM (eds) (1998). *In Flanders Fields. Museum Guide.* Ieper: In Flanders Fields Museum

Maas, B. and Dietrich, G. (1994). *'Lebenszeichen: Schmuck aus Notzeiten'* ('Life-Tokens: Jewellery for Distressing Times'). Cologne: Museum für Angewandte Kunst

Macdonald, Lyn (1993a). *Somme.* London: Penguin

Macdonald, Lyn (1993b). *They Called it Passchendaele.* London: Penguin

Masters, P. and Stichelbaut, B. (2009). 'From the Air to Beneath the Soil – Revealing and Mapping Great War Trenches at Ploegsteert' (Comines-Warneton), Belgium. *Archaeological Prospection.* 16 (4): 279–285

Mazower, Mark (2004). *Salonica, City of Ghosts: Christians, Muslims and Jews 1430–1950.* London: HarperCollins

McOrmish, D., Field, D. and Brown, G. (2001). *The Field Archaeology of the Salisbury Plain Training Area.* London: English Heritage

Meskell, L. (1998) (ed.). *Archaeology under Fire: Nationalism, Politics and Heritage in the Eastern Mediterranean and Middle East.* London: Routledge

Middlebrook, M. and Middlebrook, M. (1994). *The Somme Battlefields: A Comprehensive Guide from Crécy to the Two World Wars.* Harmondsworth: Penguin

Miller, Daniel (1994). 'Artefacts and the Meaning of Things', in T. Ingold (ed.), *Companion Encyclopedia of Anthropology: Humanity, Culture and Social Life.* London: Routledge, pp. 396–419

Miller, Daniel (1998). 'Introduction', in D. Miller (ed.), *Material Cultures: Why Some Things Matter.* London: UCL Press, pp. 3–21

Miller, Daniel (2005) (ed.). *Materiality*. Durham, NC: Duke University Press

Moshenska, Gabriel (2008). 'A Hard Rain: Children's Shrapnel Collections in the Second World War'. *Journal of Material Culture* 13 (1): 107–125

Moshenska, Gabriel (2009). *Archaeology, Material Culture and Memory of the Second World War*. Unpublished Ph.D. thesis. Institute of Archaeology, University College London

Mosse, George L. (1990). *Fallen Soldiers: Reshaping the Memory of the World Wars*. Oxford: Oxford University Press

Murray, David (2010). 'Diggers finally laid to rest in Fromelles'. *Sunday Herald Sun*, Sunday 31 January

Nash, Paul (1998). Letter by Paul Nash, Official War Artist, 18 November 1918, in *In Flanders Fields Museum, Cloth Hall, Market Square, Ieper: Eye Witness Accounts of the Great War: Guide to Quotations*. Ieper: Province of West Flanders

Niethammer, D.H. (1923). *L'Histoire du régiment d'infanterie no. 479 II, avril 1917 à juin 1919*. Stuttgart

Offelli, S. (2001). *Le armi e gli equipaggiamenti dell'Esercito Austro Ungarico dal 1914 al 1918. Uniformi, distintivi, buffeterie*. Vol. 1. Valdagno: Rossato

Omissi, David (1999). *Indian Voices of the Great War: Soldiers' Letters, 1914–18*. London: Palgrave Macmillan

Osgood, Richard (2005). *The Unknown Warrior: An Archaeology of the Common Soldier*. Stroud: Sutton

Osgood, Richard, Brown, Martin and Hawkins, Lucie (2006). 'Before the Storm: Practice Made Perfect for the Australian 3rd Division on Salisbury Plain in the First World War', *Wartime*, 34: 58–60

O'Shea, Stephen (1998). *Back to the Front: An Accidental Historian Walks the Trenches of World War I*. London: Robson Books

OVPW (2001). *Ocean Villas Project*. Website www.timetravellers.org

Paterson, A. (1997). 'Bravery in the Field?', in J.E. Lewis (Intro.), *True World War One Stories: Sixty Personal Narratives of the War*. London: Robinson, pp. 239–46

Piédalue, G. (1998). *Bilan des interventions archéologiques réalises au LHN de Beaumont Hamel: Synthèse préliminaire*. Montreal: Veterans' Affairs Canada

Prezzi, Christian and Pace, Maria (2004). *Il fronte degli altipiani: Immagini dalla Collezione Osele di forte Belvedere – Gschwent*. Cremona: Persico

Price, Jon (2004). 'The Ocean Villas Project: Archaeology in the Service of European Remembrance', in Nicholas J. Saunders (ed.), *Matters of Conflict: Material Culture, Memory and the First World War*. Abingdon: Routledge, pp. 179–91

PTA (2002). Projektgruppe Trench Art, *Kleines aus dem Großen Krieg: Metamorphosen Militärischen Mülls* (Ludwig-Uhland-Institut für Empirische Kulturwissenschaft der Universität Tübingen). Tübingen: Tübinger Vereinigung für Volkskunde

Pugh, P.D.G. (1972). *Heraldic China Mementoes of the First World War*. Newport: Ceramic Book Co.

Radley, Alan. (1994). 'Artefacts, Memory and a Sense of the Past', in David Middleton and Derek Edwards (eds), *Collective Remembering*. London: Sage, pp. 46–59

Reed, Paul (1998). *Uncovering a Great War Tank, Cambrai Battlefield, November 1998*. Hellfire Corner website www.fylde.demon.co.uk/tank.htm

Reed, Paul (2002). *Arras: Point du Jour. Discovery of Remains June 2001*. http://battlefields1418.50megs.com/point_du_jour.htm

Reznick, Jeffrey S. (2005). *Healing the Nation: Soldiers and the Culture of Caregiving in Britain during the Great War*. Manchester: Manchester University Press

Richardson, Matthew (1998). 'A Changing Meaning for Armistice Day', in Hugh Cecil and Peter H. Liddle (eds), *At the Eleventh Hour: Reflections, Hopes and Anxieties at the Closing of the Great War, 1918*. Barnsley: Leo Cooper, pp. 347–64

Richardson, Matthew (2009). Medals, memory and meaning: Symbolism and cultural significance of Greeat War medals. In Nicholas J. Saunders and Paul Cornish (eds.), *Contested Objects: Material Memories of the Great War*, pp. 104–118. Abingdon: Routledge

Robertshaw, Andrew, and Kenyon, David (2008). *Digging the Trenches: The Archaeology of the Western Front*. Barnsley: Pen and Sword

Rommel, Erwin. ([1937] 2009). *Infantry Attacks*. Newbury: Greenhill Books

Rowlands, M. (2001). 'Remembering to Forget: Sublimation as Sacrifice in War Memorials', in A. Forty and S. Küchler (eds), *The Art of Forgetting*. Oxford: Berg, pp. 129–46

Roze, Anne and Foley, John (2000). *Fields of Memory: A Testimony to the Great War*. London: Seven Dials/Cassell & Co.

R.W. (1915). 'Trench Trinkets: Souvenirs Soldiers Make from German Shells. First Anniversary of the War Special Number; August 5th 1915', *The War Budget*, 4/12: 361

Sassoon, Siegfried ([1930] 1997). *Memoirs of an Infantry Officer*. London: Faber and Faber

Saunders, Andrew (1989). *Fortress Britain: Artillery Fortification in the British Isles and Ireland*. Liphook: Beaufort

Saunders, Nicholas J. (2000). '"Trench Art" and the Great War Re-cycled', *Journal of Material Culture*, 5/1: 43–67

Saunders, Nicholas J. (2001a). 'Matter and Memory in the Landscapes of Conflict: The Western Front 1914–1999', in B. Bender and M. Winer (eds), *Contested Landscapes: Movement, Exile and Place*. Oxford: Berg, pp. 37–55

Saunders, Nicholas J. (2001b). 'Apprehending Memory: Material Culture and War, 1919–1939', in J. Bourne, P.H. Liddle and H. Whitehead (eds), *The Great World War, 1914–1945*. Vol. 2. London: HarperCollins, pp. 476–88

Saunders, Nicholas J. (2002a). 'Excavating Memories: Archaeology and the Great War, 1914–2001', *Antiquity*, 76/1: 101–8

Saunders, Nicholas J. (2002b). Interview with *The Economist* for article 'Ethics and Archaeology: Can you Dig it?', *The Economist*, 362/8266: 87–9

Saunders, Nicholas J. (2002c). 'The Ironic "Culture of Shells" in the Great War and Beyond', in J. Schofield, W.G. Johnson and C. Beck (eds), *Matériel Culture: The Archaeology of 20th Century Conflict*. London: Routledge, pp. 22–40

Saunders, Nicholas J. (2003a). 'Crucifix, Calvary, and Cross: Materiality and Spirituality in Great War Landscapes', *World Archaeology*, 35/1: 7–21

Saunders, Nicholas J. (2003b). *Trench Art: Materialities and Memories of War*. Oxford: Berg

Saunders, Nicholas J. (2004a). 'Art of War: Engaging the Contested Object', in C. Renfrew, E. DeMarrais and C. Gosden (eds), *Substance, Memory, Display: Archaeology and Art*. Cambridge: McDonald Institute for Archaeological Research, pp. 119–30

Saunders, Nicholas J. (2004b). 'Material Culture and Conflict: The Great War, 1914–2003', in Nicholas J. Saunders (ed.), *Matters of Conflict: Material Culture, Memory, and the First World War*. London: Routledge, 5–25

Saunders, Nicholas J. (2004c) (ed.). *Matters of Conflict: Material Culture, Memory and the First World War*. London: Routledge

Saunders, Nicholas J. and Dendooven, Dominiek (2004). *Trench Art: Lost Worlds of the Great War. The Trench Art Collection of the In Flanders Fields Museum*. Ieper and Bruges: In Flanders Fields Museum and Uitgeverij Van de Wiele

Saunders, Nicholas J. (2005). 'Culture, Conflict, and Materiality: The Social Lives of Great War Objects', in B. Finn and B.C. Hacker (eds), *Materializing the Military*. London: Science Museum, pp. 77–94

Saunders, Nicholas J. and Cornish, Paul (eds) (2009a). *Contested Objects: Material Memories of the Great War*. Abingdon: Routledge

Saunders, Nicholas J. (2009b). 'People in objects: Individuality and the quotidian in the material culture of war'. In Carolyn White (ed.), *The Materiality of Individuality*. New York: Springer

Saunders, Nicholas J. (2009c). 'Ulysses's Gaze: The panoptic premise in aerial photography and Great War archaeology. In Birger Stichelbaut, Jean Bourgeois, Nicholas J. Saunders and Piet Chielens (eds) *Images of Conflict: Military Aerial Photography and Archaeology*, pp 27–40. Newcastle: Cambridge Scholars Press

Saunders, Nicholas J. (n.d.a). 'Archaeology on the Front-Line, 1914–18: Site Formation in Historical Perspective', unpublished manuscript

Saunders, Nicholas J. (n.d.b). *Bodies in trees: a matter of being in Great War landscapes*. Unpublished manuscript

Saunders, Nicholas J. (n.d.c). *Archaeology on the front-line, 1914–18: site formation in historical perspective*. Unpublished manuscript

Saunders, Nicholas J. (n.d.d). *Materiality, Space, and Distance: Dimensioning the Great War, 1914–1918*. Unpublished manuscript

Schindler, John R. (2000). *Isonzo: The Forgotten Sacrifice of the Great War*. New York: Praeger

Schmidt, B. and Schroeder, I. (2001) (eds). *Anthropology of Violence and Conflict*. London: Routledge

Schofield, John (2004). 'Aftermath: Materiality on the Home Front, 1914–2001', in Nicholas J. Saunders (ed.), *Matters of Conflict: Material Culture, Memory, and the First World War*. London: Routledge, pp. 192–206

Schofield, John (2005). *Combat Archaeology: Material Culture and Modern Conflict*. London: Duckworth

Schofield, John, Johnson, W.G. and Beck, C. (2001) (eds). *Matériel Culture: The Archaeology of 20th Century Conflict*. London: Routledge

Sercu, Aurel (2001). 'Official Statement from "The Diggers" Concerning their Activities and Philosophy'. Unpublished manuscript

Sheffield, Gary (2002). *Forgotten Victory: The First World War: Myths and Realities*. London: Headline

Sherman, D.J. (1999). *The Construction of Memory in Interwar France*. Chicago: Chicago University Press

Shqiarat, M, Al-Salameen, Z., Faulkner, N., Saunders, Nicholas J., Hibbitt, D., Winterburn, J. In Press. 'Fire and water: Tradition and transformation in the archaeology of steam locomotion in a desert war'. *Levant*

Silver, K.E. (1989). *Esprit de Corps: Art of the Parisian Avant-garde and the First World War, 1914–25*. London: Thames and Hudson

Simkins, Peter (1991). 'Everyman at War: Recent Interpretations of the Western Front Experience', in Brian Bond (ed.), *The First World War and British Military History*. Oxford: Clarendon Press, pp. 289–313

Skatssoon, Judy (2006). 'Australia to be Part of 3 Nation Archaeological Survey of Gallipoli', *ABC Science Online: News in Science*, 19 September http://abc.net.au/science/news/stories/2006

Smith, Private Len. (2009). *Drawing Fire: The Diary of a Great War Soldier and Artist*. London: Collins

Smith, Richard (2004). *Jamaican Volunteers in the First World War: Race, Masculinity and the Development of National Consciousness*. Manchester: Manchester University Press

Smith, T. (1999). 'Of Ypres Battlefields – Disappearances and Discovery', *Western Front Association Bulletin*, 53: 38–9

Starling, R. (1998). 'Rethinking the Power of Maps: Some Reflections on Paper Landscapes', *Ecumene*, 5/1: 105–8

Steel, N. and Hart, P. (2000). *Passchendaele*. London: Cassell

Stephens, J. (2009). 'The Ghosts of Menin Gate: Art, Architecture and Commemoration'. *Journal of Contemporary History* 44 (1): 7–26

Stichelbaut, Birger (2005). 'Great War Aerial Photography: A Contribution to the Flemish Battlefield Archaeology', in J. Bourgeois and M. Meganck (eds), *Aerial Photography & Archaeology 2003: A Century of Information* (Archaeological Reports Ghent University, 4). Ghent: Academia Press, pp. 137–48

Stichelbaut, Birger (2006). 'The Application of First World War Aerial Photography to Archaeology: The Belgian Images', *Antiquity*, 80: 161–72

Stichelbaut, Birger (2009). *World War One aerial photography: an archaeological perspective*. Ph.D. Thesis. Belgium, Department of Archaeology, University of Ghent

Stichelbaut, B., Bourgeois, J., Saunders, Nicholas J. and Chielens, P. (eds) (2009). *Images of Conflict: Military Aerial Photography and Archaeology*. Newcastle: Cambridge Scholars Press

Strachan, Hew (1998) (ed.). *The Oxford Illustrated History of the First World War*. Oxford: Oxford University Press, pp. 134–48

Strachan, Hew (2003). *The First World War*. Vol. 1. *To Arms!* Oxford: Oxford University Press

Stratton, M. and Trinder, B. (2000). *Twentieth Century Industrial Archaeology*. London: E & FN Spon

Summerfield, Chantel. (n.d). *The archaeology of a soldiers identity in the Twentieth Century: A comparative investigation of Polo Wood and Half Mooon Copse, Salisbury Plain*. Unpublished B.A. dissertation, Department of Archaeology, University of Reading, 2009

Tarlow, Sarah (1997). 'An Archaeology of Remembering Death, Bereavement and the First World War', *Cambridge Archaeological Journal*, 7/1: 105–21

Terraine, John (1992). *White Heat: The New Warfare 1914–18*. London: Leo Cooper

Thierry, J.-P. (2001) (comp.). *Petites Histoires de la Grande Guerre: Les Objets insolites de L'Historial*. Péronne: Historial de la Grande Guerre

Tilley, Christopher (1994). *A Phenomenology of Landscape, Places, Paths and Monuments*. Oxford: Berg

Tomczyszyn, Pat (2004). 'A Material Link between War and Peace: First World War Silk Postcards', in Nicholas J. Saunders (ed.), *Matters of Conflict: Material Culture, Memory and the First World War*, London: Routledge, pp. 123–33

Tweedie, Neil (2000). '"Sacred" Battlefield Still Gives up its Dead', *Daily Telegraph*, Saturday 11 November, p. 10

Tyson, P. (2000) (prod.). *Battlefield Scavengers*. London Weekend Television, broadcast 12 November

Van Meirvenne, M., Meklit, T., Verstraete, S., De Boyer, M., Tack. F. (2008). 'Could shelling in the First World War have increased copper concentrations in the soil around Ypres?' *European Journal of Soil Science* 59 (2): 372–379

Vermeulen, B. (1999). 'Ieper is a lie', *Flanders Fields Magazine*, 1/1: 9–11

Viazzi, L. (1981). *I diavoli dell'Adamello*. Milan: Mursia

Virilio, Paul (2003). *Art and Fear*. London: Continuum

Von Lichem, H. (1995). *La Guerra in montagna 1915–1918*. Bolzano: Athesia

Walter, T. (1993). 'War Grave Pilgrimage', in I. Reader and T. Walter (eds), *Pilgrimage in Popular Culture*, Basingstoke: Macmillan Press, pp. 63–91

Warin, Patrice (2001). *Artisanat de tranchée et briquets de Poilus de la guerre 14–18*. Louvier: Ysec Éditions

Warin, Patrice (2005). *Artisanat de tranchée de la Grande Guerre, Tome 2*. Louvier: Ysec Éditions

Warin, Patrice (2009). *Les Objets du Tabac de la Grande Guerre – Artisanat de tranchée*. Louvier: Ysec Éditions

Watkins, M. (1998). *Technical Investigation and Neutralisation of the Durand Mine in the Canadian Memorial Park, Vimy Ridge, Artois, France 6–10 February 1998*. Durand Group Report

Webster, D. (1994). 'The Soldiers Moved on; the War Moved on; the Bombs Stayed', *Smithsonian Magazine*, February: 26–37

Webster, D. (1996). *Aftermath: The Landscape of War*. New York: Pantheon Books

Wenzel, Marian and Cornish, John (1980). *Auntie Mabel's War: An Account of her Part in the Hostilities of 1914–18*. London: Allen Lane

Whalen, R.W. (1984). *Bitter Wounds: German Victims of the Great War, 1914–1939*. Ithaca, NY: Cornell University Press

Williamson, Howard (2003). *The Collector and Researchers Guide to the Great War II: Small Arms, Munitions, Militaria*. Harwich: Privately Published by Anne Williamson

Willson, Lt-Col. H.B. (1920). *Ypres: The Holy Ground of British Arms*. Bruges: Bayaert

Winter, Dennis (1979). *Death's Men: Soldiers of the Great War*. Harmondsworth: Penguin

Winter, Jay (1995). *Sites of Memory, Sites of Mourning: The Great War in European Cultural History*. Cambridge: Cambridge University Press

Woollacott, A. (1994). *On Her Their Lives Depend: Munitions Workers in the Great War*. Berkeley and Los Angeles: University of California Press

Zimmerman, Larry (1989). 'Made Radical by my Own: An Archaeologist Learns to Accept Reburial', in Robert Layton (ed.), *Conflict in the Archaeology of Living Traditions*. London: Unwin Hyman, pp. 60–7

Index